Niamh Ann Kelly was born in Galway and is a lecturer in Visual Culture at the Dublin School of Creative Arts, Dublin Institute of Technology, Ireland. At the National College of Art and Design, Dublin, she studied Fine Art Painting and the History of Art at BA level and the History of Art at MA level by research. She received her PhD at the Amsterdam School for Cultural Analysis, University of Amsterdam. She has published widely on her ongoing research interests of contemporary art, the history of art and commemorative visual cultures of monuments, museums and heritage practices.

'A crystal potato – what kind of an artwork is that? Niamh Ann Kelly's book offers a fresh look at the visual culture surrounding the cultural memory of the Irish Famine, caused by the 1845 potato blight. But beyond that, in doing so she sets an example of the difficult but important task of today's developing methodology of cultural analysis. This entails an integration of historical research and contemporary reflection on how the enduring memory of the disaster continues to affect us, and hence, requires thinking about the "politics of food". In other words, it brings not only history to the present, but also art and other visual expressions together with political issues. This balanced interdisciplinary study of an event with many social and historical tentacles shows everyone how to do this.'
Mieke Bal, Professor Emeritus in Literary Theory,
University of Amsterdam and co-founder of the
Amsterdam School for Cultural Analysis

'Visual representations of the Irish Famine range from surviving artefacts and contemporary drawings to modern sculptures and canvasses. Some are disturbingly graphic, others quite abstract; some accusatory, others merely prescriptive. Some were originally intended for private consumption, while more are located in commemorative public spaces. Some would have resonated more with people in the past than they do today – and vice versa. What motivated and motivates artists to depict the Famine? Which representations best convey the injustices and sufferings of the 1840s nowadays? In this pioneering study of the Famine in visual culture Niamh Ann Kelly provides us with a highly original and subtle discussion of the material at the centre of such questions. Her erudition and aesthetic understanding is supported by a wealth of illustrations, much of which will be unfamiliar even to specialists.'

Cormac Ó Gráda, Professor Emeritus of Economics,
University College Dublin and author of *Famine:*
A Short History and *Eating People is Wrong, and*
Other Essays on Famine, Its Past, and Its Future

'Niamh Ann Kelly's lavishly illustrated book throws new light on the visual culture commemorative of hunger, famine and dispossession in mid-nineteenth-century Ireland. Located within the discipline of International Memorial Studies, the text and images both challenge and extend our understanding of Famine history. Examining the visual culture since the time of the Famine until the present, Kelly asks, how do we view, experience and represent the past in the present? To what extent does the viewer insert themselves in this complex process? Is there such a thing as ethical spectatorship? Kelly's sophisticated yet sympathetic study of the "grievous history" of the Great Famine is a powerful addition to Famine history, Irish Studies, Memory Studies and Memorial Studies.'

Professor Christine Kinealy, Director of Ireland's Great Hunger Institute
at Quinnipiac University, Connecticut

'*Imaging the Great Irish Famine* is a vital book on an important topic that continues to haunt the cultural imagination in Ireland and beyond. Addressing the interrelations between visual culture, memory, heritage, museums, and archives, Niamh Ann Kelly's interdisciplinary study offers uniquely perceptive insights into the deep history, contested meaning, and evolving afterlife of the Great Irish Famine.'

Christoph Lindner, Dean of the College of Design, University of Oregon

'Extensively researched and theoretically informed, Niamh Ann Kelly's illuminating study of visual representations of the Great Famine critically surveys the recycling of evocative recollections of dispossession, which run deep in Irish historical consciousness and have emotive universal resonances.'

Guy Beiner, Senior Lecturer, Department of History, Ben-Gurion
University of the Negev and author of *Remembering the Year*
of the French: Irish Folk History and Social Memory

Imaging the Great Irish Famine

Representing Dispossession
in Visual Culture

Niamh Ann Kelly

BLOOMSBURY ACADEMIC
LONDON • NEW YORK • OXFORD • NEW DELHI • SYDNEY

BLOOMSBURY ACADEMIC
Bloomsbury Publishing Plc
50 Bedford Square, London, WC1B 3DP, UK
1385 Broadway, New York, NY 10018, USA

BLOOMSBURY, BLOOMSBURY ACADEMIC and the Diana logo
are trademarks of Bloomsbury Publishing Plc

First published 2018 by I.B. Tauris & Co. Ltd.
Paperback edition first published by Bloomsbury Academic 2020

ISBN: HB: 978-1-7845-3710-4
PB: 978-1-3501-4568-9
ePDF: 978-1-8386-0872-9
ePub: 978-1-8386-0871-2

Series: International Library of Visual Culture

Typeset by OKS Prepress Services, Chennai, India

To find out more about our authors and books visit
www.bloomsbury.com and sign up for our newsletters.

For Aoife and Aisling

Contents

List of Illustrations

List of Illustrations

List of Illustrations

List of Illustrations

Acknowledgements

The research interest realized in this book first took form at the Amsterdam School for Cultural Analysis in the University of Amsterdam, with my good fortune to have the brilliant, inspiring and tireless Mieke Bal as my promotor. Also, at ASCA I had the privilege of the peerless close reading and critical perception of Esther Peeren whose reviews greatly helped shape the first outings of these research themes. I would also like to acknowledge the encouragement of Nancy Pedri and Hanneke Grootenboer in the early stages of this project.

More recently, I owe a debt of gratitude to my anonymous peer reviewers for their encouragement, rigorous observations and constructive criticisms. I greatly appreciate the work and patience of the team at I.B.Tauris, including editors Lisa Goodrum and Baillie Card and in production, Arub Ahmed and the designers of the book. Thanks also to Ken Moxham for his copyediting work. I am very grateful to Anna Coatman (now of *RA Magazine* and 3 of Cups Press) in her previous role as an editor of Visual Culture at IBT for her enthusiastic response to my initial proposal which has resulted in this book.

The research and images produced here have been assisted by scholarships and a research funding award from the Dublin Institute of Technology, Ireland. In particular, I want to acknowledge: the support of Dean John O'Connor, Kieran Corcoran (Head of Dublin School of Creative Arts), Prof. Noel Fitzpatrick and Prof. Brian O'Neill. I also appreciate the interest and advice from my colleagues at DSCA, DIT on various aspects of the book: Dr Mary Ann Bolger, Dr Tim Stott and Dr Brian Fay.

A number of individuals and organizations have helped in various ways by sharing their research on and pursuing images and copyrights of my selected sites of memory, while others have provided insight and inspiration along the way. Many went far beyond their professional requirements, generously spreading their passion and knowledge about the past, the Famine and visual culture. These include: Fergus Keys (Director of The Montreal

Acknowledgements

Irish Monument Park Foundation), Perry McIntyre (Historian and Vice-Chair of Great Irish Famine Commemoration Committee, Sydney), The Architecture Archive, IVARO, Crescence Maranda-Parent (Promotion officer, Quebec Field Unit at Parks Canada), William B. Peat (Executive Director, Ireland Park Foundation, Toronto), Niamh Curran (Community Coordinator, Ireland Park Foundation, Toronto), Terri Kearney (Manager, Skibbereen Heritage Centre), Eimear Whittle of Failte Ireland, Pat Doherty at Doagh Famine Village, Trevor Stanley (Secretary of Donaghmore Museum), Moses Alcorn and Yvonne Friel (Manager) at The Workhouse, Dunfanaghy, Catherine Kilbane at Achill Tourism, John O'Neill (General Manager of Jeanie Johnston Tallship), Sean Connick (Chief Executive of John F. Kennedy Trust), Michael Loughran (Visitor Services at the Office of Public Works), Matt Wheeler (Curator/Manager of Irish Agricultural Museum at Johnstown Castle), Claire Ní Dhubhcháin and Bairbre Ní Fhloinn at the National Folklore Collection UCD, Niamh O'Sullivan and Claire Puzarne at Ireland's Great Hunger Museum in Connecticut, Audrey Whitty, Valerie Dowling, Richard Weinacht and Finbarr Connolly at National Museum of Ireland, Mary MacCaffery at the Royal Ulster Academy, Johanne Mullan and Christina Kennedy at the Irish Museum of Modern Art, Rosemarie Noone at the Claremorris Gallery, The George Moore Society, Michael Dempsey at Dublin City Gallery: The Hugh Lane, Nick Tromans at the Watts Gallery, Martin Bob O'Dwyer and Bernard Minogue at Cashel Folk Village, Peter Beirne of Clare County Library, Sr Alphonsus and Sr Elizabeth Maxwell of the Presentation Sisters, Dianne McPhelim of the Clones Famine Memorial Group, James Gorry (Director of Gorry Gallery), Colleen O'Hara at the Irish Heritage Trust at Strokestown Park, John O'Driscoll (Curator and Manager, Strokestown House), Brendan Rooney and Donal Maguire at the Centre for the Study of Irish Art, National Gallery of Ireland, Patrick Wingrove at the *Illustrated London News*, Brian Clyne of Brian Tolle Studio, Susan Keating at Irish Arts Review, Derville Murphy, Séan Watts (Killenaule Historian), Gary Ward, Gina O'Kelly, Catherine Marshall, Tom Dunne, Fionna Barber, Fintan Cullen, Michael Kenny, Jacqueline Borsje, Christine Kinealy, Cormac Ó Gráda, Luke Gibbons, Christoph Lindner, and Guy Beiner.

My thanks also to the artists who readily and kindly gave permission to print images of their works: Dorothy Cross, Patrick Graham, Hughie O'Donoghue, Carolyn Mulholland, Brian Tolle, and in particular Alanna O'Kelly, who generously provided a new compilation image of her work.

Finally, I am deeply grateful to my family: my siblings, Sinéad and Brendan, for listening to and supporting aspects of this research project in many ways over a long time and my parents, Des and Mary for their support, which runs too deep to categorize, of all it took to complete this book and for, well before any of that, instilling in my siblings and I an invaluable appreciation of heritage, visual culture and the history written on the landscapes of Ireland and elsewhere.

Last but not least, my thanks to my wonderful daughters, Aoife and Aisling, to whom this book is dedicated and to my husband, John: thank you for everything, especially for the hillwalks, site visits and quiet house.

Preface

Over a decade ago, during the course of researching Famine sites of memory, I came across a poem by Irish poet Eavan Boland, called 'That the science of cartography is limited'.[1] Her text resonated across my time spent visiting historic sites, attending exhibitions, monuments, partaking in memorial events and perhaps most of all, walking in the Irish landscape in search of Famine history.

'That the science of cartography is limited'

> – and not simply by the fact that this shading of
> forest cannot show the fragrance of balsam,
> the gloom of cypresses
> is what I wish to prove.
>
> When you and I were first in love we drove
> to the borders of Connacht
> and entered a wood there.
>
> Look down you said: this was once a famine road.
>
> I looked down at ivy and the scutch grass
> rough-cast stone had
> disappeared into as you told me
> in the second winter of their ordeal, in
>
> 1847, when the crop had failed twice,
> Relief Committees gave
> the starving Irish such roads to build.
>
> Where they died, there the road ended
> and ends still and when I take down
> the map of this island, it is never so
> I can say here is
> the masterful, the apt rendering of

the spherical as flat, nor
an ingenious design which persuades a curve
into a plane,
but to tell myself again that

the line which says woodland and cries hunger
and gives out among sweet pine and cypress,
and finds no horizon
will not be there.[2]

– Eavan Boland

The poem first came to my attention in the context of a 1995 Famine exhibition at University College Cork, Ireland and it was since printed at the start of the expansive 2012 edited volume, *Atlas of the Great Irish Famine, 1845–52*.[3] Throughout years of exploring various sites of Famine memory, in Ireland and elsewhere, both urban and rural, as well as formal and informal, Boland's text seemed to echo through my central and driving question: what use has representation outside of testimony?

The Irish Famine of the mid-nineteenth century was of seismic demographic impact but the witnesses who survived at that time in various ways and various places were not asked for their testimony and may, in any event, not have wished or been able to provide it. There was no recording of experiences until the 1930s when, what is now the National Folklore Commission began interviewing rural communities through a range of questionnaire projects. This process secured a rich repository of the memories of adults, some of whom had experienced the direct impacts of the Famine as very young children and others who recalled it as a shaping aspect of their childhood passed down from a parent generation who, in turn, had lived through it. But survival of catastrophe is manifold indeed: by what means did people endure such personal ravage as precipitated by sustained hunger; at what cost; and to whom?

The horror of hunger is inscribed on the suffering body alone, while societal experiences of famine are conditional on circumstances of economic and social dispossession. These contingencies, and the lack of much immediate testimony on the Famine, pose enormous challenges for the material cultures of art, museum, memorial and heritage practices. How best to describe a history defined in the first instance by material poverty and precarious living? Can the temporal intangibilities of exhibitions and the viewing of images and objects ever adequately indicate experiences had by others?

Notwithstanding this, the landscape of Ireland holds traces of many aspects of Famine history: shadows and palimpsests of Famine-era experiences that remain as potential and potent sites of memory right across the island of Ireland. In what ways can such sites where empty cottages, re-purposed and derelict workhouses and the footprint of structures built as part of labour programmes are found; paths that starving people trod in search of relief; and not least places where the dead are buried, by the hundreds, reflect on a landscape of historical dispossession and widely felt suffering?

The spaces that lie between human experience and the writing of history are the sites of representation. These are presented where testimony is absent or muted and so can compellingly contribute to the mapping of a grievous history.[4] Gaps in rendering that Boland writes of remain: it is not possible to fully recount experiences of the past, or of others, on paper, in paint or by stone, less still to communicate these to another person. Even so, it is crucial to perform a secondary kind of witnessing when the primary or ultimate witnesses who might provide testimony are now absent.[5]

The artist and writer Trinh T. Minh-ha recognizes a fallacy within documentary conventions that might presume to fully reflect the reality of others. Instead, she describes her filmic practice as one in which she 'speaks nearby' her subject. This she defines as:

> a speaking that does not objectify, does not point to an object as if it is distant from the speaking subject or absent from the speaking place. A speaking that reflects on itself and can come very close to a subject without, however, seizing or claiming it. A speaking in brief, whose closures are only moments of transition, opening up to other possible moments of transition – these are forms of indirectness well understood by anyone in tune with poetic language.[6]

What follows is an account of a selection from the many forms of, what I term, commemorative visual culture that speak nearby a grievous history of hunger: the Irish Famine that began in the 1840s.

Introduction
The Great Irish Famine: Dispossession and Spectatorship

In the mid-1990s, Galway Irish Crystal Ltd produced a clear crystal paperweight in the shape of a potato. (Figure I.1). *Crystal Spud* was designed to commemorate Irish immigration to the USA, and the accompanying text card in its gift box set emphasizes a positive rhetoric about Irish contributions to nation-building there. Despite no reference to the Famine included in the text card, the object's memorial function relating to the extent of Irish emigration and its chosen from are caught up in a complex historical legacy of Ireland's dietary dependency on the nutritious stem tuber. *Crystal Spud*'s form further resplendently echoes the critical crux of the aesthetics of difficult heritage,[1] pointing to the tension between the contemporary presence of commemorative visual culture and the historical absences it seeks to illuminate.

In the Famine Exhibition room at the Irish Agricultural Museum and Johnstown Castle Gardens, County Wexford, is a display of potatoes on plates (Figure I.2). A wall panel above it details average daily potato consumption by men, women and children in pre-Famine Ireland of the early 1840s. It reveals the extent of the high volume of this historic vitamin-rich reliance: an adult male consumed 6.4 kg, an adult female 5.1 kg and a child under 11 years, 2.2 kg.

In its spread of appearances across the breadth of commemorative visual culture of the Famine, the potato is alternately iconic as an object, exemplified by the commercial gift culture of *Crystal Spud* and implicitly indexical by proxy, as at Johnstown. The prevalence of both real and

1

represented potatoes and related artefacts of diet, such as soup pots, in Famine exhibitions points to the core facet of this expansive and troubling history: the politics of food. David Lloyd phrased it: 'We may say that the problem of Ireland was paradoxically not scarcity, but *abundance*: abundance of population and abundance of means to support that population, an abundance notoriously supplied by the potato.'[2] The carbohydrate- and vitamin-rich tuberous crop that promoted and sustained healthy bodies was most likely introduced to Ireland during the last quarter of the sixteenth century through either Spain or Britain.[3] By the nineteenth century, it represented an aspect of a catastrophic dependency that imparted a landscape of disease, death and cultural decline.

The Famine was precipitated in 1845 when the potato blight arrived in western Europe. A fungal spore called *Phytophthora infestans* caused repeated potato blights, infesting crops through the second half of the 1840s.[4] John Feehan notes that though the crop partially failed in 1845, the near-complete decimation of the 1846 crop left many without seed tubers to plant for the following year.[5] The following year was widely

Figure I.1 *Crystal Spud.* Galway Crystal Ltd. © Gary Ward.

Figure I.2 *Potato Display in Famine Exhibition Room.* Irish Agricultural Museum, Johnstown Castle, County Wexford. Image provided by author. By permission of Irish Agricultural Museum, Johnstown Castle.

known as 'Black '47', when food shortages were piercingly felt and the cumulative effects of deprivation were harshly in evidence. The situation augmented widespread poverty, instigating hunger-related diseases and death across Ireland on an unprecedented scale. Abruptly, the vulnerability of a multitude was horrifically evident as a sustained and devastating grievous history unfolded.

In the 1840s, Ireland was part of the British Empire. There were about 300,000 cottier households and over 600,000 labourer households.[6] Collectively, these households made up over 3 million of the over 8 million population of the 1841 census information,[7] which suggests that the population may well have been, by 1845, close to 8.5 million.[8] Some were tenants of landlords with large estates and many were disastrously dependent on conacre farming: renting tiny plots for the growing season, to grow potatoes as a central aspect of diet,[9] which was typically augmented by buttermilk and, in coastal counties, fish. Christine Kinealy states that over two-thirds of the labour force continued to depend on agriculture, the majority of whom held little or no land and traded 'their labour for a small plot of land',[10] comparably to sharecropping, as experienced for example by African American slaves in the post-Civil War period. In Ireland, this fragile economic system was underpinned by a persistent over-reliance on a single crop, the potato, as an affordable staple food and, importantly, one which could be stored during off-season months.

Kevin Whelan describes a great 'shifting underclass in Irish society in the immediate pre-famine years', whose livelihoods were defined by the effects of divisive social structures as more solvent tenants emigrated amid a growing Irish economic depression and an increasing dependency on reduced varieties of potatoes.[11] Problems accruing from practices of subdivision, or fragmentation of landholdings within families, were accentuated by a rapid increase in population prior to the arrival of the blight.[12] It was a perilously balanced subsistence culture.

By 1852, the population had been depleted by over 25 per cent.[13] Lack of sustenance had viciously extended to circumstances of eviction, forced and economic emigration and abandonment of home in the search for food and basic means of survival. With a population depletion of 3.1 million between 1845 and 1855 – 1.1 million dying from hunger and related diseases and 2 million emigrating[14] – the precarious family lives of Famine sufferers were further disadvantaged by Poor Law amendments and dispossession orders. There had been earlier crop failures in Ireland, but without such devastating consequences. The mismanagement of the situation before and after the blights of 1845 and 1846 contributed to the extent of the Famine, leading it to be heralded, above earlier Irish famines, as the Great Famine.

Terming it 'the greatest demographic catastrophe in European history', Lloyd argues that cultural perception facilitated the Famine as a catastrophe:

> The intersection of policy-making and political economy in effect transforms a subsistence crisis into a famine by regulating the perception and interpretation of Irish conditions along terribly determinate lines [...] at least in part because the condition of Ireland up to the famine itself presents a theoretical anomaly, and at times even a critical abyss, for the British political economy as a discourse, just as it does for British Colonial government in practice.[15]

Lloyd identifies two principal anomalies as 'land and population, the distinct but related and recurrent objects of colonial governmentality'.[16] Ireland's double reproductive abilities – population and social formations – were considered outside of the normative progressive process of capitalist modernization. Patterns of traditional distribution of land and use of holdings such as rundale farming and subdivision were 'recalcitrant to capitalist economic and political transformation'.[17] Stuart McLean links nineteenth-century British perceptions of Ireland with earlier, broader formative perceptions of Ireland as at the edge, or marking the 'westernmost limits of Christendom, and, later, Europe,' and the Irish as '"wild" human counterparts to a newly aestheticized landscape of mountain and moorland'. This line of thinking would 'reinforce perceptions of Ireland's anomalous status in relation to the orthodoxy of economic reason that was gaining ground in a swiftly industrializing Britain'.[18]

Further to this, connotations of terminology related to 'The Pale' – a term in usage from the fourteenth century to describe an area inclusive of and surrounding Dublin city that was under English rule – suggested that those who ventured or dwelled 'beyond the pale' were not only outside of British territory, but outside of civilization itself. A legacy of these implications extends to common parlance today, and also reached into inflections within representations and depictions of Famine-related experience qualified as rural-based relative to a metropolitan centre such as Dublin, notably engendering a lexicon of primitivism, in both text and imaged accounts.

Ireland was thus doubly dispossessed: firstly, through an extensive programme of plantations in the seventeenth century and then again on the eve of the Famine by way of cultural interpretations of the fertile social abundance of pre-Famine Ireland, epitomized by the nutritious potato.

Following the potato blights, local, national and voluntarily coordinated relief schemes were set up intended to temporarily counter the central dietary position of the potato, with the provision of grain-based meals, particularly Indian meal and corn, as well as maize and oatmeal. Public works schemes and access to workhouses were the mainstay of relief projects. The building of workhouses had begun in earnest in the late 1830s, but with the advent of the Famine many rapidly became overcrowded and incapable of adequately responding to the local situation, while also struggling to contain the illnesses spreading through their rooms. According to Thomas Bartlett, by 1842 'around 120 workhouses had been built and indoor relief was being offered to some forty thousand destitute', and by 1849 some '900,000 Irish poor were being relieved' in workhouses that had been designed to accommodate 'a ceiling of 80,000' people.[19] Paschal Mahoney notes that from the outset each Irish workhouse was intended to accommodate more than those in England, 'highlighting the greater scale of pauperism even before the Famine'.[20] As the Famine progressed, workhouses were overwhelmed by the scale and spread of infections during the worst of the Famine years. John O'Connor writes that in August 1846 workhouses were only half-full;[21] by March 1847, 'with all 130 workhouses opened they were crammed to capacity with 115,000 occupants', and by 1851, 217,000.[22] Laurence Geary comments:

> While mismanagement and negligence were a feature of some institutions and while the conditions in many were appalling it would be wrong to attach the entire blame to administrative indifference. The system was simply unable to cope with the demands made upon it by the Famine.[23]

The public works programmes were similarly unable to cope with demand, and early in 1847 a Temporary Relief Act known as the Soup Kitchen Act was prompted to alleviate the dawning failure of the public works schemes. This strategy was meant to provide safe, edible food for the starving as it had been identified that many people were dying as a result of inadequately cooked food.[24] Soup kitchens, in particular voluntary ones, had another consequence, as, even in the decades prior to the Famine, religious tensions played a role in charity work, where proselytizing became associated with relief efforts.[25] In any event, soup kitchens during the Famine, both formally funded and voluntarily run, did not last long.

The prime minister from the end of June 1846, John Russell, was less lenient than his predecessor, Robert Peel, had been in implementing his relief policies – with terrible results. For example, in Russell's variation on relief works, the poor could only apply to work on various building schemes once the local workhouse was full.[26] The two key figures in charge of relief provision were Sir Charles Wood, the Chancellor of the Exchequer from 1846 to 1852, and Charles E. Trevelyan, the assistant secretary at the Treasury, whose promotion by Russell advanced his influential hold over relief policy in Ireland.[27] The notorious Quarter Acre Clause implemented as an extension to the Poor Law in 1847 decreed that there was no relief for anyone who occupied more than a quarter-acre,[28] while a £4 Rating Clause meant landlords were responsible for holdings under £4.[29] Those caught in between these descriptors became 'a parasitic encumbrance' for landlords, being neither self-sufficient nor usefully dependent.[30] This further complicated the heightening tensions between landlords and tenants, augmenting widespread displacement, eviction and, eventually, for many, emigration.

While an increase in the number of unions nationally, as a result of the Poor Law Amendment (Ireland) Act of June 1847,[31] redefined, at local levels, the allocations of workhouse places, this positive shift in recognition of a differentiating population spread was dogged by the clause that collected local rates should cover the costs of running the local workhouse. Subsequently recognized as untenable, slow redress of the funding deficits through extended government loan schemes was rolled out.[32] Even so, for many tenants and their families, repayments on their rented land were impossible to maintain in the face of continued crop failure, with the added problem of the destruction and depletion of crop stores.

A consensus has emerged in retrospect that the Famine was not simply a natural disaster but overwhelmingly a political one. Peter Gray writes: 'By December [1847] the failure of the public relief works was indisputable. Reports of mass mortality and inquests attributing deaths to the Board's [of Public Works] negligence became common.'[33] The sustained impact of failed relief policies was clear: in June 1849, there were 200,000 inmates in workhouses, 770,000 receiving outdoor relief and 25,000 in workhouse infirmaries and that year an estimated 220,000 emigrated.[34] Formal relief measures were clearly inadequate to counter the flow of displacement effected by localized forced evictions and countrywide attempts at emigration.

Successive Tory- and Whig-led governments had sought to utilize the Famine as a means to radically modernize Ireland's economy: putting an end to potato dependence, revamping a blatantly irresponsible landlord system and excluding absent or ineffectual systems of management.[35] The issue was further complicated by sectarian conclusions suggesting Ireland's Catholicism was at the root of the problem and a vengeful God had decreed a levelling of the population in the form of the Famine to cure the west and south of Ireland of its general malaise and industrial inaction.[36] L. Perry Curtis Jr, cites three connected factors accounting for the severity of the impact of the potato blight on the poorest inhabitants of Munster and Connacht: capitalism, racial and religious prejudice and socio-economic structures, including the Poor Law.[37] And through it all, death from hunger-related illness, contagious diseases and fevers and malnourishment continued apace.

As the single most definitive event for the demographic alteration of Ireland in modern history, the Famine was a history of poverty and hunger defined by the violent exercise of political power; a history more complex and impacting than can be indicated on the page. As in many histories of poverty and related systematic dispossession, the context and effects of the Irish Famine are intertwined in telling. The resulting social conditions were acutely felt for at least six years, with ongoing ramifications for cultural, political and economic life in Ireland thereafter.

The means by which this history has been presented and thus constituted through commemorative forms of visual culture is the subject of this book. There are already many histories of the Famine. Local histories have been produced by historians, librarians, archivists and interest groups throughout Ireland. Broader accounts are contextualized in variously economic, political and cultural texts by writers of Irish history including David Valone, Kevin Whelan, Alvin Jackson, Thomas Bartlett and Roy Foster. Other historians have written thematically focused Famine histories, such as Enda Delaney, James S. Donnelly, Peter Gray, Margaret Kelleher, Breandán Mac Suibhne, Christine Kinealy, Cormac Ó Gráda and Ciarán Ó Murchadha.

Texts and projects by David Lloyd, Oona Frawley, Luke Gibbons, Marguérite Corporaal, Jason King and the far-reaching Atlas of the Great Irish Famine project have encompassed wider cultural forms as both reflective of and contributive to understandings of Famine history and Irish Studies. In relation to visual and material culture of the Famine, both in Ireland and its diasporic presence, the field is emerging with in-depth scholarship in work cataloguing key memorial examples by Emily Mark-Fitzgerald and art by Niamh O'Sullivan, along with the Famine Folio Series commissioned by O'Sullivan in her role as curator at the Connecticut Irish Hunger Museum.

Building on these invaluable sources, this text extends beyond strictures of Famine history and Irish Studies to instead lodge a discussion on commemorative visual culture of the Irish Famine within a wider international field of memorial studies. Animated discourses on grievous histories and related representations of dispossession are taking place across national, historic and cultural spheres, exemplified in the works of Giorgio Agamben, Silke Arnold-de Simine, Athena Athanasiou, Ulrich Baer, Jill Bennett, Judith Butler, Marianne Hirsch, Andeas Huyssen, Susie Linfield, Pierre Nora, Paul Williams, Emma Willis and James Young.

These debates are amplified in edited projects by Jenny Kidd; William Logan and Keir Reeves; Leanne White and Elspeth Frew; Iain Chambers, Alessandra De Angelis, Celeste Ianniciello, Mariangela Orabona and Michaela Quadraro; and Philip R. Stone and Richard Sharpley.

The depiction of historical humanitarian disasters in art exhibitions, news reports, monuments and at heritage sites has framed the harrowing images associated with dispossession in the early twenty-first century. Examining a wide range of commemorative visual culture from the mid-nineteenth-century Irish Famine until the early twenty-first-century reveals the importance of how artefacts of historical trauma affect understandings of conflict, poverty and famine as ongoing forms of political violence. To reappraise the viewer's role in representations of dispossession, images, objects and locations are thematically presented. These themes are organized around, firstly, the dispossessed body suffering hunger and undertaking emigration; secondly, display cultures generated by museums and temporary exhibition projects; and lastly, the lingering landscape of this grievous history at burial grounds, heritage sites and relief works structures.

The commemorative visual culture of the Famine examined includes art, illustration, monuments, exhibitions, museums, cemeteries, tourist trails and heritage locations.[38] These span a geographical range from Australia, Canada, USA, Great Britain and Northern Ireland, with the main focus on Ireland. They are not intended as a survey – national, islandic or diasporic – rather, they have been chosen as indicative of tropes and trends within the cultural performance of Famine memory.[39] These choices have given rise to the utilization of a range of information sources from textual, visual, conversational, print and online sources to walking through designated touristic sites, as well as lightly mediated and unmarked places.

The methods of engagement throughout this exploration are drawn from a practice of cultural analysis. Methods, as described by Mieke Bal, 'are part of the exploration. You conduct a meeting between several, a meeting in which the object participates, so that, together, object and methods can become a new, not firmly delineated field'.[40] Jill Bennett's conception of intermedial aesthetics which can be 'traced through the distinctive operation of images inhabiting the interdisciplinary field' is also pertinent to the visual cultural forms presented as productive of representations of the Famine.[41] The spirit of reading sites of expression as 'gestural rather than communicative'[42] implicates viewers of other people's experiences, either past or present, as more than mere spectators of history. Furthermore, the methods used here to represent sites of Famine memory take cognizance of Sharon Macdonald's notion of 'past presencing'. Past presencing, she suggests, 'is the empirical phenomenon of how people variously experience, understand and produce the past in the present'.[43] This, among other things, indicates 'the elision and indeterminacy that is so often involved [between perceptions of past and present], and the disruption of linear notions of past preceding present preceding future' and 'necessarily gives attention to temporality'.[44] In this sense, viewers are participants in complex productions and reproductions of history, memorialization and commemorative modalities, as they are in any representation of others.

The Horror of Hunger

Famine, a form of dispossession, occurs with the failure of infrastructure to provide the most basic of needs for livable lives.[45] The first two chapters explore visualizations of Famine experience centred on the hungry body and economically forced migration as forms of dispossession. The production of subjects of history through visual and heritage cultures and modes of spectatorship that regard dispossessed others connects to David Campbell's exploration of the constitutive relation of geopolitics and visuality. Of photojournalism, Campbell writes,

> when we are dealing with photographs we are concerned with the visual performance of the social field, whereby pictures bring the objects they purport to simply reflect into being. We are not concerned with the (in)accurate representation of already existing objects, but with the ways in which sites (and people in those sites) are enacted through sight.[46]

Chapters 1 and 2 investigate this premise in relation to a set of historical representations which, though outside of photography, suggest a comparable visual performance of the social field. The resulting geopolitical relativities established between spectator and subject are made complex, however, by differentiating modes of witnessing suffering from different locations in both place and time.

The primal site of hunger is, of course, the body. Painful outcomes of hunger occur in a physical body and are consequently known to its subjective psyche. Like much physical discomfort, hunger has external triggers, but pain, such as the severe effects arising out of related illnesses, is realized in and by the body. Elaine Scarry proposes that such inner awareness of pain is simultaneously the point at which language is destroyed,[47] and further suggests that imagination and pain share a state of being objectless. Both pain and imagination are interior to the body but exist at what she terms opposite ends of the terrain of the human psyche.[48] Scarry argues that attempts to express pain, to externalize internal sensations and arising concepts, along with efforts to understand or acknowledge the pain of another, are at the heart of our engagement with the material world. Her study is centred on what she describes as 'the unmaking and making of the world' and connects internal suffering with externalized desires to alleviate it.[49] Though her exploration focused on literature, it indicates the depths of the difficulty facing artists and illustrators depicting the suffering hungry body through figurations of Famine, then and since.

Susan Sontag has explored the ways in which suffering is viewed through visual culture, focusing on the divergence between documentary and artistic practices. Using terms such as 'the antistudy of a document' and 'visionary', Sontag makes a sympathetic case for the interpretive and imaginative role of art in imaging suffering and points out the difference of expectation (and assumption) between a camera 'showing' and art 'evoking' situations of distress.[50] Though differentiated, both Sontag's and Scarry's ideas suggest the material making of the world of representation is simultaneously the making of meaning, irrespective of mechanisms of externalization. Scarry links this idea of artifice to an equivalent scale of imaginative possibility, as objects of artifice allow imaging to become collective.[51] Concluding that the work of the imagination makes the inanimate world animate-like, the world outside the body becomes, in Scarry's terms, as responsible as if it were not oblivious to sentience.[52]

Scarry and Sontag's suggestions relate to thinking through the affect, or otherwise, of images of hungry bodies: how de-sensitizing some dramatic images of suffering others can be, in news media for example. Margaret Crawford describes the expectation of particular types of images as cues for the now commonplace recognition of starvation, in Ethiopia and elsewhere, on TV screens,[53] which are also, to the viewers, images of the bodies of others.[54] This gives rise to the quandary of how ethical spectatorship, the responsibility of looking at or watching over others, might be formulated. Marianne Hirsch focuses the problem in terms of commemorative practices: a challenge for any postmemorial artist is 'to find the balance that allows the spectator to enter the image, to imagine the disaster, but that disallows an over-appropriative identification that makes the distances disappear, creating too available, too easy an access to this particular past.'[55]

The resonance of ethical spectatorship for commemorative visual culture at sites where acts of conflict and terror took place in particular generates much debate on potentially perilous them-and-us paradigms of representation. These can, at times problematically, as Marita Sturken points out, conflate 'narratives of innocence' with atrocious acts.[56] In drawing attention to aspects of initial and spontaneous popular memorial practices at Ground Zero in New York, for example, Sturken outlines the dual potential of kitsch objects and sentimental resonance in that paradigm of memorialization. To commemorate a terrible event, as Sturken indicates, may well include a synthesis of kitsch that is both locally and temporally defined. In her example this synthesis was socially expressed at Ground Zero as objects, both personal and commercial, left at the site amassed. The social production of commemoration further travelled through families and friendships, by way of traded and gifted objects of kitsch, such as teddy bears and snow-globes, invested with meaning along the way. Sturken's critique indicates that these practices heterogeneously contribute to comprehension of the event memorialized in various times and places. Such paradigms and conflations were subsequently highlighted in tensions surrounding the competition and formal commissioning processes for the memorialization of Ground Zero and subsequently in fraught debates on levels of access to the burial places of those who died there as a site for personal mourning rather than a public memorial. Finally it is perhaps the popular usage of the site that serves most affectively as an enactment of memorial culture.

It is in the wake of widening experiences of conflict, terror and consequential unsettlement, in the broadest sense, that Adriana Cavarero promotes a new term – horrorism – to encapsulate the experiences of others that routinely escape adequate conveyance in words and images.[57] She outlines that, though the threat may be more widely prevalent, those that are struck often have little shielding them: violence strikes the defenceless. A consequence of such defencelessness, as preconditions dispossession, is the violence that constitutes bodily hunger: an attack on the physical being against an individual's will resulting in the malfunctioning and disintegration of the body. Contemplating the scale of deprivation that accounts for situations of famine is the privilege of spectators. With recognition of this kind of horrorism comes an enormous onus to carefully consider what might constitute witness to a state seemingly beyond capacity of usual lexicons of description.

However, the temporal distance of the mid-nineteenth-century Irish Famine accentuates the limitations of witness that attend all such experiences of bodily deprivation, dispossession and death, where retrospective, or a kind of secondary, witnessing has firstly to negotiate a post-colonial terrain of cultural history. Though in many senses a well-documented famine, those who suffered the most died and many of the rest were socially and culturally muted, and so contemporary accounts of the Famine are predominantly reliant on those who managed relief, mismanaged relief and those who observed, such as journalists, philanthropists and travellers. While direct experiential accounts exist, mainly in the form of letters to and from emigrants,[58] it is Irish workhouse records, census information, shipping logs, as well as medical, burial and immigration records at sites in the UK, Canada, USA and Australia, that most poignantly account for qualitative experiences of life and death, many of which are latterly utilized in Famine memorials at sites across these countries.

Of the surviving contemporary accounts in Ireland, many were produced by observers outside of the social and cultural descriptors of Famine sufferers. Though Margaret Kelleher makes a case for the American writer Asenath Nicholson's work as less distanced than some male narrators on the Famine, since she literally entered into the homes of sufferers and engaged some in reciprocated social gestures,[59] Nicholson remained *other* to her subjects, as is definitive of observers.

A lasting significance of Nicholson's role during the Famine was her recognition of voice as attendant to social agency. Her writing posits the lack of speech as contingent to the condition of those who suffered during the Famine: 'They stood up before us in a speechless, vacant, staring, stupid, yet most eloquent posture, mutely graphically saying. "Here we are, your bone and your flesh, made in God's image like you. Look at us! What brought us here?"' [60] As Kelleher recounts Nicholson's ethical motivations along with her struggles to address her subjects outside of the dominant attitudes of her class, it seems Nicholson saw her role as the speaker for those without the means to be heard, or perhaps understood in another language.

Maureen Murphy suggests Nicholson's commitment to social reform, as a 'health reformer', was influenced by her austere upbringing, training as a teacher and later her firsthand experiences of 'the deprivations of life in Erris [County Mayo] in the winter of 1847–48', lending her a 'sense of divine mission to relieve the suffering of the Irish poor during the Great Famine'.[61] The passage quoted above indicates a confrontation between the 'eloquent' body inscribed by pain and the challenge for the non-sufferer to convey such experience. Nicholson later reflected on this dilemma:

> And now, while looking at them calmly at a distance, they appear, even to myself, more like a dream than a reality, because they appear out of *common course*, and out of the order of even nature itself. But they *are* realities, and many of them fearful ones – *realities* which none but eye-witnesses can understand, and none but those who passed through them can feel.[62]

From that time and in retrospective views since, a number of historically and socially specific codes of representation on themes of hunger and migration have respectively found visual and material form in figurations and ship motifs. The artworks, illustrations, memorials and heritage sites discussed in Chapters 1 and 2 connect perceptions of otherness with considerations of location in ways that variously transpose experiences of those suffering hunger and migration in particular into subjects of visual culture.

Grievous History, Difficult Heritage

> The history and culture of the vanquished and the oppressed is rarely embodied in material objects. They bequeath words rather than palaces, hope rather than private property, words, texts and music rather than monuments. They leave heritages embodied in people rather than stones. Songs, words, poems, declarations, texts often constitute the archive through which to evoke their past. Their itineraries retrace the history of struggles, of migrations, of the global organization of the workforce rather than the accumulation of wealth. It is world of the intangible, of the unexpected, of what has been untimely, sorrowful, hopeful.
>
> Françoise Vergès[63]

A dearth of artifactual evidence presents a clear challenge to curators and artists representing a grievous history such as the Famine. The homes of those most affected by the Famine were typically mud cabins with thatched roofs, with the main focal point an open hearth. The 1841 Census described four types of houses: fourth-class houses were mud-walled and consisted of one room, while third-class houses were of similar construction but more cottage-like with two to four rooms and windows; a second-class house had five to nine rooms and windows, and was typically in a town or on a farm; while a first-class house had more than ten rooms and widows.[64] The fourth- and smaller third-class houses provided little space or their function little opportunity for material possessions, as the family, often along with a treasured farm animal, such as a pig or a cow, would all sleep at night on the floor to benefit from the heat from the fire. Island-wide, the fourth-class house constituted 37 per cent of all houses, and third-class houses 40.1 per cent, the density of the fourth-class housing along Ireland's western seaboard links the impoverished living conditions with concentrated population loss during the Famine.[65] Following displacement from their homes, some lived in *scalps* or *scalpeens*: inverted mud cabins where the very poor and destitute lived. Scalps were temporary dwellings burrowed into the ground and roofed with wood, mud and grass; scalpeens were even smaller than scalps.

Added to this paucity of material culture, those retrospectively representing the Famine through curatorial cultures of exhibition do so in a contemporary context of news spectatorship saturated with media accounts of dispossession, relating to conflict, displacement, famine and hunger. As outcomes of systemic conditions, such circumstances are often described as humanitarian 'crises'; terminology that actively undermines more longterm complexities of geopolitical realities, past, present and ongoing. Museums, heritage sites and temporary exhibitions have variously addressed related commemorative challenges. Chapter 3 looks at display tactics in the subject–object triangulation between objects of difficult heritage, curatorship and museum visitor. Chapter 4 focuses on temporary exhibitions that placed the Famine within their historical subject focus, outlining the potential of art to indicate grievous history.

A history of dispossession seems an anathema to museum and exhibition practices, with poverty defined in the first instance by an absence of material matter, negligible political presence and diminished personal empowerment, as Vergès elucidates. As exhibition practice trades in codes of visibility and voice, and so in many readings is reflective of the common adage that history is written by the powerful, or at least by those with access to material wealth, it is the spaces created by the deprivation of agency that pose curatorial challenges for its remembrance in museum and gallery formats. Further, historical representations involve, like any representation of others, a subject – object construction trading on codes of empathy, and even ethics, for the summation of affect. In many analyses of representations of grievous histories (such as death camps) rhetoric of lack and absence is evoked to relay writer experiences and to explain curatorial actions. Explored in terms of performative memory and theatricality, recurrent tensions arise in some of these accounts along a perceived fault-line between reality and representation. The past cannot be re-lived and so the experiences of others will remain outside of sentient knowledge. Reflections on curatorial devices to encourage visitor identification with now missing subjects of history have revealed complex zones of theatrical representation where fact and fiction seem continually enmeshed and are linked to ethical imperatives. Juliet Steyn suggests:

> The conventions of history, in which truth-value is based on empirically verifiable evidence gleaned from primary texts (objectivity), are always in friction with subjectivities that are already invested in both the writing and the receiving subject. It is the position of author and reader, of museum curator and visitor in relation to the past that is crucial, in that it provides the pivot of the ethical, demanding decision and judgement.[66]

Intercepting the breach between the past and present are interpretative concepts such as postmemory, vicarious past, secondary witnessing and prosthetic memory.[67] Hirsch outlines postmemory, through recourse to second-generation World War II survivors' invested viewing of photographs of those who directly experienced the machinations of that war's Holocaust. This creates what she terms 'the visual space of postmemory':

> [T]he relationship of children of survivors of cultural or collective trauma to the experiences of their parents, experiences that they 'remember' only as the stories and images with which they grew up, but that are so powerful, so monumental, as to constitute memories

in their own right. The term is meant to convey its temporal and qualitative difference from survivor memory, its secondary or second-generation memory quality, its basis in displacement, its belatedness. Postmemory is a powerful form of memory precisely because its connection to its object or source is mediated not through recollection but through projection, investment and creation.[68]

Ideas of postmemory offer a means of recall for events that were not directly experienced by the subject in contemporary life. James Young has described 'vicarious past': 'by calling attention to their vicarious relationship to events, the next generation ensures that their "postmemory" of events remains an unfinished, ephemeral process, not a means towards a definitive answer to impossible questions.'[69] For Young, the distinction between artists who emphasize their generational remove from direct experience of the past and those who witnessed the events highlights a need to recognize a two-tiered approach to history. He suggests that the past as it is perceived from tracks of testimony should coexist with its representation at a remove, making historical inquiry 'the combined study of both *what happened* and *how it is passed down* to us'.[70] Young's phrasing iterates the perception that the present day is subordinate to the past: the past is both behind and stands over today. This also implies that memorialization, as it is manifested in cultural forms, has a history, and links to what Campbell describes as 'recasting visual culture as visual economy',[71] where visual economy is the production, circulation and interpretation of images, which are part of an organization of people, ideas and objects.[72]

The belated witnessing of the past perpetuated through cultural forms and highlighted in exhibition practice is shaped by the curatorial contexts of collectivized representations. Jenny Kidd outlines a double witnessing for museum professionals: 'the role of "witness" involves daily embodiment and navigation of a complex internal paradox, a double witnessing necessitating navigation of individual identity on the one hand, and professional and institutional identity on the other'.[73] Inherent tensions to this witnessing are part of the visual economy, and in the imaging of the Irish Famine have been notably rehearsed through altering Anglo-Irish relations. For example, at some museums and heritage sites, representations of the Famine are contextualized in terms of collective national identity – tied up with a history of political rebellion – and local histories.

Both overlaps and contradictions between national and local identities at such sites have at times reflected debates on historical revisionism in Ireland. Emerging with force during the period of the Peace Process in Northern Ireland, the revisionist debate on Irish history, and within it the discussion of the Famine's political legacy, was not simply an esoteric academic or intellectual exercise. Tangible repercussions were felt for the official state attitude to commemorating the Famine in the mid-1990s. The records of Dáil Éireann (Ireland's House of Parliament) for October 1995 delineate animated debate between the Government and the Opposition. The individual contributions of a number of TDs (*Teachta Dála*, Gaelic for Elected Members) reflect the tone and substance of the fraught discussion on how best to commemorate the Famine.[74] In her role as chairperson of the National Famine Commemoration Committee, Avril Doyle (also minister of state at the Department of the Taoiseach (Prime Minister)) stated in the opening remarks of her address to the Dáil on the 150th Anniversary of the Famine:

> Between 1845 and 1850, the potato crop in Ireland was destroyed by blight. Out of a population of 8 million people, over one million died from the starvation and starvation related disease. A further one million emigrated under appalling conditions, with many dying in the coffin ships or soon after landing. This is fact, not fiction, and it is not open to historical revisionism.[75]

A bald statement, which drew in response from Michael McDowell on the Opposition bench the following:

> We are not entirely a Gaelic peasant society; we never were. There is a sense in which we like to airbrush out Anglo-Irishness or the mixture of Englishness and Irishness, and not view it as authentically Irish [...] I hope we do not hear that without the Famine Ireland would have been a huge country of 8 million people, could have participated in the industrial revolution and everything would have been different; only the cruelties and indifference of others frustrated us.[76]

Later, Noel Andrews, also of the Opposition, said, 'I agree [...] that we are not in the business of apportioning blame, but for goodness' sake let us not forget from where the problem emanated, which was, beginning and ending, with our then colonial masters. Let us make no mistake about it.'[77] Likewise, Opposition member Bertie Ahern (later Taoiseach, 1997–2008) described the Famine as representing 'the nadir of Anglo-Irish relations'.[78]

Joan Burton (minister of state at the Department of Foreign Affairs), in her answer to McDowell, indicted what was to be the Government's memorial focus in her comments: 'Famine and starvation are to a considerable extent the consequences of political decisions [. . .] The Irish Famine was a consequence of political decisions, in the same way recent and current famines are.'[79] In 1995, the Irish taxpayer's contribution to the Irish aid programme was higher than ever before at IEP 89 million. Andrews described Ireland's Overseas Development Assistance as 'a real and living memorial [to the Irish Famine]'.[80]

During the debate veiled references were made to the Peace Process in Northern Ireland as a possible cause for fuelling revisionist or 'sanitizing' (Andrews)[81] histories. Kinealy suggests, 'the revisionist domination meant that intellectual debate in Ireland was effectively constrained, and to take a counter-position was tantamount to declaring support for the national struggle.'[82] This was not a desirable political alignment to make during the delicate stages of a Peace Process between the Republic of Ireland and Britain in the run-up to the Good Friday Agreement of 1998.[83]

Within Northern Ireland, indeed, commemorations of the Famine through memorial forms and practices have been restrained relative to the Republic. As Mary Daly notes, the impact of the Famine varied throughout Ulster, with the story complicated by the collapse of the linen industry. Cavan, for example, had a higher rate of population loss than Galway, while north-east Ulster 'fared better'.[84] Successive historical experience and consequential tensions left the Famine rarely represented in permanent forms in Northern Ireland. One of the most notable exceptions to this is the *Famine Memorial* at Enniskillen, County Fermanagh, Northern Ireland, designed by Irish artist Eamonn O'Doherty.[85]

In the Dáil debate of late 1995, Burton made comparative reference to the remarkably silent period of the centenary to suggest, 'In a sense it is a tribute to our general well-being, that we now feel free to remember what we did not feel free to remember when we were doing less well economically.'[86] Her claim to commemoration as a signifier of cultural confidence was somewhat undermined by the Famine Commemoration Committee's general hesitancy over permanent visible memorial forms.

Also, underlying other aspects of the Dáil debate was the suggestion that Ireland, in the midst of economic prosperity, and as a 'Celtic Tiger',[87] might prefer to distance from its Third World past, even at the expense of fully engaging with an imperial history.

In March 1997, the committee reported on how it spent its budget.[88] Included was a the award of £115,000 to a major historical research project with University College Dublin and Trinity College Dublin which led to deep scholarship in the history of the Famine and many noteworthy publications. College scholarships and a schools essay competition were instigated to promote research and writing on the Famine. Two substantial Irish Famine ship memorials were financed by the Government: a sculpture by John Behan in County Mayo and the building of the replica *Jeanie Johnston* Famine ship. The Irish national broadcaster, RTE (Rádio Télifís Éireann), received £79,562.04 for documentary work. A number of Famine graveyards throughout Ireland each received £1,000 toward their renovation costs, and sums of £5,000 went to various local commemorations such as memorials, maps, exhibitions, village renovations and plays.[89]

Overseas Irish Famine commemorations in Liverpool received over £51,000, and in Australia/New Zealand £85,141.80. Food relief in Ethiopia received £50,030 and water relief in Lesotho received £15,030.

These figures suggest that at that time the Irish government was comfortable with commemorating the Famine via overseas aid programmes, as 'the living memorial', and promoting monumental memorials in countries with a strong Irish diasporic presence, while at home emphasis was more keenly placed upon historical and documentary projects of remembrance rather than upon permanent, public or repetitious forms of commemorative visual culture. It wasn't until 2008 that the National Famine Commemoration Committee was established by the Irish government to formally inaugurate an annual national Famine memorial day.[90] Thus, in answer to the predicament of how to materially commemorate the Irish Famine amid revisionist outlooks in the mid-1990s, ideas of similarity were accentuated across historical and geographical boundaries, reflective of post-colonial concerns with international affiliations.

Appropriating the history of the Famine into universal paradigms of suffering was similarly sustained by other groups, such as nongovernmental organizations (NGOs), in their commemorative projects. Gray notes, specifically in relation to the rhetoric of some NGOs' references to the Irish Famine as raising consciousness of global injustice and poverty, that

> globalising rhetoric leaves little room for examination of the historical specificities of the Irish case – perhaps legitimate in the polemical enthusiasm of humanitarian campaigning, but problematic with respect to a memorialization process in which making justifiable truth-claims about the past is seen as essential,

and that this 'construction of the memory of the famine has become a potent political weapon in Irish political culture – a discursive construction with a grammar only partially cognate with that of academic history'.[91]

Roy Foster commented in 2001 on the 'dangers of historical interpretation that tend towards self-congratulation, tub-thumping or professional victimhood, all of which unwelcome characteristics have surfaced in aspects of recent commemoration fever'.[92] Foster's discussions on what he termed a 'commemorative binge' in the latter part of the 1990s in Ireland draw attention to the alacrity with which the sesquicentennial commemorations of the Famine made way for the bicentennial markings of the 1798 Rebellion.[93] Cormac Ó Gráda remarked that official Government-sponsored commemorations held in 1995 'jumped the gun' as there was no famine in 1845 since 'many did not perish until autumn 1846'.[94]

Luke Gibbons suggested that previous to the 150-year commemoration, 'failure of the government to commemorate the Famine need not be put down to bad faith, but may have been due to the fact that the memory was still too close to the bone.'[95] He makes a case for considering the Famine in terms of Judith Shklar's notion of 'passive injustice', which she defines as a mass suffering with low visibility (a lack of stated author to the catastrophe) and sponsored by tacit complicity. Gibbons infers, 'one of the consequences of the low visibility of passive injustice, the facility with which it eludes the nets of criticism or accountability, is that sense of outrage remains unrequited, and the voices of victims are simply not heard.'[96] On a national education level, Kinealy described reluctance, up to this point, to engage directly with the historical impact of the Famine on a national educational level as indicative of the influence of revisionist debate and events in Northern Ireland.[97]

Thus, by the 1990s, a generalized wariness of iterating historical understanding of a grievous history by way of consolidated memorial practice was reflected in tentative attitudes toward visual culture modalities of commemorative practice; and other than RTE, national cultural institutions appear to have been largely reticent in their approach to commemorating the Famine in any in-depth or sustained manner. In the context of this as well as earlier national cultural climates, Chapters 3 and 4 consider the ways in which grievous history gives rise to difficult heritage underpinned by the strategies of a number of exhibitions on the Famine.

Chapter 3 focuses on artefacts and locations that assume a power of witness as a means to reading the story of the absent subjects or the others of history. Chapter 4 explores the potential of artworks, publicly exhibited as after-images, to act as triggers for empathic comprehension of experiences of those who have gone before. Across these permanent, longterm and temporary exhibition practices emerge interdependent formulations indicative of collective identity and calls for individual empathy in representations, as Vergès listed, 'of the intangible, of the unexpected, of what has been untimely, sorrowful, hopeful'.

Landscapes of Mourning and Dark Tourism

Irish artist Alanna O'Kelly described the Famine as 'a very dark place'.[98] Her stated interest in the Famine as a subject for her art practice was informed by the reluctance she had experienced as a child among those around her to discuss it. Growing up in County Wexford, she noted fields were left fallow and though no one in the community spoke of why, it was thought they held Famine dead.[99] Reckoning grievous history as a dark place, as a psychological locus from where past events are interpreted and present-day identities negotiated, is not uncommon.

Karen Wells describes a process of 'melancholic memorialization' that follows on initial negotiations of personal tragedy such as the timely or unexpected death of a loved one in 'process of ordering and containment through visualizing and materializing practices'.[100] Though this period in turn gives way to the construction of permanent memorial forms that 'close down political space opened by tragedy and melancholia', Wells suggests '[t]his final testimonial to loss may be resignified by events, intervention and practices that return loss once again to melancholic memorialization and reanimate its political potential'.[101] While the term 'tragedy' is problematic when applied to largescale systemic suffering as in that context it can imply a lack of specific culpability, the framework of Well's melancholic memorialization of loss has resonance for sites of Famine memory. Chapters 5 and 6 consider the various means by which a range of historical sites and locations of mass burial associated with this dark place in Irish history are constituted as melancholic memorialization: landscapes of mourning across Ireland and beyond.

Thomas Laqueur writes, 'precisely because [landscape] is so resolutely atemporal, so resistant to closure, so open to all manner of reverie, it stands in such sharp contrast to history. Space is the ground for remembering – against time.'[102] He cautions against too easily advocating memory's alignment with space over a comprehension of history as integrated with the passing of time: 'Memory is a means of making the loss survivable but it is also therefore a means of allowing the past to have closure.' Accordingly, it might be useful to 'concentrate on the task of representing temporal contingencies rather than spatial absolutes'.[103] Engagement with commemorative sites, much like public mourning, is complexly inter-defined by temporal and spatial experiences (as in 'past presencing') and connectively, individually felt and collectively declarative.

Judith Butler's suggestion that interdependence of a self and an other pervades all aspects of life, from unknown others to ones close by, gives rise to a consideration of whose lives become grievable and, relatedly, whose suffering is 'speakable'.[104] The cultural aftershocks of 9/11, in her example, undermined assumptions of security attendant on notions of the First World, highlighting 'geographical vulnerability'.[105] She suggests that in a panicked response, public mourning for particular lives lost can declare the process of obituary as an act of, often exclusionary, nation-building,[106] at the expense of deeming other lives relatively non-grievable, even connoting them as unreal or somehow less human. The potential of representing suffering, and by implication death, is core to what Butler terms 'reciprocal exchange' that constitutes the global sphere of community. 'To ask for recognition, or offer it, [...] is to solicit a becoming, to instigate a transformation, to petition the future always in relation to the Other. It is to stake one's own being, and one's own persistence in one's own being, in the struggle for recognition.'[107]

Such fluidity in subject positions underlines the ethical responsibility associated with all forms of representation, including retrospective views of past others formulated through spatial cultures associated with grievous history. Into the quiet spaces of previous unmarked sites of remembrance across Ireland and further afield came community-driven acts of commemoration. These have taken the forms of cemetery restoration, demarcation of mass burial sites, trails and maintained relief works structures and commemorative walks.

When also enacted as tourist destinations, visits to these sites are implicated in wider developments in tourism, specifically predicated upon a politics of mourning and realized through physical engagement with locations and concepts of destination. With reference to the writings of R. J. Johnston, Greg Ringer cites destination as 'both a psychological state of arrival and a process of spatial movement [...] around which individuals construct and reconstruct ways of life that express "who they are and what is expected of them"', as well as a 'culturally-defined geography of places'.[108]

As both a response to and a practice of modern life, tourism is an expression of a desire to be elsewhere; to move outside where one usually lives, with historical associations between enrichment and pilgrimage.[109] This ties tourism to a dual purpose of discovering more about one's own cultural or community lineage and also of seeing how others live. As Ringer underlines, 'destination [can] be understood [...] as a phenomenon of personal experience'.[110] Further, as a consequence of modernity's urban pressures, the association of places of natural beauty with personal satisfaction has remained linked to many different types of touristic inclinations.[111]

Tourism then is a layered occupation, driven by a range of incentives that alter according to social circumstance, age, economic capacity and cultural and nature-related interests and one which has sustained impact on local or host communities. Mimi Sheller and John Urry describe sites of tourism ('places to play') as 'places in play' that 'involve performances by various kinds of "hosts", and especially by "guests"'. Organized by 'complex systems of diverse intersecting mobilities [...] [t]hese systems involve networks of "hosts – guests – time – space – cultures" that stabilize certain places as "places to play", but only contingently'.[112] This changeability implies that place (any place) is also a potential situation of variable tourism. Ringer warns that 'to conceive of the cultural destination as a stylized vignette of local history, rooted in time and space, and lacking the dynamic conditions necessary for change, is to render mute the actions, motivations and values of local participants in the ongoing social construction of their place'.[113]

Mediations between global and local contexts are realized in interchanges between tourists and residents on two levels. Firstly, as Thomas Blom points out, the global involves mediation of place, often prior to visitors actually visiting a site.[114] Emma Willis describes the twentieth century as the 'century of the tourist: economic and technical changes opened the world up for viewing'.[115] John Lennon and Malcolm Foley allude to perceptions of death (as a tourism interest or subject) as a commodity for consumption in a global communications market,[116] as well as emphasizing the extent to which mass media shapes perceptions of particular sites as emblematic of key historic events.[117]

Secondly, and as a consequence of the first, affiliations across various formations of identity are forged that Lennon and Foley outline define the commodification of anxiety and doubt about modernity and its consequences as a particular tenet of 'dark tourism', for example.[118] This, they argue, is evident in both interpretations at and design of sites, such as mass death camps and places where famous people died, which produce or reflect on uncertainty, fear and social failures or vulnerabilities.

To stratify such experiences, Philip Stone employs the notion of shades of darkness to distinguish between various so-called dark sites. The darkest type refers to 'Sites of Death and Suffering,' while at the lighter end of the chart are 'Sites Associated with Suffering and Death'. The darker group is, among other descriptors, endowed with 'higher political influence and ideology' and 'have an education orientation and location authenticity', and the lighter extremity has 'lower political influence and ideology, entertainment orientation and non-location authenticity'.[119] Evoking the concept of 'authenticity' as a qualifying characteristic, Stone suggests the closer to death the site and the less commercialized or enjoyable the visit, the darker it is. This is elaborated by Peter Hohenhaus's references to 'place authenticity' in memorials to the Rwandan Genocide. He notes the most accessible rural memorial site (at Gisozi) as the least graphic and relatively less 'raw' than comparable sites that are less commercialized.[120] Further, the urban Kigali Memorial Centre is 'geared towards foreign tourist visitation' and 'its "consumption" is the least demanding with regard to "temporal place identity"'.[121] By Stone's assessment, representations form the 'lighter' side when posited against 'darker' sites, typically tied to visible evidence and historical certainty, or so-called place authenticity.

This gap between reality (darkness) and representation (light) is complicated when some level of mediation is recognized at all sites of memory, once they are acknowledged as such. Leanne White and Elspeth Frew emphasize the significance of both personal reflection on location and collective identity formation in the process of visitor engagement with such sites: 'the respectful interpretation of [...] dark tourism sites may assist in creating a place where visitors can pay their respects to those who have died, and better understand past events within the context of the site and indeed the nation'.[122] Across the landscape of Ireland, numerous unmarked burial sites and unmapped relief works are represented off-site, through photographic and art processes, while others are lightly mediated at location or signposted, literally, or by way of reference in related local heritage sites. Some places have been overtly and strongly defined by representational practices, and include formal cemeteries, mapped heritage trails and ritualized commemorative events at clearly designated locations.

Allusions to the constructed (and thereby inhabited) emptiness of landscape and the historical absences suggested by human presence form the focus of the final two chapters of this book. Across a range of Famine heritage sites specifically associated with burial, the history of relief works and the development of heritage trails, tourism tropes of expectation and surprise are generated through various geographical, material and visual signs and augmented by symbolic gestures such as time spent in these places. Acts of walking, following trials and discovering apparent interruptions in the landscape delineate a territory – in space and time – mapped by a grievous history.

1

Figuration and the Site of Famine

The Place of Pain: Vulnerable Bodies and a Portrayal of Starvation

> In a short time the face and limbs become frightfully emaciated; the eyes acquire a most peculiar stare; the skin exhaled a peculiar and offensive foetor, and was covered with a brownish filthy-looking coating, almost as indelible as varnish. This I was at first inclined to regard as encrusted filth, but further experience has convinced me that this is a secretion poured out from the exhalants on the surface of the body.
>
> Dr Daniel Donovan, Skibbereen, 1848, article for Dublin Medical Press[1]

Bodies suffering starvation degenerate from the effects of hunger following internal malfunction and even disintegration, the signs of which eventually become externally identifiable. Margaret Crawford details the visible symptoms of hunger and diseases among children, such as marasmus and kwashiorkor arising out of nutritional deprivation.[2] Some outwardly obvious symptoms of these are, respectively, shrunken frames with premature marked ageing, and oedema in the stomach and lower limbs. Both illnesses in advanced stages give rise to browned pigmentation of the skin and the appearance of downy facial (lanugo) hair. At the Johnstown Famine exhibition room in a wall panel titled 'Disease Epidemics' oedema is described as follows: 'swelling of the limbs until the body finally bursts'. The connection between starvation and vitamin deficiencies is in evidence.[3] By extension, the susceptibility of famine victims to fever epidemics as well as more ordinarily avoidable conditions increases, such as scurvy, described at Johnstown as: 'Also called "Black Leg", caused joints to become enlarged, teeth to fall out and the blood vessels under the skin to burst. *(Lack of Vitamin C)'*. Laurence Geary notes that so-called 'famine fever' had several names, but included typhus fever and relapsing fever, noting that 'subsistence crises and famine create the ideal environment for the generation and dissemination of fevers and other infectious diseases'.[4] Though the Fever Bill of April 1847 was aimed at reducing spread of epidemics by promoting burial of bodies and related hygiene practices,[5] by this time, an over-dependence on a limited pattern of food consumption prior to the Irish Famine in the 1840s had in part predetermined the starkness of the effects of bodily deficiencies from its outset.[6]

In Famine folk history there are witness accounts of desperate actions arising out of starvation, such as the frantic searches for food cited in Cathal Póirtéir's collection of accounts gathered by the National Folklore Collection (NFC, initially known as the Irish Folklore Commission, 1934–71), housed at University College Dublin.[7] The archive's 'oral narratives', to use Niall Ó Ciosáin's term,[8] are the memories of mostly elderly informants who had a vicarious sense of this history, given their generational closeness to the events of the 1840s. Mícheál Briody writes that by the mid-1940s the commission 'had as a result of its extensive collecting, undertaken on an unprecedented scale, amassed a very large archive of folk tradition, reputedly one of the largest in the world'.[9] Kevin Danaher instigated the format of the questionnaire used for many of the informant interviews in the archive.[10] In an evaluation of the relation of folk memory to historical understanding, Cormac Ó Gráda argues that such 'evidence, despite and sometimes because of, its biases and silences, has something distinctive to contribute to our understanding of the Great Irish Famine'.[11] Of the NFC specifically, he suggests, 'At its best, the record is vivid, eloquent and compelling.'[12] Guy Beiner writes that the 'primary value of folklore sources is not only what they can offer for a study of historical events but rather the interpretative insight they allow into how people throughout Ireland subsequently recalled their past',[13] and notes that 'such vernacular historical engagements' do not simply 'complement existing historiography' but are 'inherently polyphonic'.[14]

Quoted in Póirtéir is Dáithí Ó Ceanntabhail, national teacher, Croom, County Limerick, who heard of 'by the wayside, emaciated corpses, partly green from eating docks and nettles and partly blue from the cholera and dysentery'.[15] The hope of finding sustenance was in many instances, such as these, defeated by undernourished and physically weakened bodies. The antisocial, or even dehumanizing, effects of hunger are also indicated in the NFC's collection. Crawford describes this as a total breakdown of family ties and discusses Dr Donovan's Famine-time accounts of mothers snatching food from the hands of their children and a son and father engaging in a fatal struggle over a potato.[16]

As the effects of severe hunger are highly visible on a starving body, and internally impacting on physical and psychological health, resulting in enormous changes in social behaviour, how have representations of the place of pain, the famished body – its appearance, actions and context – been developed during and since the nineteenth century? To explore this, it is helpful to look first to a twenty-first-century imaging of hunger through the medium of film: *Hunger* (2008, 96 mins), by British artist and film-maker Steve McQueen. While the film is not about famine, the depiction in it of a hungry body reflects and trades on representational strategies apparent since nineteenth-century work on the Famine: the primary response of horror, the stirring of empathy and linkage of geo-specific cases with universalized concepts of the suffering body. The film does so through innovative medium-driven techniques, but as film is usually also cinematic, its locating of hunger as spectacle links it to a wider politics of perception. Any circulation of images, including filmic, constitutes spectatorship, or social viewing, as part of a visual economy which relates representations of a specific suffering subject to the making sense of a hungry body.

In the final sequence of *Hunger*, 27-year-old Irish Republican prisoner Bobby Sands dies after 66 days of hunger strike in the Maze/Long Kesh prison near Belfast in Northern Ireland on 5 May 1981.[17] Scenes of a remembered rural landscape of Sands's boyhood as alluded to earlier in the film are interspersed with abstracted sonic and visual representations of his agonizing death. Viewers catch glimpses of lively breathless boys running in verdant countryside as Sands's adult body degenerates in a blindingly bright white clinically sanitized atmosphere. The death of Sands was a watershed moment at a very violent point in the history of the Troubles in Northern Ireland.[18] He was the first of nine hunger strikers to die at that time, and his subsequent iconic status in nationalist ideology is echoed across murals, flags, art, ephemera and clothing. He was elected an MP in April 1980 and reportedly 100,000 people attended his funeral the following month.[19]

The film's 'three-act structure'[20] denotes the firstly incarcerated and then wilfully starved body 'as site of political warfare'.[21] Punctuated silences and abstracted noise in the latter parts of the film accentuate the affective nature of the vivid visual portrayals of prison brutality, a series of protests undertaken by Republican prisoners and, finally, of the terrible failings of Sands's body in the drawn-out painful death throes of starvation. McQueen's intense representational style, including abrupt structural turns, situates his visceral depiction of the hungry body in the contested space between mainstream narrative cinema, documentary style and art film which is, arguably, a reflection on the gap between events and their mediation. Barbara Pollack notes that McQueen 'blurs the distinction between documentary and art film'. The final filmic moments seem to defy the very gap between representation and realism: '[i]t is as if the very act of dying were transpiring in real time before the camera'.[22]

Hunger stretches the medium of film in lieu of conventional cinematic narrative disclosure. In the film's claustrophobic prison world, there are unflinching passages of violence, ritualized degradation, utilization of orifices for covert communications amid surprising moments of empathy alternately with prisoners and prison guards. In the absence of ambient music to guide emotions, disconcerting viewpoints, lingering close-ups, sonic fluxes and impressionistic imagery of spaces and bodies give rise to uncomfortable viewing.[23]

The only context provided of the political circumstances is presented in background radio clips of Margaret Thatcher's unmistakable voice. The main departure from McQueen's then stated resistance to language in film is the prolonged dialogue of the 'middle act' scripted by Irish playwright Enda Walsh.[24] Sands and a visiting priest debate the ethics of wilful self-dematerialization resulting in suicide.[25] The 22-minute sequence is centred on Sands' prophetic philosophy of martyrdom.[26]

Figuration and the Site of Famine

John Lynch writes that McQueen 'operates on the ground between what we can define as meaning and sense, where meaning is what is shared in a communication, but sense has to do with the grounds of intelligibility as such'.[27] These grounds are first roughed up by the film-maker's reluctance to provide explication through language or adherence to narrative norms in order to focus on the production of affect with unexpected and often uneasy sensory effects. While this clearly displaces the work from a historical theme or a portrait of, to appropriate Lynch's term, a 'militant subjectivity', it emphasizes a wider politics of spectatorship. This occurs both in its maker's stated imperative and the sense its viewing public makes of it.

International print media interest in and televisual spectatorship of the Northern Ireland conflict was at its height in the 1980s, with the conflict then at its bloodiest.[28] McQueen recalls having watched, as an eleven-year-old boy, the news coverage of the hunger strikes and Sands in particular and cites this as a compelling inspiration for making the work. The film's title denies a specific political narrative in favour of a more universal, even humanist, consideration of the hungry body, as does reduction of the ethics of a complex political situation to a bare conversation between two men. Described as 'humanist' rather than political in approach,[29] McQueen's film has been linked in its subject matter to Abu Ghraib and Guantánamo, which were much in the news at the time of the film's early circulation.[30] The film's association with generalized incarceration and struggles over the body as a site of political freedom accentuates its meaning as decidedly shaped by an unavoidable politics of perception.

With the body in pain constituting the grounding force of *Hunger*, the work discloses how representations of suffering bodies are contingent on the historical, social and political circumstances of the circulation, as much as on the making, of their image. While Elaine Scarry and Susan Sontag raise useful complexities attendant on thinking through the impact of images of hungry bodies discussed in the Introduction, and in particular implications of ubiquitous representations for so-called 'compassion fatigue', *Hunger* seems to answer that concern by questioning the very efficacy of spectacles of suffering. The framing lack of language in *Hunger* may relate to Scarry's observation that pain is the point where language breaks down and so is inadequate to the task of description.[31] However, it is the overall prioritizing of experimental filmic possibilities that nonetheless forms a cause-and-effect narrative – situation, decision-making and death – and, most importantly, highlights the contingency of spectatorship. Perceptions are then at once located and temporally contingent, connecting the secondary witnessing of the image-maker to the social process of making sense of the scenes presented.

Comparable to this reading of *Hunger*, concepts of secondary witnessing, audience awareness and cultural and geographical relativisms have shaped representational strategies deployed in imaging the hungry body in the commemorative visual culture of the Famine. A selection of figurations of the Famine produced across the nineteenth and twentieth centuries demonstrate how some aspects have endured for more than a century-and-a-half, alongside significant changes in strategies of depiction. Art and illustrations from the mid- to late-nineteenth century were not only geographically but also politically and socially contingent, utilizing a range of artistic styles and tropes of stereotype, universalism and cultural relativity. The altering iconographies and perceptions of the hungry body in subsequent artistic and monumental practices include altered emphases attendant on political and artistic developments during the course of Ireland's transition from a colonial to a post-colonial culture, with more recent aspects of body cultures reflecting on concerns of an increasingly somatic society.

From the mid-twentieth century onwards, figures of emaciated men, skeletal women and dead children appear in public Famine memorials.[32] Why then in the art and illustration of the nineteenth century are emotively portrayed starved figurations seemingly infrequent? Though many Famine-era artists and illustrators obeyed artistic, visual and journalistic conventions, they also developed subtle strategies designed to appeal subversively to their viewers. Furthermore, the depth of the symbiotic relationship between news illustrations and text of accompanying articles suggests the more powerfully inscribed images were in fact illuminated by accompanying text inscriptions and articles. With comparatively less useful critique or expository information available than on a twenty-first-century visualization, such as *Hunger*, the historic works nevertheless reflect on various correlative politics of geographically rooted perceptions at a time of charged colonialism.

Locating Representations of Irish Poverty: History Painting and Illustration in the Nineteenth Century

Reading nineteenth-century figurations of Famine is a discussion on points of view, where perception of location is a dominant signifying factor.

Stuart McLean indicates how the poorest (and largest) section of Irish society could, within a climate of racial tension, be seen as 'wild';[33] somehow existing outside of modern society in a location of primitive beauty. His comment elucidates the popular reach of a moralizing romanticism operating in conjunction with modernity's appellation of otherness. Ireland's lack of modernization in terms of the religiousness of its society and the general state of its agriculture and industry was perceptually associated with racial characterizations by observers mostly from outside of the island. Ireland's high population was construed as additional evidence of an innate racial laziness and primitive lack of sexual or at least procreative inhibition.[34]

A set of social conditions and sectarian alignments was in oppressive motion from the seventeenth century onwards, significantly endorsed by the Penal Laws at the end of that century, aimed at the suppression of Catholicism in Ireland,[35] and further accentuated by the tensions resulting from a bloody and defeated insurgency in 1798.

By the nineteenth century, these perspectives became vehicles for colonialist fears expressed through a variety of racial stereotypes under the guise of a wondering about a lack of so-called modernity in Ireland. The British government's failure to recognize, as David Valone explores, that it was the economic condition of Ireland that shaped its people's perceived identity and work ethic (not the other way around) meant that Britain 'had long imagined the Irish as a people of the verge of a cataclysm',[36] and so, reacted inadequately as disaster unfolded.

In exploring the effect of various forms of Anglicization on the Irish, notably the suppression of the Gaelic language, L. Perry Curtis suggests that over time this imperial attitude 'hardened into a form of racial prejudice',[37] as evidenced in popular cartoon images in news media circulated across Britain from the mid-nineteenth century onwards. Writing on Famine-era eviction rates, Curtis suggests: 'Sooner or later this popular image of witless and feckless Paddy was bound to affect British attitudes towards the use of public funds to relieve the victims of famine across the Irish Sea.'[38] Mahoney notes that the pre-Famine rise in pauperism was 'attributed to the indolence and primitiveness of the people themselves rather than to the accelerated modernization of agricultural improvement and industrialization in Britain'.[39] In his analysis of photographic images of 'Irishness' of the latter part of the century, Justin Carville draws on the wider visual paradigm of illustration to note a particularly insidious development:

> Such imagery established a visual code and grammar of the Irish face through utilization of not only popular conceptions of race and cultural behavior, but also theories drawn from the social and human sciences to render their illustrations immediately legible and familiar to the Victorian public.[40]

These observations shed light on an aspect of image-making which functioned in the face of such negatively inscribed political perceptions of Irish identity. Some nineteenth-century painters and illustrators promoted Ireland as a place to be viewed sympathetically by trading in differing concepts of the location of suffering. Some depicted and named specific locations where suffering occurred, while others pursued highly aestheticized concepts of allegory. How likely were the mainly British viewers of the art market and readers of news weeklies to engage with depictions of rural Ireland, given wider political and cultural perceptions of Irishness? Furthermore, to what extent might wider artistic interests and personal career motivations have influenced these choices? This section explores the ways in which some artists and illustrators reached out to their audiences on what would have been an unpopular and uncomfortably close subject for a contemporary audience. These works indicate a web of artistic and spectator perspectives involved in making social sense of suffering: a layered politics of perception.

In Irish artist Daniel Macdonald's painting *The Discovery of the Potato Blight in Ireland*, 1847, a group of nine figures and a dog are staged around a focal point of rotting potatoes in an unspecified rural area[41] (Figure 1.1). In varying states of distress, the group consists of three generations of an extended family. At a Christie's auction in London in 1966 the novelist Cecil Woodham-Smith purchased the painting and donated it to the NFC at University College Dublin.[42] The work's title suggests the visualization of a moment of great significance portrayed through a genre subject. While this reflects Macdonald's ambitions as a young artist in London, to paint and exhibit an image of contemporary Irish poverty was potentially a personal economic risk and open to interpretation as a political gesture.[43] Niamh O'Sullivan notes that when it was exhibited at the British Institution in 1847, among 561 works, it received only one comment in the Art Union.[44]

Figure 1.1   *The Discovery of the Potato Blight in Ireland,* 1847, Daniel Macdonald. Oil on canvas, 84 x 104 cm. © National Folklore Commission, University College Dublin.

Macdonald's attention to the traditional dress of the impoverished class implies a genre interest dominating the work. The white one-piece linen shirt worn by the man is typical of Ireland's cottier class, and the woman's red skirt and cape are traditional in style and colour.[45] At the same time, the white-shirted male figure has Romantic connotations: a tragic focal point echoing Francisco Goya's figure in *3rd of May, 1808/14*. Macdonald has painted him in both shoes and socks, which were usually worn only on a Sunday,[46] and in so doing, along with his rendering of the torn trouser leg, creates positive signifiers of poverty, irrespective of historical probability. Similarly, the crouched weeping woman dressed in bright colours seems unusually well groomed, with yellow trimming on her white upper garment, a striking turquoise blue. The clothes are in keeping with a trend among the poorer classes to buy second-hand items in town outlets,[47] which may too explain the tattered grandeur of the clothing on the child standing to the left. Arguably, the fashionable empire hairstyle may also render the figure familiar to contemporary viewers. These elements suggest Macdonald had some awareness of European art. The girl, as Tom Dunne notes, might have walked out of a Thomas Gainsborough painting.[48] The weeping woman is reminiscent of Jacques Louis David's mourning women in *The Oath of the Horatii*, 1784.[49] She adds pathos to the scene for, like David's women, she mourns what is yet to come on foot of the devastating discovery.

O'Sullivan accounts Macdonald's lack of professional training as 'unfettering his considerable originality' and notes his 'unusual acuity for his age and times' in his 'study of Irish folklore, county life and customs'.[50] And this lack of convention may have contributed to his bravery in mixing pictorial languages and references in this work, in light of his broader subject interest in observing Irish folk life and customs.

That the discovery of the blight marked an abrupt disruption to a way of life, and the beginning of uncertainty, familial disintegration and uprootedness is suggested by Macdonald in Romantic stylistic strategies. In literature and art, romanticism draws on picturesque formats, ideas of which pre-date the nineteenth century. Donald Crawford outlines the picturesque as a point of view derived in reaction to, and against, the formalism of classical conceptions of beauty.[51] Identifiable by its concern with ruin in all its forms, picturesque art forms usually focus on examples of outdoor disintegration, asymmetry and implied notions of the passage of time. Figurations of people typically show beggars or raggedly dressed rural workers. Playing upon such tropes, Macdonald placed his figures in a triangulation echoing the rugged mountainous formations of parts of rural Ireland, thus implicating the land in the destiny of these people.

The theatrical depiction of landscape and climate, implying narrative indicators alluding to past, present and future, is typical of the era.[52] The background is an idyllic scene of calm pale blues and purples, contrasting with the dark foreground as a cloudy storm-front approaches. Macdonald's positioning of his figures thus highlights a judicious concern with landscape and climate. In her study on creation as the 'very projection of aliveness', Scarry proposes fallacy as 'animism' comparable to that in 'old mythologies or religions'.[53] Macdonald rendered the climate to provide a visible instance of animism of the protagonists' suffering: he 'employed the sentimental clichés of English narrative painting to elicit the sympathy of his London audience for the victims, using the magnificent scenery to accentuate the pathos of the peasant family's plight'.[54]

Points of view are the life-force of the picturesque, one such being a rendering of nature typically created by someone passing through, or looking in. Rural Ireland as a site of the picturesque is not simply non-urban but also an other to an imperial (British) centre. While Macdonald illustrates his familiarity with the landscape of southern Ireland where he grew up and began his artistic life, *The Discovery of the Potato Blight in Ireland* reflects his status as both insider and outsider to the scene he paints. This seems symbolically evident in the rendering of the two faceless weeping women, who function as a recuperation of tragedy. Neither of these women can look directly at the rotting potato pile, which is a harbinger of their suffering to come. Further to this, by not showing the viewer the women's faces, Macdonald resists a claim on visualizing the suffering other that he, as an artist, and his viewers are in a position to gaze on.

The Irish Famine (also known as *An Irish Eviction*), 1849–50, by British artist George Frederic Watts also focuses on an out of doors extended family figuration (Figure 1.2). Watts's landscape and figuration, however, contrast profoundly with those imaged in *The Discovery of the Potato Blight*. Facial expressions, bodily gestures, a bleak terrain and bare grey stones converge to produce an affective portrait of destitution with a claim on universal suffering. Like Macdonald, Watts has emphasized the younger man as the most visually arresting figure – at this time typically an Irish family's provider.[55] His gaze challenges the viewer, while to his side a woman and baby make a pieta-like composition. Her demeanour suggests a lack of hope, reinforced by the weeping bowed head of the elderly figure behind them.

Watts travelled a good deal during his lifetime but did not visit Ireland until 1850.[56] Though friendly with the Pre-Raphaelites, he was renowned for his portraiture and allegorical works, which were both less decorative and poetic than many Pre-Raphaelite works. He is best regarded perhaps, as Simon Poe suggests, as more of a 'symbolist' than an 'aesthete', within the Aesthetic Movement of the late nineteenth century.[57] Emaciated forms of skeletal Irish peasants, with browned downy skin, and dying children doubled over in agony of illness would not likely appeal to his audience. Instead, Watts's choice to present this Irish family as potentially familiar to a British audience was achieved by linking his composition to artistic

Figure 1.2   *The Irish Famine*, *c.*1848/50, George Frederic Watts. Oil on canvas, 180.3 x 198.1 cm. © Watts Gallery Trust.

formulations of earlier and contemporary artists. Claiming both familiarity and universalism in the depicted plight might well elicit sympathetic identification from viewers.

Watts deploys a biblical allegory, and the figuration has echoes of migrating Holy Family images by John Valentine Haidt (*Rest on the Flight into Egypt*, 1754–74) and Rembrandt van Rijn (*Rest on the Flight into Egypt*, 1647), for example. This reflects his interest in the harmony of pictorial composition 'absorbing all parts into a systematic unity of forms',[58] derived from Watts's close study of so-called Old Master conventions. It also bears comparison to works on similar themes by his contemporaries such as Erskine Nicol and Robert Kelly.

In contrast to textual accounts of dispossessed families, Watts's visualization is not a visceral one: the figures seem well-fed and their clothing, though accurate to the time, is rendered in good condition. While this suggests a painterly interest in textiles winning over documentary description, and presumably reflects on Watts's lack of firsthand witnessing of Famine conditions, his figuration may represent more than squeamish avoidance of tough subject matter. The range of Watts's writings and oeuvre reveal an interest in expanding history painting outside of the received idioms through his preferred symbolic language: 'The poetic fact may be put together by careful observance of the beautiful elements, the ideal rendering may be less true as to the [ordinary] facts, but more true to the mental impression, and this will be the greater thing.'[59]

In *The Irish Famine* Watts's social consciousness in approaching his theme and his concern for beauty were demonstrated in his mixture of portraiture and allegory, which he subsequently pursued as segregated pictorial forms, as argued by Lewis Johnson. Portraits, Watts was later to declare, should be monumental but devoid of actual action.[60] By contrast, in works that 'suggest ideas belonging to the human conditions', or allegory, and in which he used human forms, Watts stated, 'I have purposefully abstained from any attempt to make the figures seem real, [...] feeling the necessity of the atmosphere of remoteness, and knowing that familiarity produces a sense of the commonplace.'[61] His desire to portray a universal theme of sufferance suggests an aesthetically inscribed heroic victim narrative. Though the figures in *The Irish Famine* would have been recognizable as ordinary people, the overall beatified depiction distances the scene from the viewer in its evocation of a mythic timelessness associated with allegorical compositions.

This is accentuated by the no-place of the figuration's location. While in *The Discovery of the Potato Blight* Macdonald utilizes picturesque tropes of a clearly Irish landscape, Watts constructs a starkly symbolic fictional landscape. Unlike any Irish terrain, this is a poetically construed barren desert-like plain. Watts's out-of-place figuration is devolved from the circumstance of homelessness foisted upon his protagonists in the first place, as the dual title of the work emphasizes.

Lack of contextual specificity in Watts's painting allies it to universal tales of dispossession, which can either open up reception of the representation to a wide audience or enter the image into an ideologically contentious terrain of de-specifying suffering. Representational time-lessness can contribute to a lack of concern about the specific nature of the

Famine: its causes, effects and legacies lost in a treacherous aestheticization of suffering that might reductively imply all instances of dispossession are the same. More convincingly, Watts's no-place positions the likely forced migration of this family into a state of unbelonging – between universal and historic experiences – lending his figuration of Famine an allegorical function. Balancing the familiarity of the look of the figures with a universalized paradigm of dispossession suggests a gravity to Watt's pictorial endeavour.

Watts's initial knowledge of the Famine would likely have been shaped by contemporary newspaper accounts and in illustrated reports, such as printed in the *Illustrated London News* (*ILN*). A number of traits in line with the artistic trends outlined above were apparent in two series in particular. These images have been widely reproduced since, with some defined by attention to local detail and others dominated by implications of universalism. The first series was produced in February 1847 by Cork-born artist James Mahony (*c*.1810–*c*.1859) in a report on the effects of the Famine in West Cork in the south of Ireland.[62] The second was a weekly series of editorial reports called 'Condition of Ireland: Illustrations of the New Poor-Law' from December 1849 to February 1850 and focused on County Clare in the west of Ireland.[63]

Mahony's articles included 12 illustrations, predominantly place-specific in title. One was an image of a tiny funeral procession called *Funeral at Shepperton Lake*, and another, *Mullins' hut at Schull*, pictured a local vicar, Dr Robert Traill, visiting the sick and dying Mullins family. Mahony described the area around the small town of Skibbereen:

> [N]either pen nor pencil could ever portray the misery and horrors [. . .] there I saw the dying, the living and the dead, lying indiscriminately upon the same floor, without anything between them and the cold earth, save a few miserable rags upon them.[64]

O'Sullivan critiques Mahony's struggle to represent his experiences of the Famine, noting his repeated use of tropes such as the turned back of his subjects and the closed doors and citing 'his eloquence lay in his restraint'.[65] Obliquely, through his emphasis on naming people and townlands, Mahony drew attention to the fact that the economic shaping of landscape was a factor in the extent to which people suffered during the Famine. Arguably, this was a risky representational approach, as, in the contemporary political climate, geographically rooted representations had potential to alienate the mainstay of *ILN*'s British readership: rural west Cork is a long way from the main readership's metropolis of London.[66]

The graphic language of one of Mahony's much reprinted images appeals simultaneously to a different and broader visual code: the quasi-biblical notion of the suffering mother. In *Woman Begging at Clonakilty*, he emphasizes the realism of where starvation was felt but simultaneously exceeds the limits of geography (Figure 1.3). His text tells the reader that the woman with her dead baby in her arms was among 'the vast number of famished poor who flocked around the coach to beg for alms'.[67] She begged for money to buy a coffin in which to bury her child.

The absence of imaged context and lack of textile reference in the sketch allow her patched hooded cape – though conventional in Ireland – to potentially appertain to a number of places and times throughout history. She is a mother – any mother – lamenting the death of her baby, alms bowl in hand. Against the negative alliances outlined by McLean and Valone in contemporary perceptions of Irishness, the serene dignity of Mahony's *Woman Begging at Clonakilty* becomes apparent. The isolation of her rendering partially removes her image from a politics of relativity and towards one of artistic universalism, not unlike Watts's figuration. Though her face and that of her baby are directly depicted, the question of portrait likeness is eradicated as her identity in the image's caption renders her a beggar and a woman of Clonakilty.

Like Mahony, the author of the series 'Condition of Ireland: Illustrations of the New Poor-Law' stressed the need for locating suffering at the outset and focused on the Kilrush Union, County Clare.[68] He described the people in the village of Moveen:

> They are prostrate and helpless. The once frolicsome people –
> even the saucy beggars – have disappeared, and given place to
> wan and haggard objects, who are so resigned to their doom, that
> they no longer expect relief. One beholds only shrunken frames
> scarcely covered with flesh – crawling skeletons, who appear to
> have risen from their graves, and are ready to return to that abode.
> They have little covering than that nature has bestowed on the
> human body.

Figure 1.3 *Woman Begging at Clonakilty*, James Mahony, *The Illustrated London News,* 13 February 1847. Portrait of a destitute mother holding her baby in one arm and a begging bowl in the other. © Illustrated London News Ltd/Mary Evans.

The articles include both generalized comment and aspects of Irish living conditions explored in evocative detail. In an introductory article on 15 December 1849, the author wrote qualitatively about men who live in scalps or scalpeens, and provided illustrations.

On 22 December 1849, he described a scene he witnessed of a seven-year-old girl distributing clothing to 'the wretched children brought around her by their more wretched parents'. The illustration, *Miss Kennedy Distributing Clothing at Kilrush*, was printed page-width at the start of the article, with the explanatory text later, by way of redemptive hope (Figure 1.4). The action of 'young Miss Kennedy', daughter of Captain Kennedy, Poor-law Inspector in Kilrush Union, 'shows that, amidst this world of wretchedness, all is not misery and guilt. Indeed, it is a part of our nature that the sufferings of some should be the occasion for the exercise of virtue in others.' In his description of 'wretchedness' he drew attention to 'one woman crouching like a monkey, and drawing around her the only rag she had left to conceal her nudity'. In the sketch, this woman is shown from a side view, her face hidden by a bonnet from beneath which strands of long dark hair are visible.

Figure 1.4 *Miss Kennedy Distributing Clothing at Kilrush. The Illustrated London News*, 22 December 1849. Here a charitable Miss Kennedy is distributing clothing to destitute women and children in rags. © Illustrated London News Ltd/Mary Evans.

In the writer's sympathetic observation there is an enactment of cultural relativity. The woman's rag, which she gathers around her, serves to distinguish her state of destitution from the excess of clothing at the disposal of the well-dressed young girl. The woman's crouching posture accentuates her position as powerless and unnamed in this encounter, contrasting with the standing position of the benevolent named girl in the cart.[69] The implications of naming and unnaming through the process of image-making have since become part of a wider debate on the spectacle of dispossession, on which Sontag wrote: 'to grant only the famous their names demotes the rest to representative instances of their occupations, their ethnicities, their plights'.[70]

The writer's monkey simile allows for a further dehumanizing implication in a representation of a body in pain. This may well have echoes of Dr Donovan's and others' accounts of social breakdown and animal-like behaviour arising from severe deprivation, but must also be considered in the context of representations of the Irish possessing animalistic physiognomic traits in illustrated news in nineteenth-century Britain. Curtis examines visual constructions of Irish males as 'bestialized Paddies', highlighting the complex relationship between the two islands put under strain by the movement of people between them.[71] Peter Gray discusses how *Punch* and *The Times* developed simianized features in their cartoon depictions of Irish politicians and leading religious and cultural figures and included animal-like attributes in textual descriptions. One example in 1849 refers to the natives of Connacht as 'biped livestock' in the context of Peel's proposal for a new plantation there.[72]

While in political cartoons it was usually men who were 'bestialized' in appearance, the animal comparison made by the *ILN* correspondent raises the spectre of an established perception of Irish people as generally primitive. In journalistic accounts the virtuous charitable woman was often presented in counterpoint to accounts of women who seem to, as McLean notes, 'enact the effacement of human personhood by extreme hunger [. . .] animal-like, creatures of instinct and appetite'.[73]

However, in this text and image regarding *Miss Kennedy Distributing Clothing at Kilrush*, the depicted hungry body of the woman is dehumanized by her reported encounter with the contrasting portrayal of the child's upstanding civilizing presence: all within the rural habitat of the colonized subject, situated well beyond the pale. Such a representation potentially fosters a lack of empathy among readers and viewers, by differentiating visualizations enacted through the spectatorship model of primitivism.[74] In this way, a woman 'crouching like a monkey' appears before a well-dressed child in Moveen.

Perhaps the most familiar of Famine illustrations today, *Bridget O'Donnel and Children* was a smaller image printed beneath the *Miss Kennedy* sketch, with a direct quotation from O'Donnel in the same article (Figure 1.5). Readers learnt of her situation: her ill health, the deaths of two of her children and her social vulnerability in the absence of her husband:

> The *Sketch of a Woman and Children* represents Bridget O'Donnel. Her story is briefly this: 'I live,' she said, 'on the lands of Gurranenatuoha. My husband held four acres and a half of land, and three acres of bog land; our yearly rent was £7 4s.; we were put out last November; he owed some rent. We got thirty stone of oats from Mr. Marcus Keane, for seed. My husband gave some writing for it: he was paid for it. He paid ten shillings for reaping the corn. As soon as it was stacked, 'Blake' on the farm, who was put to watch it, took it away to his own haggard and kept it there for a fortnight by Dan Sheedey's orders. They then thrashed it in Frank Lellis's barn. I was at this time lying in fever. Dan Sheedey and five or six men came to tumble my house; they wanted me to give possession. I said that I would not; I had fever, and was within two months of my down-lying (confinement); they commenced knocking down the house, and had half of it knocked down when two neighbours, women, Nell Spellesley and Kate How, carried me out. I had the priest and doctor to attend to me shortly after. Father Meehan anointed me. I was carried into a cabin, and lay there for eight days, when I had the creature (the child) *born dead*. I lay for three weeks after that. The whole of my family got the fever, and one *boy thirteen years old died* with want and with hunger while we were lying sick. Dan Sheedey and Blake took the corn into Kilrush, and sold it. I don't know what they got for it. I had not a bit for my children to eat when they took it from me.

Printing her words echoed the author's earlier-stated intention to use microcosmic examples to emotively challenge his readers, and in this case a testimonial account. O'Sullivan notes in the image of Bridget O'Donnel, that her 'distended body and concave chest, was the antithesis of the Victorian feminine ideal, but she became in iconography a powerful metaphor for the devastated and sorrowing country'.[75] The pictorial

BRIDGET O'DONNEL AND CHILDREN.

Figure 1.5 *Sketch of a Woman and her Children. The Illustrated London News,* 22 December 1849. This is Bridget O'Donnel with her children. They are barefoot and dressed in rags. © Illustrated London News Ltd/Mary Evans.

removal of O'Donnel from her physical context marks the illustration out from other images in *ILN* articles, where considerable attention is typically given to rendering landscape and details of habitation. Shading delineates the shadows cast by the two scrawny children huddled on either side of their emaciated mother, and illuminates her as a parent unable to feed her children. O'Donnel's oscillation between narrator and icon was presumably triggered by the correspondent's attempt to affectively convey the poverty he encountered, as Mahony had done and Watts would later, wittingly or otherwise, emulate in a related pictorial paradigm. This has since become one of the most commonly reprinted images of Famine reportage.

Clearly, the biological susceptibility of women to Famine-related disease probably contributes to the prevalence of women and children in Famine imagery,[76] but as signifying chameleons in figurations of the Famine, the image of women has been repeatedly transformed. In nineteenth-century Famine imagery the allegorical female functioned within portrayals of family units and/or as a separated independent stereotype: abstracted from her home or depicted in counterpoint to thus relatively constructed civilizing elements or figures.

These artworks and images, however, also relate to a more generalized cultural legacy of stereotypes in which Ireland is depicted as a woman. What Paula Murphy termed woman as 'a patronized, powerless and propagandist symbol'[77] was imbued from a number of stereotypes in Irish history and myths, though some are considered empowered, particularly in matriarchal legends. One example is Cathleen Ní Houlihan, a personification of Ireland usually as an old woman in need of the aid of young Irish men to free her from British rule: she is often represented as homeless and sometimes referred to as 'Sean-Bhean Bhocht' (Irish for poor old woman).[78] Ireland as a deserted female lover was invoked by male poets in the *aisling* (Irish for vision), a form of visionary poem in the late seventeenth and eighteenth centuries in which the troubled country took the form of a woman: *an spéirbhean* (sky woman) who typically appeared to poets in a dream lamenting Ireland's colonial state. She was usually young and pretty, but sometimes old and haggard.[79] Later, in nineteenth-century British illustrated news and cartoons, Ireland appears as a coquettish young woman seeking attention from a male-personified British power.[80]

Since then these tropes, and others, have been both sustained and challenged in a long and complex interisland artistic history, across literature, music and visual and performance art. Marina Warner wonders if, in the 'use of the female as sign, in text and image', it is possible to 'generate a philosophy of possibilities [...] a broadening [...] through the creative energy of imaginative empathy, to draw us into the subject of a figure, make us feel inside the body on whose exterior we have until now scribbled the meanings we wanted'.[81]

The breadth of 'scribbling' upon a generic Irish female body in figurations of Famine has its foundations in reactions to local political situations and conventions of wider cultural ideologies, including ideas of primitivism. Though in some cases, such as the *Miss Kennedy Distributing Clothing at Kilrush* illustration, these configurations imaging Famine scenes may be been deployed to indicate an authorial aim of fostering sympathetic spectatorship, yet sustained problematic notions of cultural difference. A century-and-a-half later, an installation artist and memorial sculptors were to pre-empt and answer Warner's call as they refigured the hungry bodies of Famine times in representations that 'broadened' the context of such figurations.

Somatic Society: Hunger in Art of the Late Twentieth and Early Twenty-First Centuries

The universal readability of the unsettling incongruity suggested by parents unable to feed their children, and the figuration of hungry bodies more generally, are taken up in different ways and reclaimed as subjects of contemporary relevance by artists in the twentieth and twenty-first centuries. As in nineteenth-century images, the context of Famine sufferer in extended family groupings and the location of figurative representations remain pivotal through twentieth- and twenty-first-century visualizations and the related production of spectators of Famine history.

Post-Famine-era figurations of the Famine in art and memorials have been produced in a climate of contentious photojournalism and presented to an overtly somatic society, 'a society in which our major political and moral problems are expressed through the conduit of the human body'.[82] Two distinct approaches to situating the hungry body in twentieth-century art are reflected across the work of three Irish artists. The first approach centres on subjective experience symbolically transformed into an immersive art encounter for audiences in a gallery and the second on the languages of open-air monuments. The monumental sculptures employ divergent languages of figuration reflecting the artists' distinctive visions on the role of public art and interests in formal aspects of sculpture, functioning within their subject portrayals.

Margaret Kelleher analyses contradictory literary representations of women during the Famine as both life-givers and life-takers;[83] by extension, mothers, like Bridget O'Donnel, as unable to feed their children. Alanna O'Kelly's video installation *A'Beathú*, 1996, draws its inspiration from such a condition[84] (Figure 1.6). *A'Beathú* is Irish Gaelic for nurture and also refers to Catholic baptism. Suggested by Murphy as one indication, within later twentieth-century Irish art, of an 'attempt to comprehend what it is to be Irish on a bigger stage [than nationalism], in a global context'. Murphy notes that O'Kelly had read about the Famine when pregnant and so sought a 'new understanding of her position as an Irish mother'.[85] The opening and closing imagery of the work is developed around a close-up of a breast emitting milk underwater. O'Kelly, as then a new mother, unexpectedly expressed breast milk when in the bath.[86] In the video this action is restaged and interspersed with images of a breathing belly, a newborn baby's rapid eye movement and moments of darkness, with an audio of sounds of birth and those made by a sleeping baby. The work was initiated as a performance piece with earlier audio and video recordings contributing to its final outcome and it specifically includes references to a 1994–5 performance, *Ómós*, (*ómós* is Irish Gaelic for respect).[87]

For O'Kelly, *A'Beathú* reflects upon notions of nourishment of the spirit,[88] and everyone's potential to nurture.[89] Despite the motifs, this implies a non-gender-specific perspective to her exploration of the power of subjectivity to approach difficult themes of loss and starvation.[90] Revealing her own body, O'Kelly appropriates a private and subjective experience to complicate ideas of difference.

Also at this time, primarily through the medium of television, O'Kelly became aware of women unable to feed their children in various parts of the world. She saw images of nursing women whose breasts were drying following lack of adequate food during and after political upheavals and quotes a Kurdish woman refugee during the Gulf War: 'tell the world I hold my dead baby in my arms because my breasts have dried up'.[91] As mother to a newborn baby, O'Kelly was intrigued by the

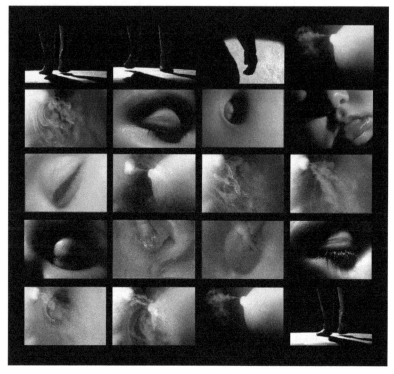

Figure 1.6   Alanna O'Kelly, *A'Beathú*, 1996. Compilation of Video Stills from Video Projected Installation. Image courtesy of Alanna O'Kelly. © Alanna O'Kelly.

symbolic power of plenitude associated with a nursing breast, and the dual implications of fecundity and waste that arise when a mother emits milk outside of feeding times. *A'Beathú* self-consciously incorporates O'Kelly's response to a global televisual landscape of shared news about deprivation in places outside of Ireland, at a time of great personal change.

The work followed on a series begun in 1992 on the theme of the Irish Famine, 'The Country Blooms... A Garden and a Grave', exhibited at the Irish Museum of Modern Art in Dublin.[92] Examining mass emigration and the relationship of Ireland's present to its past, O'Kelly developed a number of photo-text works, multimedia installations and performances, presenting what Catherine Marshall has described as 'an articulate, alternative, feminist approach to the subject'.[93] As Marshall notes,

Figuration and the Site of Famine

O'Kelly's 'multi-faceted process both embodies and symbolizes the expansive effects of the original event and its ongoing effect on Irish people'.[94]

After a period of travel, including studying art in London, and returning to live in Ireland, O'Kelly was keen to address ideas of contemporary Irishness in her art.[95] Exposure to the complexities of British–Irish relations provided O'Kelly with a renewed interest in her identity, and a curiosity about the fracturing of Irish identity both at home and abroad.[96] Ireland experienced considerable emigration as a response to economic recession throughout the 1980s and early 1990s. The growth of diasporic communities of Irish defined in the mid- to late nineteenth century seemed to have a partial echo in the emigration patterns of the 1980s.

By the end of the twentieth century, as Ireland was also in a newly reversed position as aid giver, rather than receiver, O'Kelly's work suggests a consciousness regarding senses of otherness that might reinforce casual primitivism. As Watts's apparently determined fluctuation between portrait and allegory indicated, perceived distancing of a suffering subject can be a potentially reductive outcome of universalizing images of dispossession. When horror is overly beautified through its visualization, indignation can be diluted, as explored by Sontag who noted that in photographs of atrocity the taint of artistry is often equated with insincerity and even contrivance.[97] Sontag's argument on depictions of pain in visual culture revolves around a perception of art as necessarily and usefully distinct from conventional documentary. This concept links to Scarry's argument for the place of fiction as imaginative realization, in the material world. In other words, ideas of witness, interpretation and aesthetics have varied inter-complicity in the culturally inscribed relativity of spectatorship.

O'Kelly's development of a series of subjectively derived moving images and an intimate soundscape in A'Beathú accentuates the propinquity of the subject to the viewer and underplays ideas of difference. The close-up and cropping of the motif of mother and baby undermines the sense of distance that might occur with televised panoramic spectacles of famine happening elsewhere. The form of her piece also engenders a bodily intimacy a close physical proximity is necessary to be sublimated by its sounds and images. This embracing gesture and the bodily references within the work ensure that easy differentiations of self from other are destabilized, but without

51

Imaging the Great Irish Famine

Figure 1.7 Edward Delaney, *Wolfe Tone Monument: Famine Fountain*, 1967. Bronze. Detail: Famine Fountain. St Stephen's Green, Dublin, Ireland. Image provided by author.

simplified negation. O'Kelly presents a female body and a baby as a process and consequence of being human and a metaphorical means to thinking about interpersonal responsibilities of the body politic, irrespective of gender or location.

Tension between experiences of hunger and spectacles formed in its representations are differentially explored in reflections on artistic engagements with both body politics and the historic modernist legacy of outdoor public urban memorials. On a corner of St Stephen's Green is a fountain comprising a set of thin cast bronze figures facing towards the pleasure garden[98] (Figure 1.7). Beyond two walls behind it, that make up an exit point from the park and facing Baggot Street, a busy commercial and leisure area, is a large sculpture of Theobald Wolfe Tone (Figure 1.8). Wolfe Tone was a founding member of the United Irish Society in 1791 and a leader in the 1798 Rebellion.[99] Together these figures make up the *Wolfe Tone Monument*, 1967, by Edward Delaney.[100]

The three figures are a Famine representation. An upright, standing figure leans upon a stick with one hand, and the other hand feeds a seated middle

52

Figure 1.8 Edward Delaney, *Wolfe Tone Monument: Famine Fountain*, 1967. Bronze. Detail: Wolfe Tone. St Stephen's Green, Dublin, Ireland. Image provided by author.

figure with a soup ladle.[101] The seated figure clutches at the leg of the standing one, and to the back a third figure stands with arms clasped in desperation around the back of his/her neck. An animal lies wearily by the group.[102] The figure of Wolfe Tone, which originally stood behind the fountain, was blown up four years after it was unveiled and subsequently the walls were erected between a reworked Tone sculpture and the Famine figures.[103] As the title suggests, Delaney's public sculpture contravenes conventions of heroic commemorative commissions. In a blatantly emotive strategy, alongside the named national hero, Delaney planted his unnamed victims of history.

A year earlier, Delaney adopted a similar strategy in his *Thomas Davis Memorial*, 1966, at College Green Dublin, a busy city-centre thoroughfare.[104] A subsidiary fountain references the Famine in a bas-relief plaque along its base among other images of historical events. Róisín Kennedy stresses that the inclusion of the second sculptures in both these public monuments

Figure 1.9 Rowan Gillespie, *Famine*, 1997. Bronze. Dublin Docklands, Dublin, Ireland. Image provided by author.

'allowed Delaney to link the heroic version of history to a much wider narrative of human struggle and triumph'.[105] Symptomatic of his discomfort at the weight of monolithic historical sculpture, Delaney's idiosyncratic style is more pronounced in these secondary fountain elements than in the primary figures represented. Judith Hill implies that the two main figures independently were of so little interest to Delaney that he rendered them practically impossible to distinguish;[106] the rough textures of his figures do not differentiate between body and clothing.[107] It seems that while Delaney presents a complex notion of history, he was also determined to fashion a language of modernist form. Delaney's interest in agrarian and rural motifs is encapsulated by the animal's presence in the *Wolfe Tone Monument* and further symbolically alienates the figures from the ordered urban environment in which they stand.

On Dublin Docklands Rowan Gillespie's larger-than-life figures, *Famine*, 1997, are frozen mid-trek toward the sea[108] (Figure 1.9). Realistic renderings of loose clothing accentuate the figures' emaciated forms.

Four men and two women carry between them a small dead child, a swaddled baby, meagre bundles of possessions and are trailed by a wiry hound dog, sniffing the air. The man carrying the baby looks imploringly ahead. The others have their heads bowed dejectedly or raised despairingly as they appear to shuffle in the direction of the port. Situated on a broad cobbled walkway by the water near the Irish Financial Services Centre, *Famine* was erected when the area was undergoing significant redevelopment.

In Famine times, Dublin Port – like many ports and piers around the country – was the site of multitudes of hungry and suffering bodies, hoping to leave the country for better luck elsewhere. Now known as Dublin Docklands, this area is much changed since the nineteenth century and within the duration of the sculpture's standing.[109] It was a successful colonial port; then a partially run-down inner-city area; and subsequently a site of urban regeneration and also host to key privately run entertainment venues, including the indoor amphitheatre, the 3Arena and the Bord Gáis Energy Theatre, as well as the privately funded tourist attraction, EPIC: The Irish Emigration Museum. Originally commissioned, financed and presented to the city by a Dublin-based businesswoman, Norma Smurfit, *Famine*'s location on Custom House Quay coincided with the area's regeneration at the beginning of Ireland's so-called Celtic Tiger phase and appears an audacious reminder of a time of penury and hunger. Nearby, in 2008 The World Poverty stone was unveiled to mark the International Day for the Eradication of Poverty, sculpted by Irish sculptor, Stuart McGrath, commission by the city council and the Dublin Docklands Authority (DDA). Though the area continues to change in post-Tiger Ireland, the poverty represented in Gillespie's figures remains in stark contrast to the surrounding business, entertainment and residential life.

Roger Kohn draws attention to Edvard Munch's influence on Gillespie's figurative style:[110] gaunt bodies and tortured facial facades are designed to indicate inner torment. *Famine* also contains a subjective history within the expressive forms of its figuration.[111] The figure with her hands by her side is modelled on Gillespie's sister, who suffered anorexia for a number of years and died at the age of 24. Kohn outlines that, in the spirit in which Munch had painted his sister dying of tuberculosis in *The Sick Child*, 1886, Gillespie imaged his sister in this starving group.[112] Her emaciated body is also indicated in the figuration

Figure 1.10   Rowan Gillespie, *The Arrival*, 2007. Bronze. Ireland Park, Toronto, Canada. © Ireland Park Foundation.

of the corpse carried by a distressed man at the rear of the group.[113] By this inclusion, Gillespie moves beyond a purely historical description in his work and, like O'Kelly, brings his representation of the Famine out of the nation's past and into conjunction with a more recent and personally proximate somatic experience, one that highlights the effect of hunger for the mind as well as the body.

In Ireland Park in Toronto, *The Arrival*, also by Gillespie, was officially revealed by the president of Ireland, Mary McAleese, on 21 June 2007[114] (Figure 1.10). Gillespie's five bronze figures depict the arrival of an Irish immigrant group to Canada during the Famine. The figures are in a small tranquil city park overlooking the bay, where a public memorial is perhaps more typically expected than on a bustling commercial quayside at Dublin Port. Each of the Toronto figures bears a title – *The Jubilant Man, Pregnant Woman, Woman on Ground, The Orphan Boy* and *The Apprehensive Man* – intended to capture different consequences of and emotional responses to a situation of economic migration. Yet their identity as Irish remains intact as Gillespie has mirrored the style and figuration of his Dublin sculpture. Still emaciated

Figure 1.11 Carolyn Mulholland, *Famine Memorial Figure*, 2001. Bronze. Famine and Workhouse Graveyard, Clones, County Monaghan, Ireland. Image courtesy of Dianne McPhelim.

and raggedly dressed, the figures as representations of poverty are also provocatively at odds with their contrasting urban environment. Despite initial hesitation,[115] Gillespie notes family connection with Canada as shaping his interest in the commission: emigrating during Famine times, they made a home in Canada before returning to Ireland sometime later.[116]

Like Delaney's fountain figures, Carolyn Mulholland's bronze sculpture, *Famine Memorial*, 2001, at Famine Graveyard, Clones, County Monaghan, is a non-gendered figuration of the Famine (Figure 1.11).[117] This memorial is presented in an environment that contrasts greatly to the urban settings of both Delaney's and Gillespie's memorials and seems counterpoint to their upright figures of survival.

Eschewing the monumentality associated with heroic public memorials, Mulholland proposed that her sculpture would lie in greater isolation on the site, such as on a low bier-like platform on what was at that time a field visually defined by small bumps.[118] The area surrounding it since comprises many memorial elements echoing international languages of both cemetery and monumental formalism, with the sculpture contextualized in its graveyard setting by nearby curved walls and its waist-height curved plinth. More recently, a commemorative archway has been added to the site, constructed from stones of the local workhouse.

Laid out in rigor mortis and overlaid with a sculpted sheet, Mulholland's life-size sculpture at Clones is displayed like a spectacle reminiscent of the laying-out of the bodies of celebrated figures, and referencing the Irish tradition of waking the dead.[119]

At the site, the unsettling proximity of a realistic and unnamed dead Famine victim – as the scale of Mulholland's sculpture remains 'ordinary rather than extraordinary'[120] – invites the visitor to consider those who died as individuals, rather than a statistic. The sculpture sets the scene for eternal mourning at a site of what had been unceremonious Famine-era burial for so many.

Seeing Hungry Bodies

As McQueen's strategies of depiction in the film *Hunger* sought to humanize a political act – the wilful and voluntary starvation of a body – many of the illustrators and artists who made representations of the involuntary starvation of Famine victims sought to humanize a politically inscribed suffering written upon the bodies of others. Bill Rolston outlines a visual legacy of the 1981 hunger strikes that predates McQueen's film: dramatic interventions on the streets when Republican youths began painting murals 'literally "drawing support" for the hunger strikes'.[121] This began in the context of massive rallies taking place to support the hunger strikers, as previously mural imagery was overwhelmingly the domain of Loyalists. In 1997, a dozen murals were painted of the Famine, but alongside the 'depictions of victimhood were those of resistance', including of the 1798 Rebellion and the 1916 Easter Rising.[122] Some of the imagery of these drew on Famine-era illustrations from the *ILN*,[123] with overtly provocative text reflecting contemporary political agendas. Many of the murals painted at this time are no longer extant, because, as Rolston points out, generally 'the wall is taken for the [sic] new message' as many of these mural painters tended to be more politically than artistically motivated.[124]

The improbability of convincingly picturing pain was a definitive factor in figurations of the Famine from the nineteenth century, with depictions variously utilizing codes of allegory, documentary and stereotype, largely contextualized through relative perceptions of location. Highlighting social hardship through aesthetic practices is dependent on the viewer's understanding of the social, and later historical, contexts within the image and the related implications of its production and circulation. In retrospective analyses, these nineteenth-century illustrative examples and their relationships to accompanying captions and article texts, resound through Campbell's twenty-first-century comments on the geopolitics of photojournalism as 'the visual performance of the social field', in which 'sites (and the people in those sites) are enacted through sight'.

At the time of the Famine, visual strategies of repeated facelessness and iconic unnaming, of women and children in particular, demonstrates that affective imaging of hunger might create a generalized spectacle of dispossession. Such promotion of universalism though, arguably, intended to bind spectacle and suffering together can also generate an aesthetics of cultural distance. Transcending named subjects of suffering, as well as specifying locations, may have been reflective of the desire of individual artists and illustrators to undermine the pervading politics of difference in nineteenth-century Britain. At the same time, other journalistic insistence on naming both places and sufferers appears a comparative strategy of humanization, aimed at readers as viewers of others' fate.

While cultural relativity has remained significant in how images of hunger are read in more recent times, art examples, as arguably evident also in Macdonald's and Watt's Famine paintings, have tended to Sontag's description of art evoking situations of distress. By way of artistic and interpretative licenses, O'Kelly, Delaney, Gillespie and Mulholland have contextualized their subject in a range of somatic concerns. *A 'Beathú* for example, redresses not only historic visualizations of disempowered womanhood in Famine art, but also the wider legacy of stereotypes in which Ireland is depicted as a woman. Instead of writing on the body of an other, O'Kelly uses her own body to provide an answer to Warner's call for 'imaginative empathy' and further, and not dissimilar to McQueen's later filmic work, viscerally evoke Scarry's imaginative interior/exterior body link.

Delaney's figurations of Famine reveal his pursuit of an idiosyncratic language of sculpture and a keen sense of the duality of historical perspective, with the unnamed subjects pointedly shadowing the named heroes of history. Gillespie's works demonstrate a concern with implicating history into the present day, through a layered representation of body politics. The locations of Delaney's and Gillespie's monuments contribute to the character of spectatorship each gives rise to. As enduring signifiers of a history of rural poverty their figurations of Famine are thrown into changeable focus by altering usage of these urban landscapes.

The figurative representations discussed here illustrate that as pertinent a query as what forms representations of hungry bodies take is where famine is recognized. During and since the Famine, representational challenges to imaging suffering bodies have been channelled through stylistic conventions, expectations of the art world and strategies of news media. Comparable to the emphatically visceral exploration of a non-famine hungry body in the film *Hunger,* picturing Famine hunger has been insistently refracted through ideas of place, both as signifying trope and as geographic referent. Figurations of Famine are, and have been, mediated by the ways in which landscape was rendered, locations named, where dispossession was experienced and, finally, 'make sense' where the image of the suffering body is viewed in the relativity of spheres of spectatorship.

2

Leaving the Famine: The Spectacle of Migration

Dispossession and Teeming Berths

> Hundreds of poor people, men, women and children, of all ages [. . .]
> huddled together, without light, without air, wallowing in filth and
> breathing in a fetid atmosphere, sick in body, dispirited in heart [. . .]
> In many ships the filthy beds, teeming with all abominations, are
> never required to be brought on deck and aired. The narrow space
> between the sleeping berths and piles of boxes is never washed or
> scraped but breathes up a damp fetid stench, until the day before
> arrival at quarantine, when all hands are required to 'scrub up' and
> put on a fair face for the doctor and Government inspector.
>
> Stephen de Vere, extracts from letter to T.F. Elliott, agent-
> general for emigration, November 1847, read aloud in the House of
> Lords by Earl Grey, secretary for the colonies[1]

The text quoted above is from a complaint about conditions to the Colonial
Office in London. Described by James Donnelly as a 'Limerick landlord,
philanthropist and social reformer',[2] Stephen de Vere was a contemporary
witness who travelled as a steerage passenger to Canada in 1847. Jason
King writes that de Vere

bears witness to the grim traffic all around him of small vessels ferrying the sick and the dead to the fever sheds and mass graves on the island [of Grosse Île]. His journals recall the spectacle of sundered families, that moment of separation in which Irish children were orphaned.[3]

De Vere's reports led to the 'enactment of the reforming Passenger Act of 1847'.[4]

From the 1830s until the 1860s, Canada saw tens of thousands of immigrants arrive each year at the Port of Quebec. Most of these were from the British Isles, and of that number the majority were Irish.[5] Mark McGowan notes that one-fifth of the 97,492 who set sail to British North America in 1847 did not live to 1848, with some dying en route and some on arrival, and as many as 5,424 are buried at the Grosse Île quarantine station in the mouth of the St Lawrence River.[6] Mary Daly writes that in 1847 over 97,953 emigrants left for Quebec, with 5,282 dying at sea and a further 3,238 on Grosse Île.[7] Marianna O'Gallagher wrote that in one day in 1847 there were 67 deaths and up to 1,400 sick.[8] Mary Lee Dunn describes that summer as 'the summer of death'.[9]

According to Michael Quigley, at the end of May 1847, 36 ships were at anchor at Grosse Île with close to 12,500 passengers, and on 23 May the quarantine station's first superintendent, Dr Douglas, reported between 50 and 60 deaths per day.[10] Quigley writes: 'On June 5, the day when the Medical Commission arrived [...], 21,000 emigrants were at Grosse Île.'[11] During 1847 extra hospital sheds were built, with a total of 22 recorded by the end of the year,[12] which could accommodate upwards of 2,000 sick people and 300 convalescents, in addition to the main hospital building.

Douglas, working with a team of doctors and priests, repeatedly reported grim conditions on board arriving ships, and grossly inadequate facilities for treatment and holding on the island. Ships being forced to remain at anchor contributed to the scale of the disaster, as well as the nature of the infectiousness and spread of typhus and dysentery.[13] As the station was overwhelmed by the scale of the situation, immigrants were eventually allowed to pass unchecked through the station, resulting in fever epidemics in major cities throughout Canada, including St John, Quebec and Montreal.[14]

Colin McMahon notes that in the summer of 1847, 75,000 Irish arrived further downriver to Montreal, which then had a population of 50,000.[15]

Figure 2.1 *Ship Fever Monument*, 1859, Montreal, Canada. © Fergus Keyes, A Director of The Montreal Irish Monument Park Foundation.

These immigrants were described in an 1847 report by the city's Board of Health as 'debilitated and wretched beings [...] mostly in a sickly, and many in a dying state'.[16] As they awaited further travel or influx into the city, some 6,000 died in a typhus epidemic by October, 'most of them Irish-Catholic immigrants who were hastily buried in mass graves in the vicinity of the fever sheds in Pointe Saint-Charles'.[17]

In 1859, a boulder, called the *Ship Fever Monument*, was placed at the Montreal burial site (Figure 2.1). Known locally as the Black Rock, it stands, arguably, as the first memorial in the world to reference Famine experiences. Inaugurated by what McMahon calls an 'Anglo-Protestant elite', with an initial dedication 'To Preserve from Desecration the Remains of 6000 Immigrants Who died of Ship Fever A.D. 1847 – 18',[18] the site's subsequent history played out a fraught struggle over collective identities linked to this place and acts of remembrance associated with it. McMahon outlines a series of events, including the controversial moving of the boulder to facilitate railway construction in 1900 and its return to the site some 12 years later with a rededication ceremony overseen by the Ancient Order of Hibernians (AOH). Founded in New York City on 4 May 1836, the AOH is described by McMahon as 'a Catholic fraternal organization with a mandate to maintain a sense of history and traditions of Ireland among the Diaspora'.[19]

Before, during and since this episode various ceremonial events have taken place at the site, marking tensions between immigrant identities, sectarian alignments and national histories, as reflected in the notable absence of 'Irish' as prefix to 'immigrant' in the stone's text. The memorial's awkward location in a traffic median has also been a focus for much criticism. In 2017, plans were announced to develop a memorial park to victims of Ship Fever in an adjacent site, in cooperation with the site's new owners Hydro-Quebec.[20]

Further historical context for the experiences of Famine migrants in Montreal is provided by other sources, such as the online Irish Famine Archive. This contains eyewitness accounts of migrations to Canada in 1847 and 1848 and reveals realities of arrival, and chronicles the committed roles of religious orders in Montreal, the Grey Nuns in particular, in relation to finding homes to accommodate the influx of Irish migrants.[21] The evolution of the *Ship Fever Monument* as a site of memory, its wider transatlantic, historical context and the complex politics of identity surrounding its significance indicate the necessarily polyphonic aspects of memorial processes that commemorate migration experiences determined by dispossession.

During and after the Famine, emigration, already occurring in high numbers since the 1830s, was a widespread outcome of the living conditions faced by the majority of the population. With little holdings, land or possessions, the financial strain and the lack of food led to many leaving their homes: those who could headed to the coast in search of livelihoods elsewhere. These mass mobilizations then, were undertaken due to aggregating economic pressures and, to some extent, aided by landlords and variously financed schemes. In some cases, migration was directly forced by landlords in land clearances through systematic evictions, even using force of fire to ensure the property could not be returned to. The Poor Law of 1847, and its extensions, compounded the problems facing landlords, tenants and landworkers. By the mid-1840s, overdue rents on the land, a faltering system of crops for cover and growing social unrest contributed to the increasing number of evictions.[22]

Consequently, deserted and burnt-out cottages were widespread in the Irish countryside while ships, some filled beyond capacity, sailed across the

Figure 2.2   Deserted Village, Achill, County Mayo, Ireland. Image provided by Achill Tourism. © John McNamara.

Irish Sea and Atlantic Ocean. William J. Smyth notes that the 'fourth-class house is seen as one of the greatest symbols of poverty in pre-Famine Ireland',[23] and as a motif it features across visual cultural forms. The cottage is central to depicted moments of dispossession in a number of nineteenth- and twentieth-century art works, including: Erskine Nicol's *An Ejected Family*, 1853; Robert Kelly's *An Ejectment in Ireland* (also known as *A Tear and a Prayer for Ireland*), 1848–51; and Seán McSweeney's *Deserted Dwellings*, c.1995. In some contemporary illustrations, harsher depictions call attention to the violence of eviction, such as *Ejectment of Irish Tenantry, Illustrated London News*, 1848.

More recently in Ireland, remnants of deserted cottages have been integrated into a topography of rural heritage with so-called deserted Famine villages variously maintained as ruins, renovated and re-purposed, transformed and extended as tourist sites while some are left unmarked and unacknowledged in the landscape throughout Ireland. Notable examples include a deserted village on Aichill Island, Co Mayo (Figure 2.2);

Figure 2.3 *Irish Hunger Memorial,* 2002. Artist: Brian Tolle. Battery Park, New York, USA. © Stan Ries.

Cill Rialaig artists' residency village, County Kerry; the heritage site, Kavanagh Cottage, on Slea Head, County Kerry. Perhaps one of the internationally best-known Famine memorials outside of Ireland is a transposed cottage ruin at the Irish Hunger Memorial, 2002, by artist Brian Tolle and landscaped with architect Gail Wittwer-Laird, Battery Park, New York, which consists of a grassy quarter-acre site and a cottage that was originally situated in County Mayo, Ireland[24] (Figure 2.3). At a rising tilt to the water, the site affords a spectacular view of New York Harbour and underneath a constructed cairn-like space clad in Kilkenny limestone includes text and audio representations of the Famine and world poverty. The contrast between the material elements of the relocated old cottage, now verdantly planted with Irish flora, and the burnished space below is augmented by the high-rise buildings surrounding the memorial site and the open bay and sky facing towards Ellis Island.[25]

While the loss of home is itself a critical subject to the very definition of Famine dispossession and cottage ruins and deserted villages are profoundly evocative indexical traces of Famine-era impoverishment throughout Ireland, the focus here is on one of the significant consequences of such uprooting: leaving the homeland. As in other aspects of Famine histories, narrative stories of affected subjects are retold in accounts of homelessness and emigration, from the NFC's archives to travel diaries describing life on overcrowded ships that sailed to the USA, as well as in historical fiction.[26] In art works, at public memorials and at heritage and tourist sites, the ship's impressive form is often utilized as a strategic motif to represent the scale, depth and breadth of experiences associated with the mobilization of so many people following dispossession.

Tall ships, as they were known for their high masts, were deployed to each carry hundreds of often hungry and desperate emigrants to the USA, Canada, England and Australia. Three-quarters of the Irish who crossed the Atlantic during and immediately after the Famine came through Liverpool Port,[27] where passengers attempted to disembark, with varying degrees of success. Many of these port destinations have memorials to Irish immigrants. For example, The Liverpool Famine Memorial by Eamonn O'Doherty was erected in 1998, at the corner of Berry Street and Leece Street in the grounds of the ruins of St Lukes, a church bombed in World War II.[28] The monument is a four-meter-high granite stone and has a bronze cross centrally inscribed. Set apart in the church grounds by low black railing, text plaques to the front of the main monument element outline: 'Between 1849 and 1852, 1,242,410 Irish emigrants arrive in Liverpool [...] In Liverpool parish in 1847 alone, over 7,000 paupers were buried in mass graves.' The memorial's close proximity to the striking presence of the evocatively empty yet splendid ruins of the war-torn church accentuates its solidity and contemporary lines, and augments a scene of powerful historical correspondence.

While many Famine emigrants survived their journeys, others had their dream of escape shattered, dying on board during the voyage or when held in quarantine outside of overburdened ports, and others on arrival. The conditions, rather than the death rate, have led to these ships being, in some contexts, referred to as 'coffin ships'. There are varying accounts of how different ship owners looked after their passengers. Many of these vessels were built as freight ships for cargo such as logs, so the price of tickets for migrant journeys was high, as the ships would not collect cargo for return journeys. While many ships brought in useful cargo and exported Ireland's successful industrial produce such as linen, some, controversially, continued to export grain – corn, meal and flour – during the Famine.[29]

A range of aided emigration schemes were offered, some by landlords, in the form of allocation of tickets, making the contest for places intense. Conditions on board were grim as these ships were not designed for so many passengers. The spaces entire families were allocated were restrictive: the cubby holes, or berths, generally measured around 3 ft wide, 5 ft deep and $2\frac{1}{2}$ ft high. In these airless areas below deck, several hundred emigrants might spend up to eight weeks at sea. Typically, poorer emigrants had limited access to deck during daylight hours, and allowances for food and toilet and washing facilities were scant, compounding a general lack of hygiene below deck. On arrival at their destinations, the experiences of migrants were varied. From isolation to social success, the evolution of Irish diasporic communities abroad contains many heart-breaking tales alongside happier accounts.

The visual impact of the tall ships is thus a complex one: an aesthetically strong form which previously represented both an import-export trade and the aspirations of many for a new life outside of Ireland, the degradation and appalling conditions experienced by poorer passengers are less apparent on first viewing. Authenticity as a conceptual mechanism typically invests historical authority in representational heritage and memorial practices. As there are no surviving original Famine ships, to what extent and by what means have connotations of authenticity been invoked in monuments, art and replica ships created to memorialize the cultural and social complexities of Famine migration?

The Ship Motif in Art

The National Famine Memorial of Ireland at Murrisk, County Mayo, was commissioned in 1995 by the Government-appointed 150 Year Famine Commemoration Committee. Situated in a scenic area, Murrisk Millennium Park, at the foot of the mountain Croagh Patrick, the memorial consists of a small landscaped park in which stands *The Famine Ship* by sculptor John Behan[30] (Figure 2.4). Viewed from the roadside, the sculpture's bare outline is stark and instantly recognizable as a tall ship. Its form conjures the dreams of escape that these historic ships represented for many. Close up, it has an imposing presence, standing approximately 23 ft high and 20 ft long. Approaching the sculpture from the small landscaped

Figure 2.4 John Behan, *The Famine Ship, The National Famine Memorial of Ireland*, 1995. Bronze. County Mayo, Ireland. Image provided by author.

park, the assertive upright shape is overwritten by the representation of those that did not survive. Behan has emphasized death in his use of grotesquely animated skeletal figurations, accentuating their lack of flesh as they are tautly stretched over the ship's parts. Delineated by the dramatically gaunt forms and a stark lack of masts, the overall sculpture poetically draws attention to both the mass scale and individual bodily intensity of suffering experienced as a result of the Famine.

The location of *The Famine Ship* is one of striking natural beauty, with the mountain behind it and the Atlantic to its front. In the garden-like park immediately surrounding the memorial sculpture there is some seating to facilitate sustained reflection in the tranquil spot. Given the hardships endured by the Famine population of County Mayo, the beauty of the wider landscape belies its historical poverty and adjusts the impact of Behan's dark corpse-filled depiction of emigration.[31] At a viewing distance, the grim revelations of the ship's sculpted form are countered by the scale of its scenic setting and by the mountain with its mythic connotations for a collective Irish identity tied to Christianity and specifically Catholicism. Standing at 762 m above sea level, Croagh Patrick, meaning the Hill of St Patrick, is Ireland's best-known and most-climbed mountain and a site of pilgrimage for Catholics. St Patrick, Ireland's patron saint, is said to have climbed this mountain, and at its summit is a church where thousands gather at special times of the year for an outdoor Mass. Taken as a slave boy from Romano-Britain by Irish raiders in the late fourth- to early fifth century AD, St Patrick later escaped as a stowaway on a ship that brought him to mainland Europe. He is thought to have returned years later as a missionary and is commonly accredited with introducing Christianity to Ireland.[32]

The influence of the deeply symbolic mountain, Croagh Patrick, over the reading of the National Famine Memorial cannot be overlooked. Locational proximity shapes visitor experience of heritage sites as the spectacle of historic representation is revealed. In ideological terms, tales of St Patrick have for centuries epitomized conceptions of a Catholic Ireland and, in the modern historic era, a desire to return to an Ireland pre-dating the British plantations. Though successive series of immigrations and invasions impacted on Ireland's national heritage, the remembrance of St Patrick is nonetheless viewed as a persuasive symbol of Irish identity, to which the perpetuation of St Patrick's Day parades and festivals internationally testifies.[33] *The Famine Ship*, at once emblematic of a difficult period in Irish history, functions as an icon of a positive Irish experience by virtue of its association with the folk history of its location. In this reciprocal reading, *The Famine Ship* is linked to the ships of both the capture of the slave-boy Patrick and his later escape as a stowaway. Arguably, these associations imbue Behan's skeletal forms with the status of Irish martyrs, ostensibly deified by proximity to a sacred site.

Open-air heritage sites have become a significant locus for the re-enactment of historically affiliated identities in Ireland, as elsewhere across the globe, and are mediated through idioms of national histories and international tourism interests. Guy Beiner notes, '[c]ommemorative heritage stands in the dock, accused doubly of commercialising and of selectively inventing, in other words, falsifying, history [...] memory deceptively manipulates and misrepresents the past'.[34] Proclaiming the complexity of Irish commemorative actions and events, such as re-enactments, specifically of some battles of the 1798 Rebellion, Beiner's defence of folk memory and its evolution into contemporary popular commemorative events presents a thoughtful means to consider the impact of ideas of authenticity on formulations of Irish identity.[35] Colin Graham writes that '[a]uthenticity's origins in the colonial process as well as its radiation from the colonial context need to be comprehended and disentangled from various Irish cultural contexts'.[36] Disengaging from potentially simplistic polarities, Graham assesses authenticity's complex usefulness in both historical and contemporary identity formations. Beiner's and Graham's respective explorations of the function of contested authenticity in relation to Irish historical identity imply a reciprocal reliance underpinning a linked reading of the National Famine Memorial and Croagh Patrick.

The artistic artifice of the ship sculpture in its manicured context, the less obvious socio-historic significance of its county context and the mythic connotations of an even larger collective identity associated with its location at the foot of the mountain produce a layered commemorative spectacle. In 2000, the Office of Public Works commissioned a gift from Ireland to the United Nations: *Arrival* also by Behan (8 m high and 7 m long) is a ship comparable in form to the National Famine Memorial and is situated on the plaza of the UN headquarters, New York, with 150 figures disembarking as hopeful survivors, making the link from departure to arrival in a redemptive gesture to the despairing forms in County Mayo.

In art, some images of post-Famine emigration followed on a mid-nineteenth-century European trend when, as Pamela Gerrish Nunn notes emigration was 'one of the most resonant themes that painters of modern life could tackle'.[37] Some of these works reflect on arrivals and others on departures and, though the ship form appears in a number of them, interests in figuration are also critical. Emigration was a sustained outcome of the Famine, and the dates of most images reflect that. For example, *An Irish Immigrant Arriving at Liverpool, c.* 1871, by Scottish artist Erskine Nicol depicts an Irishman at the dockside in Liverpool as he negotiates unwanted attention from lively street boys.[38] The image's atmosphere captures the disconcerting bustle surrounding such moments after the immigrant dismbarks, with the ship a sketchily rendered spectral presence. A watercolour by American artist Samuel Waugh also focuses on arrivals: *The Bay and Harbour of New York/Immigrants Disembarking at the*

Figure 2.5 Samuel Bell Waugh, *The Bay and Harbour of New York/Immigrants Disembarking at the Battery, Castle Garden, New York, c.1853–5*. Oil on canvas, 99 x 198 in. © Museum of the City of New York.

Battery, Castle Garden, New York, c.1853–5, housed at the Museum of New York City (Figure 2.5).

Amid the epic scale of Waugh's harbour image and the vastness of the docked ship, text on a travelling trunk draws attention to the depiction of Irish travellers in this scene. Phonetic spelling and naive handwriting read: 'Pat Murfy for Ameriky'. Two women sitting on the trunk have their backs to the viewer; a position which displays their brown woolly shawls in contrast to the finer garments and bonnets worn by many of the surrounding women. The museum's website outlines that:

> [i]n 1952 a conservator treating the painting in preparation for its display in the Museum's exhibition New York Street Scene, 1852 found its nativist humor objectionable and painted over a whiskey bottle that Waugh had inserted in the back pocket of the young Irishman carrying a knapsack.[39]

Between 1855 and 1890 Castle Garden in New York was used as an immigration centre for millions arriving on US shores. The building at the Battery, previously known as Castle Clinton, is one of New York's oldest structures.[40]

Margaret Allen's *The Last Hour in the Old Land, c.1877*, is a more studied portrait of the moments before departure[41] (Figure 2.6). A family

Figure 2.6 Margaret Allen, *The Last Hour in the Old Land*, 1876. Oil on canvas, 94 x 73.5 cm. Image courtesy of Gorry Gallery, Dublin, Ireland.

group sit together in a dejected mood at a quayside. Derville Murphy notes: 'Behind the couple a poster ironically advertises *The Eviction* with a tag line "a great success", referring to a contemporaneous play at the Palais Royale,' suggesting Allen's political sympathies in codifying the scene.[42] The man is the main focal point of the work and stares directly at the viewer, seeming to implicate them in his plight, while at his knee a girl rests her head and gazes sombrely beyond the picture frame. The weeping mother and bored-looking younger child in the background complete this family portrait of migrants. Like in Nicol's and Waugh's paintings, Allen's interest in clothing serves to situate the work as an image depicting poverty and loss, though, as in the other works, the clothing is in improbably good condition.

In the background of Allen's work and Nicol's Liverpool image are hazy renderings of the masts of tall ships against grey-blue cloudy skies. In Waugh's work the ship looms large and overbearing; its scale dwarfing the flustered masses on the quay. There are few other visual representations of travel from Ireland in the late nineteenth century, and fewer that image the conditions experienced on board during these arduous journeys.

Figure 2.7 Embarkation of an Emigrant Ship, Liverpool, 1850. *The Illustrated London News*, 6 July 1850. Engraving showing a bustling dock yard scene as emigrants, with trunks and boxes, line up to board their ship at Waterloo Docks, Liverpool, 1850. © Illustrated London News Ltd/Mary Evans.

Two examples, printed in the *Illustrated London News*, are, on 1 January 1846, *Irish emigrants on board a ship bound for America in the time of the famine in Ireland*, depicting a cramped interior, and on 6 July 1850 a larger scene, *Irish Emigrants sailing to the US during the Great Famine* (Figure 2.7), showing a bird's-eye view of a cross-section of thronged upper decks.

Performed Memory: Replica Famine Ships

Against the artistic appropriation of the ship as motif has emerged an uncommon type of memorial in the form of two replica Famine ships. The *Dunbrody* was launched in 2001 (Figure 2.8) and the *Jeanie Johnston* (Figure 2.9) undertook its first voyage in 2003. The state sponsorship of these ships indicates an interest in promoting the representation of historical experiences of emigration at an official Government level, in the context of international tourism and, in the case of the *Dunbrody*, through local heritage practices. Promotional material for both vessels emphasizes a positive history for the original ships. The *Jeanie Johnston* 'never lost a soul' and 'it never had a death on board'. On-board mortality on the *Dunbrody* was 'practically non-existent'.[43] The ships both use re-enactment strategies, which are reliant upon what is presented as authentic history, to deploy personal histories as a means to imply collective experience. They also utilize the visitor's spatial and temporal experience to deliver these strategies. The interplay between staging visitor experiences and referencing authentic histories is differently negotiated onboard each ship to present two means of historical re-enactment.

The original *Dunbrody* was a freight ship commissioned by a New Ross merchant family and built in Quebec in 1845. It was principally used to carry timber from Canada and cotton from the USA en route to collect cargo. Between 1845 and 1851, the ship was also used to carry passengers to Canada and the USA. Usually there were about 176 passengers per trip, though on one occasion, in 1847, 313 travelled. The production of the replica ship, now moored in New Ross, County Wexford, was overseen by the John F. Kennedy Trust, at a cost of around IEP 4.7 million, raised from European Union, Irish state and other funding sources.[44]

Tours of the *Dunbrody* start in the Departure Exhibit of the Dunbrody Famine Ship Experience visitor centre, where a tour guide introduces the ship's historical and local relevance in the context of exhibits on

Figure 2.8 *Dunbrody*, New Ross Harbour, County Wexford, Ireland. Image provided by author. By permission of John F. Kennedy Trust.

Figure 2.9 *Jeanie Johnston* Tallship, Dublin Port, Ireland. Image provided by author. By permission of *Jeanie Johnston* Tallship.

Famine-era departures. This is followed by a short film depicting a fictionalized scenario of preparation for emigration, atmospherically filmed in a rundown cottage with a narrative provided by the reading of letters. This is followed by a guided tour of the ship's decks and an introduction to the layout below deck, and finally a re-enactment of parts of the original ship's passenger and crew history. A two-tiered approach shapes a visitor's engagement with the ship: historic authenticity is suggested by the theatrical presence of actor-guides while the contemporary attendance of the visitors is affirmed at a number of points during the tour. The experiences of nineteenth-century passengers and a member of the ship's crew are acted out by actor-guides adopting the various roles in period dress[45] (Figure 2.10).

Directly addressing the audience, in chatty and informal tones, the actor-guides separately present details of these figures through a monologue, which reveals the reasons for their travel and the difficulties and hopes surrounding each journey. On one tour, for example, a young woman who could afford first-class passage to Boston was followed by a less well-dressed woman giving an account of her contrasting experience of and expectation for the journey, and a young ship's first mate detailing food allowances and other statistical information on the ship's passage.

Visitor tickets for the tour take the form of copies of original Famine-era tickets of passage dating from 1849. Each ticket has a name or names referring to real passengers from that year, with details on their space and food allocation for the journey. Once below deck, a visitor can find the bunk space allotted to those named on their ticket. At the end of the tour, the actor-guides engage the audience in friendly dialogue and answer questions while remaining in character.

After the tour, visitors are left to roam the ship. The recreation of the interior below deck impresses on the visitor how crowded and uncomfortable these ships were during such voyages – the bunk allocation was very small considering that an entire family might sleep, sit and eat in one for weeks on end. Having visited the past, visitors are reminded of the cumulative effect of historical time as they disembark through an arrival hall, focusing on diasporic experiences in North America, with a positive tone emphasized throughout the exhibition called the Irish America Wall of Fame. These combined strategies of visitor engagement emphasize the

Figure 2.10 Actor-guides on board the *Dunbrody*. New Ross Harbour, County Wexford, Ireland. Image provided by author. By permission of John F. Kennedy Trust.

contemporary experience of visitors and actor-guides, as much as they account for historical time.

Christopher Balme's work accentuates the multiple significances of the touristic experience at heritage sites and centres as key to un-layering the workings of how history is mediated in staged events at such locations.[46] The combined focus on the *Dunbrody*'s replication of a historical space and the re-enactment of stories of individuals from the past relate to Balme's analysis of framing authenticity through touristic spectatorship. Emphasizing the importance of theatrical aspects of staging history, he accounts different types of touristic events to suggest alternate roles for the viewing tourist. These are the tourist as: witness of a ritual; spectator at a performance; and observer of an ethnographical demonstration. 'The shifts between such positions [...] invite constant redefinitions of fiction and authenticity or of fictionalizations and authentication.'[47] These shifts revolve around alternate presentations and representations of the other, in Balme's example an ethnic other.

On the *Dunbrody* Famine ship, a visitor's experience of the other is one of meeting people apparently from the past (the role-playing actor-guides): observing them and also engaging with them. Within the representations of the historical figures emerges another set of others, defined by the class difference between the historical speakers made apparent in the actor-guides' monologues. And so, a visitor becomes a spectator of the complexity of the past and is temporarily involved in a historic social distinction that erodes an awareness of the present. The dramatic and fictitious nature of the staging is then iterated as the actor-guides focus on the audience (and in particular on any children on the tour), and the visitor's presence in the present day is emphasized. In this way, Balme's conceptualization of the tourist as, at once, witness, spectator and observer comes into play during a visitor's experience on board the *Dunbrody*.

Though the replica Famine ship *Jeanie Johnston* embraces a more conventional form of museum below-deck in its representation of historical experiences, its intimate scale animates the nature of the histories referenced. When docked at Dublin port, the ship is open for tours and visits of its on-board museum, mostly from spring to autumn. When first constructed and launched, the replica ship retraced traditional Irish emigrant routes from Frenit, County Kerry, through some 20 ports in the USA and Canada before returning to Ireland. This symbolic journey in 2003 indicated an agenda of the replica ship's memorial function to be to provide, literally, a moving monument to the original ship's Famine history.

Built in Quebec and used to bring cargo to Liverpool, England, from where it was sold to a merchant from Tralee, County Kerry, the original ship made 16 voyages to North America with an average of 193 migrant passengers per trip. However, in April 1852, some 254 passengers were reported on one trip. The primary source of funding for the replica project came from the Irish government's Famine Commemoration Fund in 1995. The project ran heavily over its estimated budget, and further funding was raised from the Irish government, the European Union and various public and private sponsorships, with the total cost nearing €15.5 million. The ship, owned by the DDA and operated by a sailing company, Rivercruise Ireland Ltd, transfers to Dublin City Council on abolition of the DDA.[48]

Jeanie Johnston's history from the original ship's difficult and lengthy passages – of up to 47 days from Kerry to North America in conditions similar to those on the *Dunbrody* – to the replica ship's identity as a heritage venue is further inflected by its usage as a sail-training and corporate party venue, improvised in response to financial difficulties in sustaining the ship. Its multi-purpose functions reflect changes in Irish society over the last century-and-a-half, with economic downturns marrying with the commercial potential of the ship as a period-style vessel in a country largely surrounded by sea. Financially controversial from the outset, the evolution of the replica *Jeanie Johnston* signifies the passage of recent time as much as it recalls the historical passage made by Famine emigrants on the original namesake.

Nonetheless, the below-deck museum presents a highly evocative representation of Famine emigration. A sign inside the cabin area upstairs reads, 'This way for Passage to North America, 1848', with an illustrated hand directing the visitor down a steep stairwell to the main display area below deck. On the guide-led tour of the *Jeanie Johnston* the visitor arrives downstairs to a dimly lit and silently populated area. Sets of mannequins in nineteenth-century costume mostly typical of poor emigrants, as well as the ship's doctor and captain, are installed in

Figure 2.11   Below Deck Museum, *Jeanie Johnston* Tallship. Dublin Port, County Dublin. Image provided by John O' Neill, *Jeanie Johnston* Tallship.

the bunks, at the table and in other corners (Figure 2.11). Visits to the boat are by guided tour, which reflects on content from a previously available leaflet indicating that these figurations are 'based on real Irish people, who sailed on the *Jeanie Johnston* between 1848 and 1855'.[49]

For each mannequin tableau presented of one or more figures, a story and/or name were supplied in the leaflet.[50] The mannequin representations of James Stack and his family, for example, are packed into a bunk space sleeping head to toe. This tableau is augmented by the guide, as per leaflet text, to reveal to the visitor that James and 11 members of his family had been 'reduced to living in a mud cabin built against a ditch' (a scalp) prior to assisted passage on the *Jeanie Johnston* in 1851. Another figure, named as Young Margaret Conway, is an anxious-looking girl with an unruly mop of red hair sitting at a bunk's edge clasping a small grey cloth, suggestive of her meagre possessions. The guide outlines that she was 15 years old and travelled with her 12-year-old brother with no other family members on board, citing the common fragmentation of families during Famine uprooting.

Elsewhere, a seated man, well-dressed in breeches, waistcoat, jacket and boots, plays the fiddle for a young boy standing beside him, in a more benign representation than the ones that dominate the museum area.

The experiences of passengers who lived with strangers, in close proximity and often in progressively poor health, over weeks of travel are made palpable by the interior space and the figurations: it is not difficult to imagine a couple of hundred passengers confined for most of a journey below deck. The eerily still sustained presence of the mannequins brings home to the visitor the reality of how cramped conditions were on board such Famine ships. In particular, the heads and feet of the Stack family protruding from a small berth assert the tightness of scale and lack of personal privacy experienced on these migrant journeys, as does the crouched position of Margaret Ryal as she breastfeeds her newborn.

Emma Willis proposes the potential of 'ethical theatre' as 'a form of responsiveness', 'contingently bound to social and historical contexts'. Her study of performances that intervene in memorial forms related to traumatic histories is an exploration of 'ethical spectatorship': 'spectatorship where our relation of the performed object is not taken for granted'.[51] For her 'to identify the other (not to identify with the other), means to begin to understand the nature of one's own relationship to that other from outside of our own inside perspective'.[52]

While the Jeanie Johnston relies on the visitor's engagement with the space and guided information presented, the spatial intensity of the life-size scale they are placed in promotes a performative proximity to the history represented. As with the *Dunbrody* re-enactments, the mannequin figures on the Jeanie Johnston and their printed narratives are indicative of a truth-content behind the museum: they are purported to refer to real Famine-era experiences; the affective power of their emblematic stories of personal difficulties is evoked to indicate wider circumstances of Famine emigration. Perhaps more significantly, the tension generated on each of these replica ships, between the ultimate inaccessibility of past experiences and the insertion of the visitor into their representation nonetheless, indicate a provocative play on self and other in the spectatorship of an extraordinarily vast scale of historical economically, where not physically, forced migration.

Moving Subjects; Authentic History

The idea of colonialism as a rupture in Irish history and by extension, its cultural forms, is often accentuated as a persuasive concept by the experience and consequence of the Famine. The population depletion through death and more pronouncedly through emigration that the Famine engendered in a mere decade seems to provide evidence of an intensification of that rupture. That the nationalistic idealism that followed the Famine presented the possibility of an alleged return to Irishness, or at least the beginning of the end of British rule in Ireland, furthers the notion that centuries of British rule in Ireland were somehow an interruption in the narrative of a continuous Irish cultural identity. This line of thinking gained charge in part by the presence of migrants lending visibility abroad to an Irish cause at home. Laurence Geary suggests that the short-lived but intense American Famine-relief effort may have fuelled political feeling in Ireland among the middle classes, which 'found expression in the radicalization of members of the young Ireland movement' with its implicit criticism of British handling of the crisis during 1846–7.[53]

Certainly, Irish independence movements of the late nineteenth century actively promoted ideas of pre-colonial Irishness through the revival of what was called Gaelic life, as was evident in aspects of various cultural movements, across language, literature, theatre, art, crafts and sport.[54] An emphasis on rupture is not unusual within redemptive narratives associated with collective identities perceived, internally at least, as subjugated by imperialism of one kind or another. Exaggerated accent on rupture or break can be further linked to what is termed 'the invention of tradition' in some claims made for homelands.[55] Such modes of invention can also find expression, for example, in over-stated pre-plantation identity without acknowledgement of interim influences or assimilations, desired or otherwise.

Looking to a comparable theoretical frame then, albeit applied to a very different history, presents a useful lens for considering the link between pressured migrant journeys during and after the Irish Famine and post-colonial trading on collective identities associated with cultural rupture. In the context of Africentricity and its relationship to slavery, Paul Gilroy has suggested that retrospectively defined processes of social memory are caught up in a polemical fight between modernity and tradition in the ways in which a race re-members itself, particularly in diasporic situations.[56] In relation to black culture, he describes the desire to consider 'tradition' as pre-slavery: 'It seems as if the complexity of slavery and its location within modernity has to be actively forgotten if a clear orientation to tradition and thus to the present circumstances of blacks is to be acquired.'[57]

Gilroy points out that though the 'middle passage', the experience of the slave ships, is one defined entirely by force and concluded in the modern era, as it had begun for the passengers, in bondage, the journeys of slave ships represent connection as well as rupture. What he terms the black Atlantic – 'the web of diaspora identities and concerns'[58] – provides the substance of his argument against simplistic oppositions between tradition and modernity. He presents a meditation on the complexity of contemporary racial identity in the context of cultural forms that actively seek to negotiate a troublesome past or grievous history.[59]

By attempting to return the visitor in time, the *Dunbrody* and *Jeanie Johnston* insist that migrant journeys are worth commemorating, though what emerge are ambiguous and difficult acts of remembering. Firstly, the appropriation of authenticity as central to both memorial ships accentuates the desire to recreate history by appealing to the visitor's potential of personal identification: the individual like the one alluded to by an actor-guide or a mannequin could have been the visitor's ancestors who may have travelled in such circumstances. Secondly, and in counterpoint to this agenda, the contrast between the talking interactive actor-guides on the *Dunbrody* and the silent mannequins resisting engagement on the *Jeanie Johnston* demonstrates, though differently, the theatre of representation. Considered together, these strategies undermine rupture as the only significant means of accounting for the radical mid-nineteenth-century shifts in the Irish domestic population. As Fintan O'Toole has noted, '[s]eas don't separate, they join. The ocean is not a cultural barrier but a means of passage.'[60] The iconic Famine ships in replica present in their breadth of representational functions the potential remembrance of arrival and linkage as well as departure and separation.

A perceived islandness of Ireland has entrenched connotations that are particularly notable in early twentieth-century rhetoric on an Irish republic, often articulated through an obsession with small Atlantic islands, off Ireland's western coastline, as sites where authentic Irish culture resides:

> For the young country, the Blasket and Aran Islands had, as well as their echoes of Greek myth, a more specific aura of pre-history. They were part of the creation myth of the Irish State [...] They were a past that would also be the future. Their supposed isolation had preserved them from corruption, kept their aboriginal Irishness intact through the long centuries of foreign rule.[61]

The territorially problematic limits of the description of Ireland as an island are nonetheless relevant to the sustained symbolism of ships in Famine remembrance, across pictorial, sculptural and replica forms, and their potency as vehicles for postmemory.

To theatrically indicate the experiences of the difficult overseas and transatlantic journeys made by so many during the Famine, taking full account of geographical and cultural locations, may be the closest social memory, the linking of social identity to historical experiences, can get to an authentic artefact of Famine-era emigration. Nebulous today in the midst of local positivisms, these troubled journeys accelerated the growth of the Irish diaspora in the new worlds of the USA, Canada and Australia, illustrating both Gilroy's and O'Toole's observations of journey and seas as connecting factors in cultural dynamics. As a result, another type of link developed more recently across these seas reflects on the ongoing impact of diaspora on collective identities. The trade routes that turned hungry exiles into ethnic cargo in the mid-nineteenth century are today traversed, in reverse, by genealogy tourists. Such searches for roots are quests for 'origin' and reflective of desires to establish an 'authentic' cultural identity through connecting the past to the present day. In relation to Famine memorializations in particular, contemporary enthusiasm for genealogy may have contributed to support for some fascinating historical projects, including the *Australian Monument to the Great Irish Famine (1845–1852)*.

Unveiled in 1999 at Hyde Park Barracks, Sydney, the monument, instigated by Clonmel-born Irish-Australian Tom Power, was designed by sculptors Hossein and Angela Valamanesh, with a soundscape by Paul Carter (Figure 2.12). It is dedicated to the memory of 4,114 girls and young women who came to Australia on 20 ships from workhouses

Figure 2.12 *The Australian Monument to the Great Irish Famine (1845–1852)*, 1999. Design: Hossein Vlamamesh and Angela Vlamanesh. Soundscape: Paul Carter. Hyde Park Barracks, Sydney, Australia. Image from architectural report by Phillips-Pinkington Architects, 1999, and supplied by the Great Irish Famine Commemoration Committee. © Phillips-Pinkington Architects.

across the 32 counties of Ireland, on a special emigration scheme, Earl Grey's Famine Orphan Scheme, between 1848 and 1850. The main part of the monument takes the form of a dislocated sandstone wall of the barracks, into which is placed a glass panel, etched with 420 names. The barracks was designed as a male convict barracks, but in the mid-nineteenth century was an immigration depot for single female immigrants.

During the memorial's design phase, a newspaper advertising campaign resulted in 420 names being nominated by relatives for inclusion on the panel. A workhouse-type table with a stool and bowl protrudes from the wall on both sides, providing both a visual link and a disruption in the monument's depiction. The monument's manipulation of the site and other material elements bears witness to the enmeshed experiences of uprooting, dislocation, connection and separation that define a migrant's journey.

The website for the monument includes an illuminating representation of migration, with a revealing and moving database, The Famine Orphan Girl Database, on the girls and young women who arrived in Australia through this scheme.[62] Two entries on the same page outline the fates of two 16-year old girls, who travelled on board The Lady Kennaway in 1848:

- Surname: Boyle
- First name: Ellen
- Age on arrival: 16
- Native place: Donegal
- Parents: Not recorded
- Religion: Roman Catholic
- Ship name: Lady Kennaway (Melbourne, 1848)
- Workhouse: Donegal, Donegal PLU?
- Other: shipping: nursemaid, cannot read or write; empl. Charles Ryan at Doogalook, Goulburn River £12 3 months; married William Calnan at Melbourne 1849; 11 children born Kilmore, Longwood, Violet Town area are noted on Ancestry; died Violet Town 1896.

- Surname: Berne [Burns, Byrne?]
- First name: Mary
- Age on arrival: 16
- Native place: Tuam, Galway
- Parents: Not recorded
- Religion: Roman Catholic
- Ship name: Lady Kennaway (Melbourne, 1848)
- Workhouse: Galway, Tuam
- Other: shipping: house servant, cannot read or write. Mary Burns, see 'Melbourne Argus' 27 Feb 1849, employed by John Bland Elizabeth St., £7 1 year, complaint by Mr Bland, tinsmith, about her bad behaviour, court sent her back to employer with warning to behave.[63]

Balme's discussion on authenticity, like any framing device on the making of meaning, in a heritage context underlines the tourist position as an outcome of a series of socio-political choices. Relatedly, Graham points out: 'Authenticity may resist definition, but its materiality in textuality is undeniable.'[64] He notes Benedict Anderson's idea that 'authenticity "proves" itself through its simultaneous and contradictory textual existence and refusal to be defined',[65] in interdependent theoretical states between authenticity and imagined communities (of which national identity is one). In the forging of collective identities such as national identity, narrative time and ideas of origin are conventionally interdependent: time of origin of identity (locating the source of the myth), time of suppression of the collective group (colonial experience or imperial rule) and the reassertion of 'authentic' identity (post-colonialism, leading towards expression of independence, such as nation state).

Searching and scrolling through the Famine Orphan Girl Database, the limits of rupture as signifying a meaningful break between the past and the future are undeniable. Connectivity between past and present is generated by the – textual, visual – presentation of a series of data entries on named and located individuals both brings history home and spreads the story in a manner complemented by material and located monuments. Authenticity might then be considered less a representation of authority in presentations of history today than one of many interconnected strategies that engage the contemporary spectator within commemorative visual culture. These strategies of representing past experiences of migration that pertained to a vast set of individuals, within a broad, complex socio-economic situation, might be usefully held to Lloyd's description: 'In eviction, homelessness, death and the scattering of emigration, there is no recovery to be traced but only conditions of a transformed subjectivity, subdued but not subjected.'[66]

With a dearth of artefacts relating to Famine ships, commemorative representations negotiate and, through processes of imaging, replication and theatre, create a duality of representation in which there is both identification with the subjects of history and recognition of their otherness. An implicit critique of authenticity in strategies of remembering, this further reflects the fraught nature of memorial practice more widely, with its inherent implication of forgetting and the promise of letting go of a painful past. Affiliations are made through time between subjects and designated sites of memory through the national monument, art works, replica ships and representation of an immigration centre described here. On closer inspection, each type of site emerges, respectively, as equally artificial, mythological, populated, bridging and illuminated. The constructed nature of each representation of troubled migrations that transpired along historic trade routes thwarts simplifications about supposed rupture to instead complicate the temporal relationship of the past to the present and further imaginatively collapse the dominion of geographical distances between Ireland and the destinations of those of de Vere's description 'huddled together without light, without air, wallowing in filth and breathing a fetid atmosphere, sick in body, dispirited in heart'.

3

Sites of Memory and the Others of History

Otherness, Empathy and Post-Colonial Heritage

Experiential presence of the past at museum and heritage centres is substantially synthesized through layered imaginative geography. This interpretative space between events and their representation is also a perceptual gap between history and memorial culture, bound up in the legacies of modern tourism and emergent heritage and exhibition cultures. David Brett highlights a distinction often considered between visual and material culture: the first is the realm of images and appearances, and the latter of things and objects.[1] Visual culture, then, is considered less rooted in place than material culture, which is implied to have significant bearing within and upon geographical locations. Brett notes that in some circumstances, culture can become 'locative and placing'.[2]

Histories of exhibition practices of the nineteenth century, however, indicate that material and visual cultures are interconnected in the mediation of placed-ness. Tony Bennett's observations in his seminal text on the 'exhibitionary complex' of nineteenth-century developments in public exhibition formats in urban centres demonstrate that 'technologies of vision' are 'embodied in the architectural forms'.[3] This engendering of citizenship in terms of spectacle and surveillance, the visitor both viewed and viewing, remains partially consonant with recent heritage formats in both urban and rural contexts. Brett has commented that '[t]he heritage industry represents a further extension of the power of the manipulated spectacle over history [...] heritage is [...] a part of the more general commodification of experiences'.[4] Bennett's and Brett's analyses note that objects on display appear to be a sharing of knowledge, while a further spectacle is created by the viewers themselves moving through display areas: revelation and containment occur in the passage through space, as the placed-ness of material culture is visualized.

Museums and heritage sites broker personal and collective identity formations typically cued from viewing displayed collections. Susan Pearce's accounts of the constitutive role of museum collections in the formation of identity bear relevance to wider modes and materials of representational practices at heritage sites.[5] On an international stage, centuries of trophy plunder and twenty-first-century instances of videoed museological destruction demonstrate the continued power of heritage locations as sites of political statement, perpetuated by contestations over similarity and difference between the figures of history and forms of empathic witnessing in the present day.

Pierre Nora identifies an inherent contradiction within historical remembrance:

> From countless 'microhistories' we take shards of the past and try to glue them together, in the hope that the history we reconstruct might seem more like the history we experience. One might try to sum all this up by coining a term like 'mirror-memory', but the problem is that mirrors reflect only identical copies of ourselves, whereas what we seek in history is difference – and, through difference, a sudden revelation of our elusive identity. We seek not our origins but a way of figuring out what we are from what we are no longer.[6]

Nora suggests a complex subject-relation with individual figures of history that emphasizes the passing of time as a differentiating factor in identity formation, in effect producing a qualifying *otherness* of history. In a post-colonial context this observation has pronounced relevance, where processes of radical differentiation become central in the assertion of collective identity to forge both cultural connections and differences. Luke Gibbons has suggested that the post-colonial turn in Irish criticism, for example, 'represents an attempt to extend the horizons of the local to distant and often very different cultures',[7] and the 'ability to look outward [...] may be best served by reclaiming those lost narratives of the past which generate new solidarities in the present'.[8]

Regardless of the history, underpinning any encounters with the objects and places of heritage lie contentious distinctions between the concepts of reality and representation; the curatorial status of original and copy; and the resultant production of history and fiction. Barbara Kirshenblatt-Gimblett proposed that museums, as sites of representations of the world, create the world as 'real'.[9] She discusses 'virtuality' at the extreme end of heritage practices, such as the living history of folk villages.[10] Even in the context of such overtly entertaining and diverting tourist practices now commonplace, the modes of virtuality suggested, for example as discussed, on board the replica Famine ships – re-enactments on the *Dunbrody* and the life-size tableaux presented on the *Jeanie Johnston* – effectively erode the power of rupture as trope in narratives of collective identity to foster empathic encounters with the others of history.

In other contexts, debates have since arisen around the critical useful-ness of overly performance-based representations, where arguably the lean toward simulation may become a more memorable aspect of a museum or memorial visit than the history it illustrates. A common critique, in literature on Holocaust representations in particular, is of excessive emphasis on 'performed' memory or 'experience-based' representations of history functioning at the expense of more sedate accounts associated with the presentation of authentic artefacts. By implication, an apparent over-identification with individuals of the past may erode the terrifying banality of grievous histories as systemic occurrences.

Paul Williams notes that the emergence of the performing museum has come about from the confluence of a surge in memorialization and an increase in theatrical display techniques,[11] with the result that '[i]n the performing museum the total physical environment itself becomes the attraction'.[12] While largely referring to designed aspects of memorial museums, the statement can be applied to contemporary modes of heritage spectatorship more generally. Bodily engagements of spectators are increasingly implicated in modes of representation, from interactive tours to immersive sites: the pioneering of synaesthetic experience may problematically be assumed to result in greater cognizance by the visitor of the histories presented. Juliet Steyn phrases the curatorial challenge:

> Resting upon notions of empathy and identification, an assumption is at work which asserts that experience naturally pertains to comprehension [...] Does this mean that 'understanding' history means that one has to have had an experience of it, to be in it? That the distinction between the 'real' and the 'representation' is no longer sustainable as a critical force? That in order to overcome this 'loss' of distinction, the loss itself must be actually inscribed? That we only have recourse to the 'real' through the drama of identification? That the self is reduced so as to become merely an elaboration or reflection of the Other, in other words, the same as.[13]

However, forms of experiential heritage aligned to grievous histories can encompass curatorial strategies that engender empathic responses from visitors at location-based representations, without necessarily overwriting the subjects – the others – of history, as Emma Willis' conception of ethical spectatorship advocates. Jill Bennett develops a concept of 'interim space', which 'may be understood as the contingent place that emerges in the wake of loss and conflict, particularly as the memory of place is inscribed within a postcolonial history'.[14] This interim space she describes as 'opened up by the often volatile relationship between common memory and sense memory'.[15] For Bennett, empathic vision is 'enacted as a modality of seeing',[16] and empathy 'characterized by a distinctive combination of affective and intellectual operations, but also by a dynamic oscillation'. With these definitions, her spatial metaphor linking common and sense memory sits outside of oversimplifications of experiential-based representations:

> This conjunction of affect and critical awareness may be understood to constitute the basis of an empathy grounded not in affinity (*feeling for* another insofar as we can imagine *being* that other) but on a *feeling for* another that entails an encounter with something irreducible and different, often inaccessible.[17]

While her work specifies art's capacity to transform perception, in particular of trauma within living (and sense) memory, this chapter is concerned with historical representations at museum and heritage sites that traverse a comparable curatorial spectrum, designed to elicit empathic responses from visitors reflecting respectful comprehension of the particular otherness of grievous history.

Acknowledging the general temporal and social distance of historical subjects to present-day viewers, these heritage centres, museums and historic sites are largely to be found in small towns, at the edges of villages or on country estates. These locations aptly reflect the position of the Famine within a history of rural and agricultural poverty shaped by imperial wealth: that is to say the hinterlands of trade centres such as market towns made up of townlands and villages that were then much more populated than they are today. The Famine's present-day representations are, as a result, positioned within a paradigm of post-colonial negotiations of related, and located, heritage cultures. Though Thomas Laqueur notes, 'history taught that the past was elusive and its tangible remains were thus precious',[18] as the history of the Famine is one of poverty, the dearth of material traces relative to its scale of devastation creates a conundrum in a sector usually defined by such reification of material objects and fetishization of partial evidence. And so, Françoise Vergès' 'history and culture of the vanquished and the oppressed' find commemorative expression through the 'material objects' most of the subjects never had: Big Houses, parkland estates and land to call their own.

Within the framework of post-colonial heritage, can representations of the Famine at museums and heritage centres escape the reductive binarisms so often associated with traumatic memory formation of death and survival; horror and heroism; perpetrator and victim? Given the paucity of material evidence associated with the Famine, by what means are ideas of secondary witnessing configured through encounters with objects to portray the suffering of others? In a post-colonial context, to what extent do the physical locations and aspects of these Famine representations inform politicized loci of memorialization?

To consider these questions, this chapter focuses firstly on the role of objects in exhibition practice and secondly on the significance of visitor engagement with place in forming historic representations. The first focus is on the thematic of food relief as a primary indication of transitions from individual experiences of hunger to a description of mass dispossession attendant on a wider history of the Famine. The emphasis on place reflects on an expansive understanding of the Famine as part of a formative national narrative of civil rebellion, critically linked to the politics of land ownership. Both these aspects of Famine representations at heritage sites – personal, localized searches for sustenance and the forging of a collective identity – are emotively charged, empathically demanding and ethically resonant.

Intimate Encounters with Disruptive Objects: Food Relief in Focus

As the inadequacy of the workhouse system as a means of addressing a growing lack of access to affordable food and housing in Famine times became clear to many during the Famine, the Temporary Relief Act of 1847, better known as the Soup Kitchen Act, was rushed through Parliament in recognition of the immediate widespread need for administrated access to sustenance and outdoor relief. On the face of it, the Act was to provide provision for food distribution and rationing of food for sale to those who were able-bodied but could not afford to buy for themselves.[19] Government soup kitchens were set up around the country from mid-May 1847 serving free watery soup to thousands daily. By mid-August, soup kitchens were feeding 3 million people daily,[20] and in some parts of the west of Ireland the entire population was reliant on the kitchens for sustenance.[21] A system of differentiation between levels of destitution became key to provisions for either indoor (entry to workhouse) or outdoor relief (including food aid). In some cases, in order to demonstrate a need for outdoor relief, a family would prove pauperism by entering the workhouse for a period and, on being approved as destitute, receive food aid for up to two months after their release.[22]

Basic sustenance provided by official soup kitchens was supplemented by charitable administrations of voluntary and private relief committees.[23] Among these groups was the Society of Friends, commonly known as Quakers. James Donnelly argues that the actions of the Society in setting up soup kitchens or houses at the start of 1847 prompted the Government to address the need for the provision of food on a national scale.[24] By late 1846 the Society had formally become involved in Famine relief, and provided direct food aid for just over a year.[25] Donnelly writes that they provided 'fifty giant soup boilers' early in 1847 and in total contributed almost 300 boilers throughout Ireland.[26] Christine Kinealy suggests that the popular memory of the Society's intervention in Famine relief was sustained by their role in keeping the Famine in the press media in Ireland and England.[27] Their social standing gave them the opportunity to publish and provide eyewitness accounts, allowing them to function as a volunteer pressure group. This was borne out in images as well as in text, and on 16 January 1847 the *Illustrated London News* depicted the Society's soup kitchen in Cork city, which they established in November 1846[28] (Figure 3.1).

Within frameworks of extensive displays on the Famine, both the Skibbereen Heritage Centre in County Cork and the Famine Exhibition at the Irish Agricultural Museum and Johnstown Castle Gardens in County Wexford utilize large objects to represent the experiences and scale of Famine-related food relief. The particular contextual – curated and designed – strategies employed at these sites provide the interpretative function of the objects associated with food.

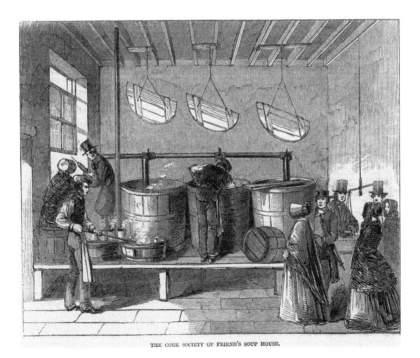

THE CORK SOCIETY OF FRIEND'S SOUP HOUSE.

Figure 3.1 The Cork Society of Friend's Soup House. *Illustrated London News*, 16 January 1847. Soup house set up by Cork Quakers to provide relief for those affected by the failure of the potato harvest. © Illustrated London News Ltd/Mary Evans.

At the Skibbereen Heritage Centre, in Skibbereen town, a series of displays recounts the Famine's history and its effect on the local area. Thematically organized around Emigration, Press Reports, Soup Kitchens, After The Famine and Why Skibbereen?, the densely filled exhibition space utilizes diverse methods of display to engender parity between different ideas of historical witness. Videos of actors in period costume recounting individual testimony are surrounded with statistical information; anecdotal knowledge is presented alongside documentary evidence; and archaeological objects are equated with simulated replicas. Recessed into the jaggedly shaped walkway is a series of display areas containing painted scenes of Famine life with three-dimensional figuration and contemporary props set behind panes of glass. Text panels explain the significance of each theme depicted in the vignettes. Between these, large wall panels with images, text and graphics underpin the exhibition route and provide information on the local history of the Famine within a national context. Among those represented by the videoed actors are a local doctor and a relief committee member: in facing the camera, they address their monologues directly to the viewer.

In the context of these layered representational strategies sit a number of large items relating to Famine-era food relief: two soup pots, a water trough, a millstone and a half-full sack labelled 'Relief . . .'. These objects seem at odds with the predominant neatness of the exhibition. Unsuitable for hoisting into vitrines or sitting safely on eye-level plinths, the objects are also unwieldy in an interpretative context. Previously unremarkable functional objects presented in a highly curated context otherwise efficiently trading on the artificial nature of display practices, they embody the conundrum of a visitor's sense of history. The stony crudeness of the water trough for horses and the millstone in particular at once challenge and emphasize the visitor's distance from the past. Unlike the other large objects, the sack is of recent manufacture, a replica, as evident from its cleanliness. Though its newness detracts from its signifying power, it points to a basic practical depiction of international aid projects and, like the other large objects, sits productively ill at ease among the cool confines of monitors, glass cases and designed wall panels.

The worn surface of the millstone and the sooty black emptiness of the pots are evocative of people long dead: respectively holding indexical traces of those who ground corn in workhouses and those who queued at soup kitchens. One of the soup pots is displayed opposite a wall panel on Soup Kitchens (Figure 3.2). The Soyer's Soup recipe is printed nearby and draws attention to the paucity of ingredients used.[29] The other pot is situated among a series of smaller artefacts in the first exhibition area. With minimal contextual information supplied for these objects – the labels give only the donor's name and the object's function – their physical awkwardness usefully disrupts the centre's narrative tidiness, rendering them effective reminders of the messy scale of history.

The Famine corridor and exhibition room at the Irish Agricultural Museum and Johnstown Castle Gardens originated from a 1996–7 touring exhibition and opened as a permanent exhibition in July 2008. Johnstown is a lush estate developed around the still-standing nineteenth-century-renovation residence of Johnstown Castle, with formal gardens, mature trees, two lakes, walkways and a deer park. The castle is not open to the public, but the museum, gardens and grounds are. Also on the site are the main offices of Teagasc, the Agricultural and Food Development Authority, its research facility, as well as the museum.

As at Skibbereen, the main Famine Exhibition room at Johnstown is densely populated and thematically organized, with wall panels featuring diagrams and charts among a range of textual and image sources. These outline the national story of the Famine with special attention to the Wexford region. There is a focus on the blight itself: how and why it started, spread and the long-lasting effects it had, in keeping with Teagasc's more general purpose of pioneering food production in Ireland.[30] Interpretative elements are apparent, such as the text panel titled *The Lessons*, which emphasizes that the politics of food (production, export, import, disintegration) and the underpinning desire to make retrospective sense of the Famine are axiomatically staged elements of representation.

Notably, a centrally-placed life-scale fourth-class cottage, or cabin, structure accentuates the blend of display techniques in the room. Surrounded by period objects including a butter churn and farm implements, the whitewashed, thatch-roofed cottage serves as an immersive introductory station to the exhibition rooms. Inside the cramped interior, an audio provides a historical context, while peat fumes complete the sensory experience. The attractive brightly painted white exterior of the cottage belies the small dark interior and images a way of

Figure 3.2 Soup Pot, Skibbereen Heritage Centre, County Cork, Ireland. Image provided by author. By permission of Skibbereen Heritage Centre.

life very different from the site it inhabits on the Johnstown Estate. Positioned within the exhibition room as a boldly artificial construct, its representational power extends across the exhibition rooms as a counterpoint to the artefacts presented elsewhere.

In a corner of the room two large artefacts are used in an assemblage presentation on workhouse experiences (Figure 3.3). A large wooden door is situated near a long wooden table with benches. *Entrance Door to Callan (County Kilkenny) Workhouse* is a dislocated object, now painted green and varnished and set in a mock stone archway and doorstep. Beside it is a long wooden table with benches to either side, *Pine Table from the Old Workhouse at John's Hill, Waterford City*, 1890s. The table is randomly set with a series of wooden plates and spoons. Wall panels provide general information on private and public relief measures and the consequences of the Famine in terms of disease epidemics. A vignette of the crude appearance of a workhouse interior, the assemblage conveys a sense of the basic nature of provision at such places.

Figure 3.3 Workhouse assemblage, *Famine Exhibition Room*. Irish Agricultural Museum and Johnstown Castle Gardens, County Wexford, Ireland. Image provided by author. By permission of Irish Agricultural Museum, Johnstown Castle.

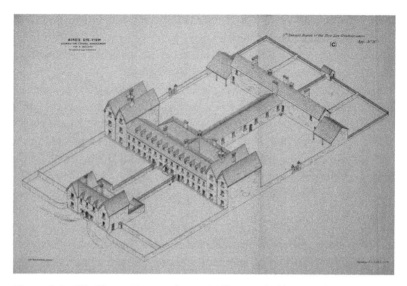

Figure 3.4 Workhouse Design: George Wilkinson, 'Fifth Annual Report of the Poor Law Commissioners. Papers relating to the Providing of Workhouses in Ireland', London, 2 May 1839, Appendix 10. Image courtesy of the Irish Architectural Archive.

British architect George Wilkinson designed the prototype workhouse complex (Figure 3.4). He modelled his generic design directly on workhouses he had built in Wales and England, and the Irish ones were similarly functional in plan. The layout typically comprised an entrance building, where inmates were formally admitted, washed down and had their own clothing taken away; main accommodation area for inmates and matrons; a centrally positioned dining hall, with kitchens and washhouses at either side: and typically, behind this an infirmary. Later, fever houses were added in separate buildings, in recognition of the contagious nature of many illnesses at this time.[31]

Though a dining room would not have been located so near a front door, the collapsing of real space on two levels as depicted at Johnstown – within a representation of a workhouse interior and the geographical sources for the artefacts – allows each element to play off the other's presence. The imposing scale of the doorway and the repetition of the place-settings impress upon the viewer the authoritarianism encountered when seeking relief work and shelter, and the programmatic system of mass feeding projects. These elements, illuminated in light of the hard-hitting descriptions on the 'Disease Epidemics' panel, successfully evoke what must have been a conflation of hope, trepidation, relief and disillusionment on the part of anyone seeking or receiving workhouse relief.

Jennifer Bonnell and Roger Simon have written on the nature of encountering the suffering of others through what they call 'difficult exhibitions':

> [W]hat defines the difficult exhibit is what happens in that moment when one receives the gift that an exhibition enacts, when one comes face to face with the troubling consequences of the 'otherness of knowledge'. What happens in this moment is an experience that mixes partial understanding with confusion and disorientation, the certainty of another's fear and suffering with one's own diffuse anxiety and disquiet.[32]

Implying that empathy is reliant on an intimate encounter, intimacy is not, they argue, 'solely a matter of physical scale leading to the narrowing of the interval between two points in space'.[33] Instead, 'an intimate encounter suggests a relation in which one inhabits the world but does not settle in it [...] Intimacy in the exhibit hall then references a moment when one becomes undone, absorbed in the singularity of another's existence.'[34] The 'mix' they describe is supplanted by a temporal erosion of distance from history or otherness resulting from a momentary loss of self, in the face of the other, and occurs in singular experiences with the past, difference or any manifestation of otherness.

By similarly regarding the creation of subjects at museum and heritage sites, this process of awareness might engender what Emmanuel Lévinas terms a 'radical passivity'.[35] Coming face to face with a vulnerable individual at each site, the visitor might become morally implicated in a present-day acknowledgement of the continued importance of the past life stories presented.[36] Lévinas retains the idea of the other as a positive and socially (ethically) useful effacing of the self.[37] A commonality between what Bonnell and Simon and Lévinas suggest is a temporary loss of self, as central to their perceptions of encounters with otherness, in order to see the other. The value Bonnell and Simon ascribe to this moment is definitive of their privileging of individuals.

The gift they describe as one that 'carries with it the demand that the visitors attend to and assess the significance of what they are being given' implies an underpinning ethical imperative made possible through an encounter,[38] such as at an exhibition, that writes the subject. However, the 'undoing of the self' is immediately overwritten by an inscription on Bennett's idea of 'interim space': in this case, where present-day experiences of the visitor's senses collide with concepts of the history of, in these examples, unspecified and unknown others. The unwieldy objects discussed here at Johnstown and Skibbereen appear as Laqueur's 'precious tangible remains', constructed as such by exhibition placement proffering by intimate proxy encounters with unnamed individuals from the past.

Blending museological conventions of objects 'in context' and 'in situ', to borrow Kirshenblatt-Gimblett terms, respectively at Skibbereen and Johnstown, a core objective of heritage (to draw attention to the past) is played out through a mix of surviving and manufactured objects of history.[39] At Johnstown, history is delineated with equal conviction via dislocated artefacts (the workhouse vignette) and artificial simulation (the cottage) with the 'in situ' displays (again, the workhouse vignette), provoking visitors to conjure a vast, complex story through stage settings. Imagine: the people that were evicted from a small dark interior like this one, knocked at such a door and sat, ill, at such a table. It seems less critical than at first glance when and how the material things were made; their instrumental power is potentially equivalent. At Skibbereen, large empty and worn artefacts have literally travelled in time to convincingly animate the scale of Famine relief, now the more compelling for strategically contrasting to the 'in context' accounts across the gallery.

Disobedient Nationalism and the Houses of Heritage

'Museums create master narratives through acting as both the constructor of present-day "reality" and through bringing into focus a memory of the past that (coincidentally) supports the present.'[40] Eilean Hooper-Greenhill outlines how visual narratives are constructed by the collation of material objects, of which site is one, and their interpretation.[41] She also writes, 'Cultural symbols have the power to shape cultural identities at both individual and social levels; to mobilize emotions, perceptions and values; to influence the way we feel and think. In this sense culture is generative, constructivist.'[42] At a number of heritage sites in Ireland, the constitutive confluence of place (location and building) and objects (internally displayed, artefacts, images and text) constructs master narratives of political rebellion in relation to Famine memory. At some, place is the defining prism through which disobedient nationalisms, as an expression of civil unrest, are refracted in post-colonial readings of Famine-era events.

At sites of Famine remembrance, international affiliations arise across time and/or across geographic terrain in modes specific to different representational emphases accorded to the grievous history. While the three museums discussed in this section – the National Famine Museum at Strokestown Park, County Roscommon, the Famine Warhouse 1848 at Ballingarry, County Tipperary and, the National Museum of Ireland's (NMI) Museum of Country Life at Turlough Park House, County Mayo – and in particular the museum at Strokestown, collectively house a rich resource of interior displays and exhibits, the focus in this reading is on the influence of geo-specific interpretations of the collections, display

Figure 3.5 Strokestown Park House and The National Famine Museum (Stable Buildings), Strokestown Park, County Roscommon, Ireland. © Strokestown Park.

architecture and sites. Specifically, this highlights the means by which each site constructs locally rooted approaches to Famine history within competing concepts of disobedient nationalisms in their inherent dispensations of space and time.

The primary museum devoted to the Famine is the National Famine Museum at Strokestown Park.[43] With its notorious history as a large landlord estate, Strokestown presents a local story through which wider Famine narratives emerge. Strokestown Park is privately owned, with the Famine museum located in the buildings of the original estate's Stable Yards (Figure 3.5). Westward Garage Group bought the site in 1979 and its founder, businessman Jim Callery, realized its extraordinary heritage value and set about the arduous task of conserving the site and grounds.[44] It first opened to the public in 1994 and since 2015 has been operated by the Irish Heritage Trust (IHT), as part of a rural regeneration programme.[45] According to the museum's website, '[i]t was designed to commemorate the history of the famine in Ireland and in some ways to balance the history of the "Big House"'.[46] Under the auspices of the IHT, the museum now has a clearer national remit, indicated by its current title as an Irish national museum dedicated to the Famine. The Big House, of splendid Palladian design, is open for guided tours and visitors are free to stroll through the extensive parkland and restored walled gardens.[47] The stately house architecture and 300-acre estate grounds provide marked contrast to the emphasis on deprivation in the museum's exhibits and information panels in the stables.

During the Famine, Major Denis Mahon was Strokestown's landlord. Ciarán Ó'Murchadha describes the ruthless dispossession policy: 'In one of the greatest single clearances ever executed, Mahon had ejected 3,000 of his tenants, and "emigrated" a further thousand, under appalling conditions to America.'[48] Mahon was murdered in November 1847 amid ensuing civil unrest, but his successor, Henry Pakenham Mahon, continued the programme of clearances. The supposed assassin of Mahon was tried and hanged. The provision of this dramatic microhistory is persuasively framed by the technology of the site's narrative function in exploring the museum and its context, and in particular, its specific history as representative of the socio-political impact of the Famine.[49]

With a wide range of visual and material sources, the museum displays are thematically organized. The Ascendency section orients the museum's context in local and wider historical terms. Alongside vitrine presentations of a pocket watch that belonged to Major Denis Mahon, a portrait drawing of him and a wall-based large family photograph of his descendants are information panels on the Landed Gentry, the Dublin Parliament and the Linen Industry.

By way of strategic contrast to this contextual information are two small images: a copy of a drawing, *A Cottier Tenant and his Family, 1830s*, and a colour photograph, *Eritrea, April 1991*. The first image depicts a family lying huddled beneath a blanket in front of an open hearth with a bullock tethered behind them sharing the heat in an Irish cottage. In the second image, three children lie beneath an old blanket on a makeshift mattress for a bed of a small mud hut and in the background is a bullock resting. The impoverished settings in the images counter the wealth described in the room and by the museum's own location at Strokestown Park.

Here and elsewhere in the museum there is another comparison made across time and geography. A three-legged Irish stool in one room bears visual relation to an African stool or *gambur*, possibly from Somalia, in the final exhibition room.[50] Connecting an Irish past with more recent experiences of famine in other countries indicates a desire to make historical experience resonate in the present and has clear uses in raising awareness of dispossession as repeated systemic occurrences. It is a delicate representational alliance to make, however, as neocolonial forms of primitivism may also serve to distance the more recently suffering subject. The double otherness at Strokestown, between historical subjects (landlord class and dispossessed) and between the present-day subject and spectator (dispossessed people elsewhere and museum visitor) are persuasive means of producing layered empathic responses.

Other exhibition rooms at Strokestown fill out the action-packed history of the estate, the horrific unfolding of Famine dispossession and hunger with explanations on the potato blight and the scientific efforts to allay it. Blended displays engage the visitor throughout including a 12-minute 1994 documentary film by Pat Murphy in one of the central areas (Figure 3.6). The film provides a caesura in the conventions of museological display, cueing an immersive meditation on Famine experiences and the nature of place. Its 'anti-documentary' style finds echoes in Trinh T. Minh-ha's approach to 'speaking nearby' her filmic

Figure 3.6 Exhibition Room, The National Famine Museum, Strokestown Park, County Roscommon, Ireland. © Strokestown Park.

subjects, and is an approach apparent in Murphy's feature film work in the 1980s.[51] Its placement suggests the museum's overall curatorial caution about over-defining Famine history.

In the centre of one exhibition room a glass case positioned at waist height displays a maquette-like scale model of the sprawling townland of Gortoose/Strokestown. In the language of a scale model, the relationship between the layout of the town and the physical extent of the estate that fed its livelihood until Famine times are depicted. Various exhibits and panels in the room are reflected in the protective glass covering of the case. This succinctly highlights the contingency of historical account to specific locations. It also encourages the visitor's awareness of their physical presence within the museum's representations of the past and the townland it references.

Across the Strokestown site – exhibition areas, the Big House and the parklands – the local history is effectively related to larger narratives of identification, both national and universal. The maquette/model in the

Figure 3.7 Famine Warhouse 1848, Ballingarry, County Tipperary, Ireland. © Photographic Unit, National Monuments, Department of Culture, Heritage and the Gaeltacht.

museum highlights this evocation of microhistory. 'In its best version, microhistory takes a singular episode from the past and makes it stand for something much bigger than the sum of its parts',[52] as is affectively demonstrated at Strokestown. On the museum's opening its first curator, Luke Dodd, noted that 'the estate has assumed a new and meaningful function in an Ireland that's completely different from the one that originally produced it'.[53] Since then, the museum has augmented its profile beyond the geographical site, for example, with a far-reaching archive-driven project: Great Famine Voices Roadshow, across the USA and Canada, represented online. Inclusive of the house, outbuildings and parkland, the Strokestown site's ongoing oscillation between index and representation is reflexively indicative of Peter Hohenhaus's 'place authenticity' and its necessary mediation.

The history presented at the Famine Warhouse 1848 in County Tipperary also centres on local civilian rebellion, but one that was politically motivated at the outset (Figure 3.7). The modest house and garden embody the notion of site as artefact, with its conservation intended to memorialize a specific political incident during the Famine and was host to the 2017 National Famine Commemoration. Located outside the small town of Ballingarry, signposted across a network of small country roads, the museum takes the shape of an attractive two-storey country house with a small yard and outhouses to the back and a well-maintained lawn at the front. Preserved by the Office of Public Works (OPW), the museum includes an introductory audio-visual in one of the converted outhouses.[54]

Throughout the farmhouse, wall panels outline the politically charged story associated with the site, its political and socio-economic context and the suggested impact of events in 1848 on and within a wider history of political struggle. The key protagonist presented is William Smith O'Brien, who was a leader of the Young Irelanders, a Protestant and the Member of Parliament for County Limerick.[55]

At this time, the Young Irelanders were working towards a social uprising, to protest against and overthrow British rule in Ireland. A defining focus of the group was their repeated attempt to unite landlords and tenants, with their temporary popularity defined by other political fallouts. 'If the Repeal Association and O'Connellite gradualism were killed by the Famine, then the militancy of the Young Irelanders was both fired and destroyed.'[56] O'Brien was a dashing figure of new Anglo-Irish thinking and a vocal critic in Parliament of British policies in Ireland. In 1848 he was, along with others from the movement, on the run from British law enforcers.

On 29 July 1848, O'Brien was in the village of The Commons, County Tipperary, having travelled in a rebel group through counties Wexford and Kilkenny inciting public protests. Barricades were set up by local people to prevent the police from arresting him. On seeing the barricades, 47 incoming policemen diverted their course across some fields, with the rebels in pursuit. The policemen entered what is now the Famine Warhouse 1848 for refuge, taking hostage the inhabitants who were in the house at the time: five young children. A crowd of locals and armed rebels gathered outside. When the children's mother, Mrs McCormack, arrived she was refused entry to the house and so O'Brien went with her to the parlour window to negotiate with the police. During this discussion, a policeman shot at O'Brien, leading to an exchange of fire lasting a number of hours. Eventually, the police received reinforcements from Callan, and the locals and rebels filtered from the scene. The events are referred to as the War of the Cabbage Patches.[57] An illustrated account of the brief uprising was published on 12 August 1848, in the *Illustrated London News*, which Niamh O'Sullivan notes 'has a demonic quality suggestive of a whole country out of control'.[58]

The narrative throughout the museum is largely focused on the national and international contexts of the day's events and the fates of the key political protagonists and other Young Irelanders. The visitor's attention is drawn to other rebellions in Europe earlier that year and to the admirable qualities of O'Brien.[59] The aftermath of the events is explored around the themes of arrests, trials, imprisonment and escape. O'Brien was subsequently arrested at Thurles railway station and sentenced, as were other leaders, to death by hanging, drawing and quartering. A feature in the museum's information panels is the role of British penal imprisonment in Van Diemen's Land.[60] Transportation was decreed in lieu of the death sentences for many of the captured Young Irelanders and others, including O'Brien.

The Famine is cited as the primary provocation for the political atmosphere of the time and locality: 'The Young Irelanders became increasingly discontented and radicalized by the horrors of the Great Famine of 1845–1850' (OPW leaflet). The failed uprising also had the effect of hardening British attitudes toward Famine relief efforts. The Famine Warhouse 1848 is thus denoted as an artefact of politics: a place where, at a time of Famine, routine domestic life converged with a symbolic incident in a wider story of political upheaval which in turn contributed to an evolving nationalism.

The site is also an artefact of place. The house and its grounds can be read in terms of what Hooper-Greenhill calls a 'critical provenance'. Assuming provenance of an artefact as simply a matter of inventory, she argues, 'naturalises processes of collection, of ownership, and museological processes of acquisition and documentation', whereas a critical provenance 'asks questions about all these matters which are ultimately concerned with relationships of power, knowledge and value'.[61] This proposition informs how moving through the house indicates much more than the first-level reading of the narrative accounted in the wall panels. While clearly pointing to a 'liberation narrative', to appropriate Roy Foster's sense of the term,[62] a literal gap in representation at Ballingarry allows the visitor space and time to contemplate the signifying power of the house and its site as partially disruptive to its representation.

Between the context, build-up and revelations of the events described on the ground floor and the explication of the consequences revealed upstairs, the large window of the stairwell encourages the visitor to look out. The contextual, interpretative layering of text and images in the rooms on the ground and first floors becomes amplified by the spatial awareness of the house and its environs as a palimpsest holding history's enthralling yet never fully legible inscription. Here, place as a politically emotive representation is explicitly revealed and a history of rebellion and resistance is linked to civil unrest in other countries and merged with a representation of Famine times.

Tension between Famine history and its relationship to Irish national identity is apparent in the NMI's approach to the Famine.[63] Beauty and awe are currencies at each of NMI's four sites – as at other national museums worldwide. The conquest over the material world presented through its galleries is drawn from wide and deep legacies of displays of power. Douglas Newton emphasizes a positive potential for museums as protectors of cultural pride:

> The museum can only work within the limitations imposed by history, and these are irrevocable. The museum can do many things; it can teach us about ourselves and 'others,' but cannot change anything except its visitors' minds. The museum cannot bring the past back to life [...] It can preserve tokens of a culture and, by displaying them cultivate and keep alive the memory of times and people that created them. That memory enriches us all, and bestows upon us culture. Without it we have no past, and thus less sense of our own individuality and worth.[64]

National heritage as a commodity of wider tourism is presented through the objects, displays, buildings and sites of national museums as part of a mirage in which history and memory are pragmatically intertwined to typically produce national culture and promote a sense of collective identity. But as a history of dispossession, such as the Famine, is significantly defined by a set of absences, how might a national cultural institution concerned with conventions of materialism frame such a set of experiences? Perhaps, as Iain Chambers highlights, '[a]bsence, not as a

Figure 3.8 Museum of Country Life, National Museum of Ireland, Turlough Park, County Mayo, Ireland. Photograph by Peter Moloney. © National Museum of Ireland.

lack, but as an interrogation, produces a slash in the temporal–spatial coordinates of an imposed History'.[65]

In September 2001, the NMI opened the Museum of Country Life at Turlough Park House (Figure 3.8). Nestled in a scenic valley just north of Castlebar town, the demense includes a preserved house built in 1865 by Sir Thomas Newenham Deane for the Fitzgerald family in a dramatic High Victorian Gothic style, and an extension designed by the OPW's Architectural Services to house the NMI exhibitions, a shop, archive and storage areas. There is a restaurant in the coach house alongside a conservatory of exotic plants. As well as access to the museum, the drawing room and library of the Big House are open for visits and tours. The small surrounding parkland is finely landscaped, featuring an artificial lake and short routed walkways along trees and green lawns. On a nearby hilltop is a ninth-century round tower and beside it the ruin of an eighteenth-century abbey.

Within this multi-layered scaffold of its location, replete with historical architectural signifiers of a fraught religious past, the NMI's rhetorical oscillation between a modernist museum and a post-museum is reflected in a number of statements about aspects of its location, its processes of acquisition and the nature of its collections. This curatorial self-consciousness signals a shift towards a post-museum as one which recognizes that, as Hooper-Greenhill put it, '[v]isual culture within the museum is a technology of power [...] used to further democratic possibilities, or [...] to uphold exclusionary values',[66] and is sustained in the interpretative emphases throughout the presentation of the collections in the galleries.

Panel texts encourage the visitor to consider how collections are made and draw attention to traditions, customs and education in Ireland. Beyond assumptions that museums conserve relics from the past and visitor expectations of a neutral revelation of history, text panels imply that collections can be arbitrary and myths are always present.[67] According to the NMI website, the folklife collection dates from the end of the Famine to the end of World War II, from 1850 to 1950.[68] With little mention of the Famine at the Dublin museum sites, at Turlough Park the museum's main reference to the Famine is in the explicit context of growing land agitation, which was, of course, a crux issue of the burgeoning post-colonial nation.

A series of richly presented permanent exhibitions focus on country life in factual terms and cite changes in political and socio-economic circumstances in Ireland.[69] Within these, methods of rural crafts and survival techniques, from making clothes to providing food and shelter, are described. Land wars, Land Acts and the evolution of the Irish National Land League movement are the key historical markers for the Famine in the museum.[70] The Land League actively sought reduced rents and increased ownership of land for Irish people. A text panel titled 'The Impact of the Great Famine' points out: 'as an outlet for grievance, some rural (and towns) people turned to the Irish Republican (or Fenian) Brotherhood, a secret nationalist army with the aim of an Irish Republic'.[71] It also states, 'the decline of the Irish language was evidence of widespread cultural change', which is usually attributed to emigration, as well as the vast numbers of deaths, during the Famine. This political fervour and cultural dilution of tradition, as a twofold outcome of the Famine, are specified as aspects of an altering nationalist landscape. The museum thus promotes the Famine as an event in which land, as well as food, was centrally at issue in a developing narrative of nationhood and changing cultural identity.

Writing on links between narrative forms and knowledge production, Mieke Bal points out, 'One only needs to think of the place of narrative in the historical disciplines, and of the reflections on the fits and misfits between the actual historical narratives and the events they purport to describe, but, also, constructed.'[72] At Turlough Park, a story of national identity evolves over a 100-year time span within which the Famine is presented as an influential spectre consolidating political and cultural change.

Between History and Memory: Manufactured Worlds

While museums generally deploy the artifice of bringing the past into the present by insistent recourse to objects, Kirshenblatt-Gimblett points out the 'virtual' aspect of heritage practices at certain sites.[73] She describes the museum beside the ruins of Cluny church in France as an interpretive interface that 'shows what cannot otherwise be seen [...] the museum openly imagines the site into being [...]'.[74] In her example, an artefact is damaged and in large part missing: so its absence is addressed through a meeting of archaeological information and speculative imagination, allowing the visitor to imagine, or re-member, the absent artefact.

In her wider study, Kirshenblatt-Gimblett suggests the experiences of the past presented in heritage practices are less about material presences than about conjuring a supra-narrative. The stories, histories and experiences of individuals and societies no longer here, hover over the things, places and people that have been ordained as conduits for the past in the present. The allusion to virtuality underscores the function of museums and heritage sites as manufactured worlds where the stories disclosed are simultaneously conjured, the past made present, with purpose, at and for that moment. A museum may openly imagine a site, and its history, into being, implying that cultural significance is produced at the moment of imaginative engagement. The meeting of expectation and representation in museum galleries lies at the heart of efforts to humanize Famine experiences through exhibition technologies, reflecting on William Logan and Keir Reeves' definition:

> Heritage conservation is a form of cultural politics; it is about the
> links between ideology, public policy, national and community

identity formation, and celebration, just as much as it is about
technical issues relating to restoration and adaptive re-uses.[75]

Histories of the Famine are variously conjured as local elements in a
national disaster and, in some instances connected to present-day
international famines and, in other places, critically tied to rebellious
schemata of nationalism formed in various acts of civil disobedience. The
difficulty of documentary, to borrow Minh-ha's insight,[76] is acknowledged
in museum practice through an awareness of how subjects of history are
constructed, rather than found. Added to this, Jenny Kidd notes the impact
of representation for the subject-formation of the visitor, '[t]he
relationship between the museum's role as an arbitrator of collective
memory and as an active constituent in the making and re-making of
individual's identities renders ambiguous any sense of an objective past'.[77]

Kirshenblatt-Gimblett suggests that the documentation and exhibition
of the subject might mark its disappearance,[78] which returns any
discussion on cultural forms representing the past to a querying of the
objectivity conventionally associated with historians and curatorial roles.
In other analyses, writers on heritage and culture turn to theorists for
clarity: Henrietta Riegal draws on Johannes Fabian's outline of a
distinction between anthropological fieldwork and ethnographic writing –
or representation generally – which creates a distance from its formerly
interactive subject.[79] Colm Tóibín quotes Seamus Deane's critique of the
discourse of the historian as presumed to be an objective account: '[s]uch a
discourse, which claims for itself a fundamental realism through which
things as they really are or were could be presented in a narrative, depends
upon a narrator who is not implicated'.[80]

Arguably then, curators, archivists and historians are implicated in the
architecture of representation that define the social memory of the Famine
as linked to museum sites and formal heritage centres, but so too are the
sites themselves implicit in the formation of such historical knowledge.
Balancing the difficult tasks of conveying the scale of the Famine, its
sustained, far-reaching effects and complex definitions with engendering a
more intimate awareness of Famine experiences is tackled variously at the
museums and heritage centres discussed here.

Interests in creating empathy at such memory sites may mean that less
socially palatable aspects of grievous histories go unrepresented. Kinealy

Figure 3.9 Exhibition Room, Ireland's Great Hunger Museum, Quinnipiac University, Connecticut, USA. Image courtesy of Ireland's Great Hunger Museum, Quinnipiac University, Hamden, CT, USA. © Robert Benson.

warns that oversimplifying the perpetrator-and-victim narrative of Famine histories leads to an overly sanitized or unhelpfully genteel version of human history.[81] Dodd similarly rejects the 'celebration of victimhood' in favour of promoting awareness of the complexity of the context of the Famine and the ongoing need to contest interpretative histories,[82] and Breandán Mac Suibhne's work draws attention to less palatable realities of human behaviour at a time of profound distress and in its aftermath.[83] The Famine precipitated vast social shifts and, some suggest effected psychological transgenerational affect but left relatively few tangible residues. It is now also beyond living or even second generation recall: thus, it occupies neither history nor memory in soliloquy.

Self-aware contemporary curatorial practice is evident in the increased emphasis placed on the potential of these museums and heritage centres to widen access to research material, as at Strokestown. This is reflected also at Ireland's Great Hunger Museum (IGHM) at Quinnipiac University, Connecticut, USA, opened in 2012 (Figure 3.9). Its collection is intended as a tool for educating 'more and more people about the Great Hunger and the lessons to be learned from this terrible human rights tragedy' and also about 'the high quality of Irish art'.[84] A library of printed materials is accessible alongside the changing displays from its pillar art collection, supplemented with active acquisitions, an active publication policy and online links to the university's research resource, Ireland's Great Hunger

Institute. Initially developed as an extension of a university art collection, the range of visual culture utilized at the museum puts forward a conceptual link between artefact and art as equivalent proxies for historical understanding, with the generation of a memorial culture that explicitly includes post-Famine art as after-images.

As zones of representation that make the world real, museums are manufactured worlds: their artificial nature at once virtual and referential. From the intimate quality of contemplating displayed objects to the sweeping narratives evoked by microhistories, museums can offer diverse means of empathic witness to grievous histories. Walking through the sites discussed here, the personal devastation produced by lack of food, the fracturing of families in searches for sustenance, and domestic dispossessions through eviction resulting in the break-up of communities are conjured. Consequently, climates of localized civil unrest are connected to wider political upheaval with a supra-narrative of land agitation defining the Famine's place in the emergent narrative of a post-colonial nation. These sites sidestep the difficulty of documenting absence in order to make suffering appear at the moment the visitor engages with the sites: the objects, images and texts, buildings and environs. Place is a significant aspect of these museums; not only shaping the appearance of suffering, before the viewer, but also as the conceptual locus for bridging the gap between sites of memory and the others of history.

4

After-Images: Temporary Commemorative Exhibitions on the Famine

The Politics of Perspective

In early April 1995, a joint proposal was sent to the National Gallery of Ireland by Catherine Marshall, then Curator of the Collection at the Irish Museum of Modern Art, and Colleen Dube, then Curator at the National Museum of Ireland. The proposal outlined the possibilities inherent to a three-way institutional collaboration for an exhibition entitled *The Art and Visual Imagery of the Famine*. According to Marshall and Dube, the exhibition would 'offer the National Gallery of Ireland (NGI) an unparalleled opportunity not only to empower the Irish nation with its survival and achievements but to enable the public to perceive the Famine's impact on Ireland's visual identity'.[1] The proposal quoted from Thomas Davis's essay 'National Art', originally published in 1843, calling for the creation of a national collection of Irish art and the recognition of a history of Irish art:

> To create a mass of great pictures, statues, and buildings, is of the same sort of ennoblement to a people as to create great poems or histories, or make great codes or win great battles. The next best, though far inferior blessing and power are to inherit such works and

achievements. The lowest stage of all is neither to possess nor to create them [...] [T]o collect into, and make known, and publish in Ireland, the best works of our living and dead Artists, is one of the steps towards procuring for Ireland a recognised National Art.[2]

Thus Marshall and Dube appealed to the NGI's sense of national duty and further suggested, 'the repercussions of the period [1845–51] are still being reconciled by the Irish nation and its diaspora'. In qualifying the potential remit of such a project, the Famine was presented as a definitively Irish event and the proposed exhibition as a prospective platform for cultural debate on Irishness.

On 11 May, the gallery declined the proposal in a letter, observing that it was 'difficult to reconcile the differing philosophies relating to the commemoration and how it should be presented at the National Gallery'. The letter suggested that 'a subject as complex as the Great Famine should be more broadly based, employing the skills of a range of experts [...] to address the many different aspects of this tragic period of Irish History'.

This hesitancy echoed the cumulative tensions of a punchy and at times divisive revisionist debate of the 1980s and 1990s. One cultural outlet was the Field Day project launched in Derry in 1980, in an effort to transcend the binaries associated with the Irish history of governance and contingent synthesis of cultural identity. Beginning with a focus on theatre, by 1983 the project expanded to the commissioning and publication of a series of discursive pamphlets, continuing until 1988.[3] Also at this time, Irish Studies was becoming a recognized academic field both nationally and internationally and was initially defined by post-colonial theory.[4] Amidst this animated focus on what constituted Irishness and academic debates on nationalisms, the reluctance on the part of the NGI to present a commemorative exhibition on the Famine is not wholly remarkable. The subsequent lack of any significant inter-institutional exhibition was, however, indicative of sustained undermining of the role of art in historical remembrance in Ireland at formal institutional levels.

The problem of how to adequately memorialize the past, in particular when little physical evidence remains, is compounded by distancing through time. The politics of perspective on grievous history was apparent in the rejection of *The Art and Visual Imagery of the Famine* proposal, as well as in the spread of the Irish government's spend of its Famine Commemoration funds outside of Ireland (though this can be argued to reflect on the extensive diasporic impact of the Famine, alongside the sense of a 'living memorial' promoted through aid packages at the time).

Despite this, individual artists, independently motivated arts committees and curators have presented representations of the Famine through temporary exhibitions. This chapter looks at five such exhibitions organized in two main commemorative time frames: one in the mid-twentieth century – the centenary of the Famine – and four in the late twentieth century at the 150-year commemoration period.[5] Punctuation points of commemoration, such as centenaries and sesquicentennials, though inherently meaningless, are nonetheless forceful in defining codes of public historical remembrance by drawing on epochal concepts of 'monumental time',[6] as traded in by institutions of history, such as museums and educational curricula. Selected artworks from these projects will be looked at in the context of prevailing political and artistic concerns of the respective periods. Considered together with curatorial strategies, the artworks indicate the potential for art to stand in where a historian's faith in materialism might necessarily be thwarted by a history of poverty.

Arguably, viewed alongside conventional historical practice, art might labour under its perceived distance from history as a mere interpretation or at best function as an illustration at a distance. When compared to artefactual evidence considered to be documentary proof of an event, by virtue of physical proximity to the past, concepts of postmemory and after-images have latterly blurred the evaluative distinctions between history and its representation. James Young writes of artistic representations of Holocaust experiences:

> The problem for many of these artists, of course, is that they are unable to remember the holocaust outside of the way it has been passed down to them, outside of the ways it is meaningful to them fifty years after the fact [...] It is necessarily mediated experience, the afterlife of memory, represented in history's after-images: the impression retained in the mind's eye of a vivid sensation long after the original, external cause has been removed.[7]

As Young suggests that events and their telling are instrumental in the construction of history in the present day, art curation also intervenes in comprehensions of the past as a form of history writing. The transitory representations occurring in temporary exhibition projects reconfigure the relationship between art and history and between commemorative practices and social memory, on an ongoing basis. Curation is also caught up, however, with the history-writing of art as a discipline and within the histories of display practices.

In examining this topic, Stephen Bann borrows Wolfgang Ernst's term 'blind spot', to note interconnections between chronologies and phenomenal display:

> [T]he art historian is in danger of registering as the definitive state of the museum precisely that form of order which has been determined by the growth of art history as a self-conscious discipline [...] [j]ust as the historiography of museums is irretrievably contaminated by art history's complicity with the museum as a form of display, so the critical study of the museum has to reckon with a significant history of museum critiques.[8]

For Bann, such blindness is most apparent when the apparatus of a history is itself accepted without question. Svetlana Alpers suggests, '[a]s scholars, art historians all too often see themselves as being in pursuit of knowledge without recognizing how they themselves are the makers of that knowledge'.[9] This implies that it is the process of pictorial analysis and taking time to look at artworks, along with research about art, that might make most sense of the art historian's work.[10]

As an interface between art history and museum studies, the notion of a blind spot points to the critical space of the history of cultural memory. Cultural memory, in this usage, refers to Ann Rigney's iteration of the nature of the 'vicarious recollection' of cultural memory, which is 'the product of representations and not of direct experience'.[11] In her critique of the limits of what she terms the 'plenitude and loss model' of memory studies, Rigney notes:

> Once cultural memory is seen as something dynamic, as a result of recursive acts of remembrance, rather than as something like an unchanging and pregiven inheritance, then the way is opened to thinking about what could be called 'memory transfer'.[12]

Such a transfer of memory implies replacements of a singular dominant narrative of history with multiple perspectives in which the past is reconceived, not as a static unchanging entity, but as a constantly shifting present-day phenomenon, with memory transfer relating to what Rigney calls cultural models which are, in turn, reliant upon 'whatever mnemonic technologies and memorial forms are available'.[13]

History writing, in any cultural form, can make past events seem closer and gives voice to people no longer present. Silke Arnold-de Simine writes that secondary witnessing 'implies listening to testimony, empathically reliving at least partly the emotions triggered by the initial event, such as shock, fear and terror, and of course forming an experience and a memory that was denied to the survivors'.[14] While she writes of exhibited images and objects pertaining to direct testimonies of traumas, the indirect relating of grievous history in art and curation is also a process of representation defined by who is now absent, what has happened in between and what has been definitively left out: in other words, the history of cultural memory itself, reliant as it is on the 'mnemonic technologies and memorial forms available'.

Given these critical contexts and the politics of perspective, both locally and theoretically contingent, what kind of imaginative history appeared at temporary commemorative exhibitions on the Famine? This chapter explores both artworks and exhibitions as after-images: transitory moments of representation that are, in Minh-ha's terms, 'a speaking in brief, whose closures are only moments of transition, opening up to other possible moments of transition'.[15]

The Silent Centenary and Imaginative History

Cormac Ó Gráda presents a fascinating account of the evolution of what was perhaps the most significant centenary product formally commissioned to commemorate the Famine: the book eventually known as *The Great Famine: Studies in Irish History*, edited by Robert Dudley Edwards and Thomas Desmond Williams.[16] Though proposed as early as 1943 or 1944 and intended for publication by 1946, it finally reached bookshelves in 1956. Disappointment with the book was reflective of a range of organizational issues along the way, but as Ó Gráda suggests, its overall tone was what rankled with many: 'That Irish historians in the 1950s should have sought to rid Irish history of its undue emphasis on the tragic is understandable; but the appalling catastrophe of the 1840s was an unhappy choice for that campaign.'[17] This very approach was evident in the earliest significant exhibition to include art remembering the Famine, organized at the time of the centenary.

The event did not prioritize Famine remembrance, but was, rather, a celebratory one, organized on the theme of Irish political freedom. In 1946 the *Exhibition of Pictures of Irish Historical Interest* was organized in connection with the Centenary Commemoration of Thomas Davis and the Young Ireland Movement. The catalogue prefaced the exhibition as follows:

> This Committee [Special Committee of the Government Committee in charge of the Centenary Celebrations] recommended that the Exhibition be held in 1946, that it be confined to exhibitors of Irish birth or origin, and that the exhibits should be illustrative of the period of Irish history from the founding of the *Nation* newspaper in 1842, connecting with the trend of events from that year through the Fenian Movement and the War of Independence to the present time.[18]

The show was held in the National College of Art and Design: 78 works were submitted and 47 of these were selected for exhibition in the Central Hall of the college building in Kildare Street, Dublin; 39 other works were loaned from the National Gallery, the Municipal Gallery of Modern Art (now Dublin City Gallery The Hugh Lane), the National Museum and Áras an Uachtaráin (the President's Residence in the Phoenix Park) and were displayed in the Entrance and Inner Halls of the college, bookending the open submission section. Of all the works, the few that did either directly or indirectly depict the Famine were exhibited in the open submission section.[19] For the most part the exhibition consisted of portraits of celebrated figures associated with Ireland's emancipation from British rule and related heroic scenes reflecting a narrative of liberation. The historical interest referred to in the exhibition's title was therefore interpreted through a survivalist reading of history and emphasized by a celebration of the life and political influence of Thomas Davis.

Gorta (Famine), 1946, by Lilian Lucy Davidson was formerly known as *Burying the Child*, is deeply expressionist in tone and palette, reflecting Davidson's education and absorption of developments in international art practice[20] (Figure 4.1). The work was painted following what Katherine Cahill describes as her 'Western peasant cycle of paintings' of the 1920s and 1930s.[21] The confrontational composition intensifies the raw human drama of the depicted scene of burial, with the central figure's direct gaze

Figure 4.1 Lilian Lucy Davidson, *Gorta*, 1946. Oil on canvas, 70 x 90 cm. Image courtesy of Ireland's Great Hunger Museum, Quinnipiac University, Hamden, CT, USA. © The Estate of Lilian Lucy Davidson.

presented as a challenge to a viewer's culpability in looking on at the scene imaged. The work is in the IGHM's collection in Connecticut, USA.

*Bliadhan na Gorta c.*1946, by Pádraic Woods focuses on a different kind of digging of the land[22] (Figure 4.2). It is an image of ominous portent, as a man and woman, seemingly unaware of impending disaster, till their lazybeds on a sunny day under the watchful eye of a small child.[23] Woods gave much attention to the rural landscape in the painting, with a considered mountainous depth of field beneath a fresh cloudy and misting sky, while the detail of the hand plough in the foreground provides a convincing account of the hard labour involved in maintaining such lazy beds. This work, along with *An Ghorta 1847 (The Famine 1847)*, 1946, by Maurice MacGonigal (Figure 4.3) and *Famine, c.*1946, by Muriel Brandt (Figure 4.4), is now held in storage at the National Museum of Ireland, Collins Barracks.

MacGonigal's and Brandt's images each have a central female figure as a focal point.[24] In MacGonigal's work the Madonna-like figure may be a

Figure 4.2 Pádraic Woods, *Bliadhan na Gorta (Year of the Famine)*, c. 1946. Oil on canvas, 64 x 79 cm. Image provided by National Museum of Ireland.

member of the local landed gentry who is sympathetic to the plight of those around her or an allegorical figure of Ireland as a woman, depicted in a densely populated picture plane. Susan Crofts terms this work a 'truly western subject painting' and 'the closest the artist came to allegorical painting'.[25] The patterns of furrows, the beauty of stone walls and an abandoned cottage imaged against the sunset accentuate the work's elegiac power over any particular documentary aspect. Reactions to the potato blight are depicted in the demeanour of defeated-looking men among the tiny fields as they contemplate the failure of the soil, and emigration in the figures on the horizon line heading toward the shore.

In Brandt's painting, the triangular composition of a woman surrounded by three children and a dog recalls a pieta configuration, associating the image with depictions of mourning and martyrdom in traditions of European religious art. In the background a group of people are taking a coffin for burial. The figures of a mourner wearing a black hooded cape and

Figure 4.3 Maurice MacGonigal, *An Ghorta 1847 (The Famine 1847)*, 1946. Oil on canvas, 75.5 x 92 cm. Image provided by National Museum of Ireland. © Estate of Maurice MacGonigal, IVARO Dublin, 2017.

red skirt and a young girl centrally placed in the composition, also in a striking red skirt, bring to mind MacGonigal's interest in rendering traditional clothing. Leach has noted that Brandt was well considered for her paintings of children,[26] which is reflected in the attention paid them in this work.

Considered in the context of their submission for public exhibition, these paintings can be read as indicators of how history was visually approached in the mid-twentieth century – exhibited together with other works as a set of after-images of the Famine. Their respective languages are each influenced to varying degrees by the Irish artistic climate of the time, local post-colonial negotiations of otherness and international contemporary art debates. In the 1940s, Irish art circles were divided by the academy traditions on the one hand and artists that supported the Exhibitions of Living Art (ELA), begun in 1943, on the other. Within the

Figure 4.4 Muriel Brandt, *Famine*, c.1946. Oil on canvas, 89 x 119.5 cm. Image provided by National Museum of Ireland. © Estate of Muriel Brandt, IVARO Dublin, 2017.

Royal Hibernian Academy (RHA) were further divisions, but the ELA produced the most hotly debated arguments about art at that time. Under Mainie Jellett's guidance the ELA provided Irish artists and the Irish public with a taste for European modernism that had not much affected academic practice of the time. Kennedy has written of the RHA in the early 1940s that 'its fortunes were at their lowest ebb since the nineteenth century'.[27] In this context, the 1946 *Exhibition of Pictures of Irish Historical Interest* was principally aligned with academy concerns of subject and portrait art. Arguably, Davidson, a friend of Jellett's, chose a more modern stylistic approach than the others viewed here. Both Davidson and MacGonigal were strongly influenced by subject interests in the west of Ireland following research trips there, and all four share a domination of figurations in outdoor settings as core to their depictions of Famine times.

In treating their subject matter as a historic theme, indicated by the emblematic titles of the works, and in particular by the busyness of

MacGonigal's and Brandt's symbolic scenes, the artists seem to have consciously positioned the Famine as a theme within traditions of European and Irish history painting. Distinct from the expectation of most history painting, however, these Famine images are centred on unknown individuals: not titled kings, queens, soldiers or religious leaders, but members of the ordinary cottier and labouring classes who were worst affected by the Famine. The events depicted are not singular coronations, battles or marriages, but a series of quotidian Famine-era experiences at unnamed locations. In place of epic historic moments arrives the slower study of a socially inscribed situation of poverty and its effects.

As pieces of history, the paintings point to an empty-feeling space in the collective Irish visual imagination in the mid-twentieth century. These artists produced pictures of a past they had not experienced, but felt they could, nonetheless, vicariously present, as after-images. The idiom of painting became more than a mere supplement where photography had been absent at scenes of direct Famine experiences: it was a self-conscious form of mediation that allowed Davidson to image an expressive charge, gave Woods the licence to observe a social realism, MacGonigal the possibility of multifarious viewpoints and Brandt the means to symbolically imbue her figures and strategically illustrate funerary rituals. Constituted as artistic proxies to a difficult past, these paintings no doubt upset the triumphalist vision of remembrance implied by the 1946 exhibition's title. Half-a-century later, the issue of commemoration had been inveigled by Ireland's status as no longer merely a post-colonial nation, but an aid-giver to other countries now suffering more blatantly from the effects of systemic poverty.

Travelling Memory and Critical History at 150 Years

Paul Ricoeur wrote of two modes of encountering a history. One is 'a ruinous dichotomy between a history that would dissolve the event in explanation and a purely emotional retort that would dispense us from thinking the unthinkable'.[28] The other mode is usefully interdependent: 'the more we explain in historical terms, the more indignant we become; the more we are struck by the horror of events, the more we seek to understand them'.[29] Similar to Young's focus on the expediency of combined modes of understanding the past, Ricoeur warns against separating the apparently objective from the personal, or a general story from individual narratives. Linking this to Arnold-de Simine's comments on memory as a way of relating to the past that requires empathy and identification, might suggest that social memory is an encounter with history by way of commemorative visual culture, such as art, as a means by which past experiences appear in the present.

The following four temporary exhibitions took place in the 1990s, at the time of the 150-year commemorations of the Famine, and, in differing modes, both reflected on and produced cultural memory of the Famine. Two large-scale touring projects, the Teagasc/Department of Agriculture, Food and Forestry's *Famine 150* and the George Moore Society's *Famine*, were begun in 1995. These included exhibitions: the former centred on agricultural history, the latter on the arts. Smaller in scale, the 1995 Famine exhibition in University College Cork (UCC), *Famines Yesterday and Today: The Irish Experience in a Global Context* and the 1998–9 Irish Museum of Modern Art (IMMA) exhibition, *Representations of the Famine*, were significantly less constrained by official governmental or overseas peripatetic burden than either *Famine 150* or *Famine*. This left their curators institutionally freer to engage in exploring the structuring of history through practices of exhibition and interpretation.

These four exhibitions, to varying degrees, pushed at the boundaries between artefact and art and between data and interpretation, and in this regard can be identified with a practice of critical history. Michael Ann Holly explores New Historicism in art as a fracturing of perceived distinctions between historians and critics,[30] defining the resulting critical history as a modality of spectatorship where the object and reader are bound together in the production of meaning:

> The trick is making what forever will be a provisional metaphorical construction at least partially consonant with that made visible in the reigning artistic metaphors of the period [...] [C]ritical history does not arise spontaneously: it is coupled with the objects about which it speaks.[31]

This section looks at the extent to which cultural memory exhibited through temporary projects produces a set of after-images of the historical period they focus on. As such, they were firstly, publicly available at the places and for the durations of exhibition and, later, potentially linger on as a sustained form of secondary witnessing through recounting, recollection or re-exhibition.

Famine 150 was developed in 1995 by Teagasc and the Department of Agriculture, Food and Forestry. The closest thing to an official commemorative exhibition on the Famine at this time, it comprised multimedia displays focusing on the social conditions that maximized the effect of the Famine on Ireland's population, and on the development of the potato blight and related scientific processes of prevention. The press release emphasized that '[a] major demonstration of how the potatoes were sown, grown and stored in the 1840's and their use in the diet of the time, will be an important part of the exhibition'.[32] An immersive aspect was apparent in the use of life-size exhibits, recreating 'live scenes from that period', such as a soup kitchen and a reconstructed and furnished 'Class 4 mud-walled house'. The exhibition was thematically devised around Population and Potatoes, Land Tenure and Land Use, Coming of Blight, Emigration and The Move to Science. The Famine and its effects were presented as occurring most prominently between 1845 and 1850, although contextual and subsequent nineteenth-century conditions were represented.

That *Famine 150* sought to delineate the Famine as a five-year event was not unusual in Famine representations at this time, though it arguably reduces both the scale of history and thwarts possibilities of wider representations. Indicative of the limits of practicalities of a large-scale touring exhibition, this reduction is countered by some historians, such as Christine Kinealy, who regularly dates the Famine as 1845–52. Estimating the duration of the Famine can also be linked to geographical contexts as different terms were used to describe experiences at different locations in Ireland. Discussing the NFC's 1945 questionnaire, 'An Gorta Mór, 1846–52', Niall Ó Ciosáin notes that the term *Gorta Mór*, meaning Great Famine, the translation more likely having been from English to Irish than the other way round, was rarely used in Irish-language folklore. With reference to Cathal Póirtéir's work on the localized naming of the Famine, Ó Ciosáin brings to light connections between time, language and place in different iterations of the Famine's duration and reflecting on local experiences.[33]

The five-year span defining the Famine for the purposes of representation may be further explained by the exhibition's timing during

Ireland's revisionist debates and the Northern Irish Peace Process. The locations of the touring exhibition are significant in this regard: *Famine 150* was shown in Dublin at the Royal Dublin Society, and early in 1996 in Derry, Northern Ireland, at The Calgach Centre, a conference and exhibition facility. It was Teagasc's intention that the exhibition would then return to Dublin for permanent display at the NMI. Though this was never realized, a form of the exhibition found a home for permanent display at the Irish Agricultural Museum and Johnstown Castle Gardens, County Wexford. As a touring project formally developed in the name of Ireland, *Famine 150* was tailored by the weight of this representative agenda. Its focus on Irish agriculture, known data and generalized comment and information on worldwide famines, as well as its presentation of to-scale representations of abstracted details of everyday Famine-era life, steered the initial exhibition on a path of politically non-controversial history which was presumably expedient to its continuance at the time. Even so, the legacy of its hard-hitting factual content continues to resonate at Johnstown, as discussed in Chapter 3.

Famine, organized by the George Moore Society in Claremorris, County Mayo, was another touring project, also large in scale though less weighted by a formal national burden.[34] Where Teagasc had sought to explain the event, the George Moore Society focused on responses to the Famine in cultural forms. Patricia Noone, chair of the society, outlined the process: 'The Society has chosen to express the deep suffering of the Irish people during those "black" years through the media of painting, sculpture, literature and music. To this end, the society invited some of Ireland's finest artists to work on the Famine.'[35] The overall project consisted of an exhibition, a commissioned suite of music and other musical performances, a number of talks and literary recitals. Elements of the commemoration toured variously from Claremorris to Dublin, Ulster and then on to the USA (including Boston and New York) and Canada over a two-year period. The project was supported by the Bank of Ireland and the Irish government, which gave £10,000. These contributions funded the main exhibition and the commissioning of a new musical score by Charlie Lennon called 'Famine Suite'.

In the exhibition catalogue, Brian Fallon, then Chief Critic of Literature and Art for the *Irish Times*, drew attention to the diversity of the art exhibition, stating that 'no intellectual study could manage to group [the exhibits] under a single label' and that 'the various works are not directly illustrative of the Famine itself, they are a collection of individual responses to it'.[36] Questioning the nature of connections between art and national identity, he wrote:

> But even if it [the exhibition] does not claim to be the whole of Irish art, it certainly represents the Irish mind and sensibility, not programmatically or nationalistically, but through an interlinked series of individual responses – prismatically, you might even say. And through its personalised reactions to the past, it also goes a long way towards explaining the complex phenomenon of modern Ireland, how and what it feels and thinks about the present as well as about history.[37]

Given his earlier suggestion that 'writers and artists, after all, are to a great extent the expression of their racial and national psyche, though sometimes quite unconsciously, and they cannot help being so',[38] his comments reflect a mode of thinking about Irish art that was in part tied to the debates of the 1940s and arguably to Davis's essay of 1843. Fallon's antipathy towards what he saw as trendy art was an evolution of arguments about what constituted modern art and where contemporary Irishness as expressed in idiosyncratic cultural forms might fit within this.

Though ostensibly a thematic exhibition, *Famine*, like the proposed exhibition *The Art and Visual Imagery of the Famine*, was viewed, by virtue of its scale (it comprised some 98 artworks) as a statement about the state of Irish art. Fallon suggests the artists in *Famine*, though wide-ranging in artistic styles and spread over three generations, share the (unspecified) characteristic that they and their work exist somehow outside of the transitory pressures of international art trends.[39] While careful to avoid endorsing previous ruralisms, Fallon in his catalogue text, which was the primary theoretical frame for the exhibition as it was presented to the public, identified the exhibition with a distinct anti-urbanist preference within art of the era.[40]

Among the 34 exhibitors in *Famine* were the celebrated painters Patrick Graham, Basil Blackshaw, Louis le Brocquy, Anne Donnelly, Seán McSweeney, Anne Madden, Hughie O'Donoghue, Sharon O'Malley, Tony O'Malley and Charles Tyrrell; and the eminent sculptors John Behan, John Coll, Edward Delaney and Conor Fallon. The exhibition was notable for the (intended or not) selectivity of the type of art it presented, by dint of the artists commissioned to participate. Practical considerations attendant on a large touring project may well have influenced the selection of work exhibited: though some were big in size, all were transportable and adaptive to alternate installation settings and so did not, and could not have, reflected on the diversity of media, attitudes and practices evident in art in Ireland in the 1990s. Therefore, while the George Moore Society presented an ambitious set of cultural responses to the Famine, that also effectively complemented Teagasc's series of explanations and lessons, *Famine* also generated a necessarily portable account of Irish culture.

On the whole, figuration and landscape-derived representations dominated *Famine*. Within this scope, many artworks reflected the tension between collective representations that occur through curatorial practice and ongoing individualism in artist's practices with variations on subject choices and stylistic concerns. For example, Coll's bronze *Famine Victims* depicted one skeletal figure horizontally placed through the hollowed abdomen of the other, opening up symbolical interpretative possibilities. McSweeney's painting *Deserted Dwellings* was, like the works of many other exhibitors, recognizably in keeping with the artist's stylistically distinctive oeuvre and simultaneously poetic in its elegiac evocation of emptiness. Madden's *The Boat*, less stringently typical of her work at the time, alludes to dispossession in a bird's-eye view of a white ship which is at once superseded and defined by a vast ocean, painted in rich swirls of textured blues and gold. Works by Graham and O'Donoghue employed more overt historical references.

Graham's *Grey Area*, *c*.1995, a large painting subsequently known as *Famine Painting*, comprises the backs of two adjacent canvases facing out, drawing attention to the image's structural base[41] (Figure 4.5). Predominantly white in colour, a bowl and a cross are the two main iconographic elements. A scrawled series of words qualify the image: an apology for the Famine. The first phrase 'I am sorry' is crossed out and replaced by 'I apologize.' The text refers to British Prime Minister Tony Blair's controversial 1997 statement on the Famine. The ground of the painting reads as a whitewash over the pictorial and text elements within it, suggestive of aspects of history concealed, not by lack of evidence, but by a subsequent lack of sufficient address.

The bowl in the bottom part of the left panel is empty, and above the striking form of the crucifix on the right a red 'tick' mark reads like an

Figure 4.5   Patrick Graham, *Famine*, 1995. Oil on canvas, 182.5 x 365 cm. Image provided by Dublin City Gallery: The Hugh Lane, Dublin, Ireland. © Patrick Graham.

ironic approval of the cross icon and perhaps of the labelling of memory. Close inspection of the painting reveals a single drop pearl-style earring hung on the centre of the cross. Graham's amalgamation of text, iconography, structural exposure, layering and materialism in *Grey Area/ Famine Painting* tenders the hope of proxy as a means to a useful poetics of commemoration by gesturing, imaginatively, towards the unsettling instability of representations of the past.

In O'Donoghue's watercolour *On Our Knees* a large kneeling figure in the foreground takes up most of the dark picture surface, dominated by deep blues[42] (Figure 4.6). The blurred figure has no gender, clothing or ageing detail and digs with their hands at a dark spot in the ground. The title refers to both the individual depicted and, in its plurality, the larger national community brought to its collective knees by a colonially constructed economic and social disaster.

There are many accounts in Famine histories of people frantically digging at the clay with their hands for potatoes, eating raw roots, turnips and even grass and nettles in desperation. Póirtéir recounts an example of this from the NFC archive:

Kathleen Hurley, Ballymoe, County Galway, in 1937: [...] Those pitiful scenes remained fresh in my father's memory. People worn

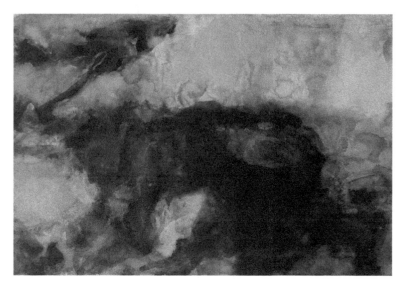

Figure 4.6 Hughie O'Donoghue, *On Our Knees*, 1995. Watercolour, 40 x 60 cm. Image provided by George Moore Society; photograph by Alison Laredo. © Hughie O'Donoghue.

> out with the untold hardship, badly clad staggering for want of food, or any kind of nourishment, wending their way back to satisfy the hungry gnawing pang with a drink of hot water or a mouthful of fresh grass or herbs they gathered by the roadside.
>
> My father said he saw people dead on the roadside, such sights, their bodies all skin and bones, with bunches of green grass in their mouths, the green juice trickling down their chins and necks. Eating such foods brought on disease on the mouth and lips.[43]

O'Donoghue conveys a sense of horrific despair through figuration, with a lack of distracting detail supplanted by a generalized suggestion of individuated distress a balance of representational devices that seems to mitigate against Ricoeur's ruinous dichotomy.

Teagasc and the George Moore Society generated after-images of the Famine framed by political and cultural concerns of the time and toured in the name of contemporary Ireland. Though physical and political practicalities dictated that aspects of *Famine 150* and *Famine* were somewhat restricted representations, each were mammoth undertakings in the absence of significant support for cultural institutions to realise projects of this scale. Considered in counterpoint as broadly contemporaneous to each other, *Famine 150* pursued ideas of explanation, while *Famine* coalesced around a series of individual artistically rendered responses to a grievous history.

Inherent to both the UCC and IMMA exhibitions was a blended approach to representation through exhibition which overtly connected explanatory and expressive approaches in relating a grievous history. Though each had a different thematic focus and terms of reference for commemorating the Famine, the two exhibitions made apparent the 'useful interdependence' of explication and empathy as a mode of encountering the past in the present.

The *Famines Yesterday and Today: The Irish Experience in a Global Context* exhibition was an initiative of the UCC's Department of Geography. Open for three weeks, it was led by an academic interest in pursuing the possibilities and potentialities of multimedia and multi-disciplinary display. The content was presented at two different locations within the campus and included the presentation of new cartographic research on the Famine, artworks, photographs of recent famines elsewhere in the world, along with information panels on selected themes and geographical areas affected by the Famine.

In his account of the exhibition's development, presentation and interpretation, John Crowley, the key researcher on the project, notes, '[w]hile the Famine was island-wide in scale, it was very much regional in terms of its impact' and also that '[i]t became necessary [. . .] to create an aesthetic platform as a means of exploring the trauma, guilt and defensiveness associated with the Famine and its aftermath'.[44] The exhibition layout expanded on this thematic thread: the gap between what is conveyed by statistics and what is felt in human experience. The first display area centred on maps indicating how certain areas were affected by the Famine, and the second area was titled *Oileán an Uaigneas* (Gaelic for 'Island of Loneliness') and included the text of Eavan Boland's poem 'That the science of cartography is limited',[45] which pointed to the inadequacy of superficial mapping, or scientific account, to explain suffering, less still to promote empathic understanding.

The maps section highlighted regional impacts of the Famine by focusing on selected townlands, including places in Mayo and Tipperary, to explore representative themes of eviction, burial and workhouses. Ideas of witness as well as selectivity were acknowledged in the presentation of eyewitness accounts from the Famine era: 'The committee decided to include a wide range of voices, however humble, from the period, in the knowledge that in allowing only certain witnesses to speak we had suppressed others.'[46] Information on and photography (from the Magnum Photographic Agency) of more recent famines in other parts of the world clearly signalled the project's titular aim to iterate a link between Ireland's history and present-day poverty and hunger.

An interest in the wider presence of the Famine as a theme in literature was sustained through the exhibition with the interspersed use of various quotations. Music also featured, and work by composer Marion Ingoldsby was commissioned as part of the project. Contemporary artworks by Annette Hennessy and Alannah Robins from a Sculpture Society and West Cork Arts Centre project that summer were also included. The blend of representational elements as core to the overall project promoted an equivalence between artefact and art in representing the past. As a representation of Famine that sought to explore the roles of witnesses, historians, artists and curators in mediating past events, the UCC project and its research reverberations convey an experiential means of actualizing the intermingling of indignation with understanding. Insistently preventing the viewer from presuming upon the authority of the display, the exhibition provoked an unsettling awareness of how partial (in both senses), changeable and fragile understandings of the past can be.

IMMA's exhibition *Representations of the Famine* crossed a comparable curatorial terrain. Though it prioritized a wide range of individual artistic responses to the Famine, the IMMA project encompassed a broad temporal range and therefore reflected diverse media and artistic scope. Comprising only 20 works, drawn from the museum's collection and borrowed, the tight scale accentuated the intentional diversity of media and time periods included. Indicative of the range of works exhibited are Cork artist Daniel Macdonald's *The Discovery of the Potato Blight in Ireland* (1847) (Figure 1.1), Elizabeth Thompson/Lady Butler's *Evicted* (1890) and Alanna O'Kelly's slide-tape installation work *Sanctuary/Wasteland* (1994). The exhibition was shown in both the Republic and in Northern Ireland and toured to counties Derry, Cork and Mayo as part of the museum's National Programme then coordinated by Carissa Farrell.

Contemporary works in various media were displayed alongside historical paintings and illustrations, and the exhibition in Cork also included work resulting from a community arts development programme. In the press release, curator Catherine Marshall wrote:

> The historical works were exceptional in their time. For well over a century the horror of the event and the guilt of the survivors meant that the Famine was rarely represented visually [...] The somewhat strained relationship between art and the Famine is an indication of the importance of bringing a particular selection of works together, both in terms of remembering the Famine and its history, and understanding a change in the role of the visual artist.[47]

Marshall's awareness of the production of meaning in the making of exhibitions expands on the suggestion in her earlier proposal with Dube to the National Gallery to focus on nationalism in relation to art. The curatorial self-consciousness of *Representations of the Famine* and Marshall's decision to move between time frames in her selection of artworks generated a microcosm within which the extent of the blind spot to which Bann alludes could be assessed. Gathering together competing artistic intentions symptomatic of a range of artistic concerns usually aligned to particular time periods activated a set of after-images of a grievous history seemingly designed to reference a gamut of cultural memory by way of an exhibitionary complex. Exploring in tandem two exhibited works, O'Kelly's installation and Butler's painting, that though produced nearly a hundred years apart share out-of-doors site-based initiation and concern with the lived landscape, indicates the powerful scope of this curatorial agenda to harness representational themes through time.

O'Kelly's work was developed on a beach site, known as Teampall Dumach Mhór (Church of the Great Sandbank), at Thallabhawn, County Mayo (Figure 4.7). Located at the base of Connaught's highest mountain, Mweelrea, and exposed to strong winds and the Atlantic Ocean, a mound of earth, rocks and bones was the site of a sixth-century monastic settlement and later a place where Famine bodies were buried, 'known as a sanctuary to 17th century map makers and [...] referred to as the Wastelands by local people in the 19th and 20th century'.[48]

While O'Kelly was recording her work, much of the mound still remained. Over time, the mound has eroded. As the ocean washes away

Figure 4.7 Alanna O'Kelly, *Sanctuary/Wasteland,* 1994. Video, dimensions variable. Collection Irish Museum of Modern Art, Purchase, 1997. Image courtesy of the Irish Museum of Modern Art. © Alanna O'Kelly.

both the bone and the stones, the layers of historical significance are exposed and disappear. In the work's installation, the mound and close-up details are interspersed with sequences of dwellings further along the coast. The poetic pull of the landscape context is temporarily offset by the revelation of human (and presumably animal) bones in O'Kelly's work: while new fauna grows on the surface of Teampall Dumach Mhór, the bones rise also, and after they have been washed away, traces of the monastic settlement will eventually come to the slowly levelling surface. Slow dull sounds permeate the darkened room, adding to the sombre visual atmosphere. O'Kelly learned how to keen, for this and other performance works, and in *Sanctuary/Wasteland* she proceeds to sing a lament in Irish.[49] The dark hues of the images mean the depictions are not easily read and, like the work's dual title, reflect on the complexity of reading place.

Fionna Barber draws attention to the 'palimpsest of meanings' which 'underpins an emphasis on montage and multivalency within the piece itself'.[50] As an artwork, with duration and spatial particularities, *Sanctuary/Wasteland* is not constantly accessible, nor is it definitive of the site's history or identity. O'Kelly's documentation of the location in the creation of an audio-visual installation is an intervention in the site's conservation. While not actually preserving the place, her work acts as an interpretative memorialization and leaves the site itself to change as per the variable programme of erosion. O'Kelly's work challenges the reliance on absolute knowledge or material evidence as the only means to negotiate the past in the creation of a secondary form of witnessing: art as after-image.

Butler's painting is a rare example of an artist directly observing an eviction in the post-Famine era, with paintbrush, literally, in hand[51] (Figure 4.8). Butler's witnessing of a turbulent social scene happening in the east of Ireland, County Wicklow, sets up a comparable, though historically differentiated, interest in the potential of the landscape as idiom. In her 1922 autobiography, she wrote:

Figure 4.8 Elizabeth Butler, *Eviction*, 1890. Oil on canvas, 131 x 194 cm. © National Folklore Collection, University College Dublin.

The 'eighties had seen our Government do some dreadful things in the way of evictions in Ireland. Being at Glendalough at the end of that decade, and hearing one day that an eviction was to take place some nine miles distant from where we were staying for my husband's shooting, I got an outside car and drove off to the scene, armed with my paints.

I met the police returning from their distasteful 'job', armed to the teeth and very flushed. One getting there I found the ruins of the cabin smouldering, the ground quite hot under my feet, and I set up my easel there. The evicted woman came to search amongst the ashes of her home to try and find some of her belongings intact. She was very philosophical, and did not rise to the level of my indignation as an ardent English sympathiser. However, I studied her well, and on returning home at Delgany I set up the big picture which commemorates a typical eviction in the black 'eighties. [...] I did not see this picture at all at the Academy, but I am very certain it cannot have been very 'popular' in England. Before it was finished my husband was appoint to the command at Alexandria, and as soon as I had packed off the 'Eviction', I followed [...] and saw again the fascinating East.[52]

Butler presents the bereft woman without obvious religious or heroic overtones. Alone beside her razed cottage, as a group of figures walks away from her, the evicted woman stands windswept on a hilltop in an unsympathetic and indifferent landscape of remarkable beauty. Butler comments on her studies of the Glendalough area and was pleased with her portrayal of the landscape, noting 'it has the true Irish atmosphere'. Indeed, a fallout from Butler's 'successful' landscape is apparent in the remark of the then British Prime Minister, Lord Salisbury, who commented '[...] on the "breezy beauty" of the landscape, which almost made him wish that he could take part in an eviction himself'.[53] The account of the work in Butler's autobiography reveals the social context for the production of the painting, with an artistic bravery emerging amid an exciting life of travel and cultural encounters.

In her curatorial determination to bring historical works into the framing institutional context of a museum of modern art and further juxtapose them with contemporary artworks, Marshall shone a light on methods of historical representation. The diversity of art practices and range of individual responses to the Famine configured an awareness of the structuring of representation within each of the works as well as through curatorial presentations on the past and present, engendering a practice of critical history. The presentation of, for example, O'Kelly's and Butler's works illustrate a direct challenge to separations of history and theory in art, indicative of Holly's later call to recognize historians as the makers of history. *Representations of the Famine*, as a curatorial project, exposed trajectories of art historiography through a critical process of negotiating the after-images of a specific grievous history.

Jacques Rancière argues that "'the logic of stories" and the ability to act as historical agents go together', as variously indicated by the curatorial practices at the time of the sesquicentennial commemorations discussed here.[54] Bringing to bear a range of strategies of representation, these four exhibition projects pointed to a useful entanglement of explanation and emotion in order to engage the reader of history, or exhibition visitor. As emissaries for Irish political maturity and artistic practice, the Teagasc and George Moore Society exhibitions were emblematic of a range of contemporary cultural attitudes in post-colonial Ireland and presented challenges to history's appeal to closure.

As curatorial and experimentally driven projects, the UCC and IMMA exhibitions drew attention to processes of representation. Framing Famine history within exhibition practice as itself an aesthetic practice, constitutive, rather than merely reflective, of the production of meaning, or social sense, links to what Rancière terms 'forms of visibility that disclose artistic practices, the place they occupy, what they "do" or "make" from the standpoint of what is common to the community'.[55] Indicative also of Rancière's conception of artistic practices as "'ways of doing and making" that intervene in the general distribution of ways of doing and making as well as in the relationships they maintain to modes of being and forms of visibility',[56] the relationships forged between art and artefact, data and cultural forms of interpretation across the four exhibitions questioned perceptual gaps between an event and its representation; and between the narratives of history and instances of their comprehension.

Artistic Intention, Curatorial Strategies and Collective Remembrance

In 2003, Kevin Whelan suggested: 'Irish historians are in thrall to [. . .] [a] striking myth – that history itself is not a form of myth, and that it alone can escape the constructive element of narrative form.'[57] Since then, the advent of the so-called 'decade of commemorations' in Ireland, central to which have been the Workers' Lockout of 1913, World War I and the 1916 Rising, this discussion on history as myth has come centre stage, leading to diverse outputs, including an extensive programme of talks, on diverging and even contradictory accounts of this period of time. What Guy Beiner calls the 'dustbin of Irish history' may yet be usefully tipped up,[58] as one clear outcome of the flurry of talk about commemoration has been a renewed debate around the value of folk history in, as Beiner phrased it in 2006, 'crafting the past'. He describes folk history as

> a 'people's history' featuring multiple narratives that refer to numerous people and are told in different versions by various storytellers to assorted audiences. This kaleidoscope complexity amounts to democratic history that was by no means free of local prejudices and politics, though these did not necessarily correspond with prevalent suppositions about 'traditional' nationalist history.[59]

Debates on folk sources restricted by academic patterns of historiography correspond to the typically demoted position of visual culture in historical understanding. Complicated by the perception of the histories of visual forms as elitist and existing in silos to wider social and cultural life, Whelan's assertion can then be translated into tensions suggested in Holly's critique of the distinctions between historical and critical art histories, or crafting of the past. This is a challenge for conventional positivist models of historical representation common to museums and much commemorative practice, especially when the contested space between history and myth is often also embedded in the construction of otherness in cultural practices through temporal and/or geographical distancing. Such conditioning of 'past-presencing' is further restricted by relegations of overtly interpretative sources, such as folk memory, or practices, such as art, within historiography.

The tentative attitude at an official national level to exhibiting the Famine at the time of both the centenary and the 150-year anniversary was indicative of contemporary politics of cultural perspectives, attendant on the respective political climates and dominant artistic dispositions. The difficulty of making a representation of the Famine pivoted not only, then, on the problem of materialism, but also on difficulties of historicism that accompanied Irish historical awareness through the twentieth century.

144

As a young nation in the mid-twentieth century, Ireland seemed unable to acknowledge more difficult memories, which is not uncommon in newly defined post-colonial societies. In this way, and notwithstanding the efforts of individual artists, the 1946 *Exhibition of Original Paintings of Irish Historical Interest*'s presentation of work in a chronological context was aimed at echoing a prescribed narrative of an established social history. All the more for their presentation in this context, the works of Davidson, Woods, MacGonigal and Brandt insisted on the significance of individual artistic intention for collective forms of commemoration and further, delineated, both within and in spite of the national and international artistic climates of the time, a vernacular of post-colonial after-images.

In the 1990s, the exhibitions organized by Teagasc and the George Moore Society produced exportable descriptions of Irish history and culture and were, in this, effective in generating a focus on the Famine through international relations and a viewpoint on Irish culture. The more permanent legacy of *Famine 150* at Johnstown Castle to some extent overwrites its function as a temporary exhibition. Some of the works exhibited in *Famine* are now dispersed across private and public art collections, and might otherwise never have appeared in the public arena.

Both the UCC and IMMA projects demurred from reconstituting linear comprehensions of the Famine, connecting instead Rancière's comment on crossovers between historical agency and the function of stories to Whelan's observation on the prevalence of narratives constructed to address the past. The UCC exhibition can now be usefully considered as signposting what Young also outlined: that only by considering both an event and its representation can appropriate cultural memory, or witnessing in the present, be realized. IMMA more directly put into practice a proposition that processes of criticism and history are intertwined in comprehending past events. By privileging each artwork as equally relevant to the present-day understanding of the Famine, *Representations of the Famine* intimated a crossover between monumental precepts of history and concepts of social forms of memory, explanation and emotion, and pointed to the usefulness of considering art exhibitions as a collation of after-images.

Integrating comprehension with affect, the UCC and IMMA projects outlined curatorial strategies for remembering past events in defiance of conventional expectations of finality in representation or disclosure of cultural identities.

To varying degrees, and reflective of temporally available 'mnemonic technologies and memorial forms' of Rigney's description, interpretative functions in all five exhibitions referenced here tie them, in different ways, to a changing practice of imaginative history. As instigators of interpretative acts of historical understanding, commemorative exhibition practices have implications for disrupting easy separations of history and theory. Looking back, it seems that in presenting works that move beyond specific illustration, literal depiction or physical representation to embrace the multiple potentialities of understanding, artists have been calling on viewers to actively imagine a scene of history in the present. This provides an opportunity for curators of history and readers of art to acknowledge art's potential as a proxy for imaginative history; one that facilitates ongoing and altering types of secondary witnessing.

5

Grief, Graves and Signs of the Dead

Famine Graveyards: Signs of the Dead or Symbols for the Living?

In Fermoy, County Cork, there are two graveyards side by side, situated between old workhouse buildings and more recently developed sports fields. One is a military cemetery which incorporates a World War I burial site and is denoted by a large headstone and punctuated by the presence of trimmed shrubbery; the other is a mass Famine graveyard with a small plaque at its entrance. The latter site is an L-shaped green field surrounded by a high brick wall (Figure 5.1). In its centre is a tall wrought-iron Celtic-style cross and at one side there are wooden seats projecting from the wall.[1] A series of small grey metal crosses are nailed to the crumbling wall of a small run-down building backing onto the site. A distinctly grim and monotone place, even sunshine cannot undermine the emphatic emptiness of the Famine burial site.

As counterpoints, the adjacent location of the two graveyards points to representational complexities associated with remembering the dead on a mass scale. The soldiers' graveyard appears formalized through commemorative conventions in comparison to the Famine grave's relative poverty-stricken under-memorialized aspect. Inscribed on the main headstone in the soldier's graveyard are the names and ranks of 22 soldiers,

Figure 5.1 Famine Graveyard, Fermoy, County Cork, Ireland. Image provided by author.

described as 'officers and men', buried there who died in 'The Great War'. Throughout that graveyard are other older headstones, notably of young children of military families buried during the late nineteenth century and poignantly indicative of Fermoy's past as a British garrison town of considerable distinction. The specificity of these grave markers underscores the anonymity of the thousands of Famine dead believed buried in the shared mass plot beside it. The gap between visibility and knowledge is starkly evident in the few paces between these two graveyards.

As examples of visual, material and spatial culture, the distinction between cemeteries and burial sites is an issue of both form and content. A cemetery is here understood as a symbolically formalized place where the dead are generally named and typically utilized as a site of ritual return for the living. A burial site is indicative of graveyards which are defined by lack of certainty over who is interred and marked with varying degrees of symbolic interpretation, operating outside of continued-use graveyards. Both types of graveyards are heterotopian spaces, in Stéphanie Toussaint's and Alain Decrop's definition of 'collective or shared places allowing overlaps within surrounding borders'.[2] Depending on the site, these borders are infiltrated by alternate ongoing rituals of everyday life, commemorative practices and heritage tourism.

In the example of the two graveyards side-be-side at Fermoy, their contradistinction casts a light on the codification of the celebration of power and heroism and the prestige associated with certain kinds of death on one hand, and, on the other, the embarrassment of pauperism. This divergence also reflects a tension between marked and unmarked sites of burial generally, and pertains to the range of memorial forms at Famine graveyards in Ireland and elsewhere.

Practices of remembering the dead as denoted by both the physical upkeep of a graveyard and the forms of visitation to it reveal how those living recall the dead as witnesses to the past, often in efforts to make sense of the present day. As the fraught evolution of the *Ship Fever Monument* in Montreal (discussed in Chapter 2) indicated, the process of memorializing a Famine burial site is laden with competing interests, and can, to adapt Guy Beiner's phrase, result in a 'crucible of memory'.[3] Contested affiliations of collective identity surround the marking of cemeteries, particularly those aligned with grievous histories. Such a politics of mourning demonstrates the sustained significance of the dead for those living.

In his discussion on what the dead mean to the living, Colin Davis draws on a number of sources that link concepts of witness to the past with practices of mourning in the present day.[4] While Giorgio Agamben's concept of the 'ultimate witness', for example, can be ascribed to the dead – as those who cannot tell us anything – to suggest their radical 'otherness' to the living, Davis explores continuance also. Following on Martin Heidegger, Davis suggests linkage between past and present, between the dead and those living: 'In mourning, and in our continuing care for the dead, the dead do in some sense remain with us, as our being-with-others becomes being-with-the-dead.'[5]

For Davis, it is Emmanuel Lévinas's notion of 'unanticipated signs' that fosters most significance, on which he writes:

> The signifying gaps through which the dead might speak do not only occur in books, of course. In fact, if we knew where to find them, they would be already lost to us [...] signs which irrupt as a surprise and which signify without any ascertainable signifying

intention. They cannot be determined in advance or attributed to a conscious subject. They may be anywhere that we don't expect them. Perhaps they are all around us.[6]

Though suggestive of limitations to what might be gained from a discourse of how the dead appear as signifying presences among the living, and by implication from reading burial sites, Davis's comments elucidate that processes of remembering the dead are discussions about the living. The counterpoints between the two Fermoy graveyards reveal contingently variant attitudes to both the past and the application of memorial signs. Issues of place, space, materialism, visibility and memorial conventions, expectation and surprise, contribute to a reconsideration of how ideas of reality and representation have shaped Famine remembrance and forgetfulness in the commemoration of Famine victims at variously formalized and visited graveyards.

The impact of poverty and rising rates of death on burial practices and the effects of an unprecedented rate of mortality compounded difficulties in realizing culturally comfortable forms of burial.[7] In Ireland, long-established conventions of wakes, which comprised several days of an organized and socially complex celebration of the life of the deceased, were pared back to virtually nothing.[8] As the Famine wore on and people were displaced in larger numbers, burials were hasty, and where coffins were used they were often reused, when the availability of wooden furniture to make coffins ran low. This gave rise to the use of coffins with sliding base panels on hinges, known as hinged or sliding coffins, recorded in County Cork. Such a coffin could bear, with some dignity, the dead to the grave, where the base slid open and the body dropped to the earth so that the coffin could be used repeatedly.[9] At graveyards where bodies were buried in such density, the term Famine pit is sometimes applied.

Across the NFC and contemporary news reports, such as in the *ILN*, accounts tell that some did not receive even this formality and shrouds were used to bury many from workhouses where disease had spread: these corpses were carried on carts to open mass graves, or pits, and showered with lime before burial. Though the Fever Act 1847 decreed greater sanitation around the burial of bodies, there are reports of hurried burials of relatives and neighbours in ditches and fields by those on the move for survival toward ports or in search of relief aid.

With these realities in mind, the symbolic divergence of the Fermoy graveyards draws attention to correlations between histories of burial and the consequentially defined practices of continued commemoration of such deaths. In this respect, war cemeteries and memorials bear some comparative relevance to the reading of the commemorative signification of Famine burial sites. The suggested individuation at conflict sites, particularly in the absence of certainty over where and how may are buried is evoked in lieu of listing the dead by name. Soldiers killed in the course of conflicts, like victims of other large-scale disasters, are often transformed into a mass on-site symbolical memorialization of their deaths. In Colleville-sur-Mer, near Omaha Beach, France, for example, the scale of the loss of life there during World War II is indicated by miles of replicated small white crosses, denoting almost 10,000 troops. The assignment of such crosses, suggesting homage by proxy to the loss of individual lives, where many of the bodies remain lost or unidentified, was a practice begun in remembrance of World War I. Writing on Sir Fabian Ware's work to establish the Grave Registration Commission on foot of the casualties of the Great War, David Crane outlines this evolution of war grave remembrance in the context of what is known as 'battlefield tourism'.[10]

Lists of names of the dead is a much-desired presentation of individuality sustained after death, and subsequently a convention in many conflict-related monuments.[11] Unusually, for a history mired in lack of certainty over burial, one Famine graveyard in Ireland has succeeded in marking a cemetery which incorporates a so-called Famine pit, in this idiom: St Mark's Cemetery at Cashel County Tipperary. Locally driven research and fundraising led to a dedicated wall within the cemetery being carved with over 1,000 names of the Famine dead thought interred there.[12] The inscription accounts names, ages and dates of death, as would have been listed in a workhouse record.

Marked Famine graves and their related monuments in Ireland and abroad commonly enunciate Western typologies of the amassing of the individual passing of life into shared symbolism, such as occurs in the memorial aspects of the cemeteries at Parks Canada: Grosse Île and the Irish Memorial National Historic Site of Canada. The development of this particular site indicates provocative struggles over competing claims to history defined by tension between immigrant and national cultures at what is perhaps one of the best known sites with a large number of Irish Famine migrant dead interred. Other places, such as unacknowledged burial sites throughout Ireland, present an inverse means of staging the past and in doing so question assumed historiographical links between visibility and knowledge. The production of photographic images of such sites further contributes to this commemorative visual culture, highlighting overtly documentary and representational practices as contributive to this field of public mourning.

Across Ireland, the location of many memorialized Famine graveyards indicates a history of the depletion of the rural population. That sites of mass Famine burial in Ireland are largely outside of cities – at the edges of small towns and villages, often near workhouses, in what are today less populated rural places – is a reminder that rural Ireland was, relative to European descriptors, quite densely populated before the Famine.[13] This bears out the need to consider sites of history, as indicated also at the museum and heritage sites discussed in Chapter 3, beyond today's conception of urban or rural descriptors: as social sites of a Famine cultural memory performed at particular places.[14]

Place is described by Toussaint and Decrop as 'more or less stable, absolute, occupied and provid[ing] the possibility to experience sensations in relation to the area', against 'space' as 'changing, moving and [...] no-one's property'. Thus, place, they write, is 'a tried and consumed space' and its meanings 'belong to the realms of experiences'.[15] Bearing this in mind, many Famine graveyards are maintained as sites of memory by a meeting of vernacular and national processes of historiography where multifarious experiences of place, are engineered by a breadth of formalized commemorative elements.

Marked Remembrance: Cemeteries and Anticipated Signs

In 1909 at what is now called Parks Canada: Grosse Île and the Irish Memorial National Historic Site of Canada, the AOH displayed conspicuous 'evidence of the currency of the nationalistic rhetoric in Canada'[16] by unveiling a memorial on the highest part of the island. The 15-m-high Celtic cross stone monument has three text panels in English,

French and Irish, which do not bear the same text, with inflections of varied cultural allegiances apparent in each. The Irish inscription translates:

> Children of the Gael died in their thousands on this island having fled from the laws of foreign tyrants and an artificial famine in the years of 1847–48. God's blessing on them. Let this monument be a token in their name and honour from the Gaels of America. God save Ireland.

The Irish and English versions have nationalist overtones echoing language employed by revolutionaries of the nineteenth century. The primary form of the Irish stone memorial – a Celtic cross – has clear Christian symbolism and Irish cultural relevance.[17]

Described by Mark McGowan as a 'cultural battleground',[18] Grosse Île is a small island, measuring 3 miles in length and 1 mile in breadth. Between 1832 and 1937, from May to October each year, it was a point of entry into Canada and North America and a quarantine station. Little remains of the associated mid-nineteenth-century structures. For tourists, visits to Grosse Île are possible with or without interpreters and there are also costumed animators at various renovated and preserved buildings, such as the disinfection building. Of interest to this account are the memorials and graveyards on the island as forms of commemorative visual culture, synthesized through processes of fraught debate and dogged by controversy over false claims to historical accuracy.

A 1832 cholera epidemic decimated the immigrant population at the site, and in 1847 catastrophic under-resourcing and inability to cope with the numbers of arrivals in serious states of ill health led to another devastating population depletion for the Irish. Memorials to the Irish who died there have been controversial, not least due to contemporary and subsequent reluctance on the part of some governments to acknowledge both the reasons for and the fact of conditions on the island and ships on its shores during the worst-affected years.

While in 1832, individual plots were used to bury the dead in 1847, the speed of death, many from typhus, engendered mass burials. In July, Dr Douglas (the quarantine station's first superintendent) reported, 'six men are constantly employed digging large trenches from five to six feet deep, in which the dead are buried'.[19] This refers to the island's main six-acre burial site, the Western Cemetery, but there are also burial sites in other parts of the island, including on the eastern side. Witnesses reported 'bodies stacked like cordwood' on the shoreline awaiting burial and that, presumably due to the mentally unsettling nature of the illnesses, some immigrants wandered away from the sheds, died and may well have been buried by companions in random unmarked parts of the island.[20] Mary Daly has noted that 'four Catholic and two Protestant clergy, four doctors, three stewards and twenty-two cooks and orderlies [...] died'.[21]

Douglas had a marble Monument to the Physicians erected on the site in 1852, which primarily commemorates his peers who worked and died in 1847. This takes the form of a cornet with an urn on top and lists the doctors' names and homeplaces. On a base panel the following text appears: 'The mortal remains of 5,424 persons who fleeing from pestilence and Famine in Ireland in the year 1847 found in America but a grave.'[22] In the early 1980s, white crosses were placed throughout the field in front of Douglas's memorial, and so the burial site is now visually reminiscent of a war cemetery. While the crosses do not mark individual graves, they point to a desire to plot individual memory.

However, it was a 1991 proposal by Parks Canada to transform the island into a tourist-oriented theme park that triggered years of debate and consultative hearings on the ownership of the memorial process associated with the site. Two diaries purporting to recount experiences of Irish Famine immigrants on the crossing to Canada but later revealed respectively as fraud or outright fabrication,[23] and as dubious in contemporary authenticity or historically weak at best,[24] became associated with the fractious debate. The first, known as Gerald Keegan's *Famine Diary*, a fiction written by Robert Sellar in 1895, was much cited in the debates of the early 1990s on the dedication of the Grosse Île, and in 1997 Parks Canada quoted the second, Robert Whyte's *The Ocean Plague* published in 1848 (republished in 1994 as *Robert Whyte's 1847 Famine Ship Diary: The Journey of an Irish Coffin Ship*), in a book on the site's history.

In the context of yet another false diary claiming to account ill behaviour of religious orders in Quebec, Jason King argues the accounts of Limerick landlord Stephen de Vere (quoted in Chapter 2), who reported his 1847 travel in steerage to Canada to Parliament, and of John Francis Maguire can be understood as a refutation of the suggested reputational damage to the religious orders who cared for incoming immigrants. King observes that in Canada 'the recuperation of famine memory was [...] crucial for the creation of communal identity',[25] to the extent that

[t]here was implicit in these controversies a sense of creative tension between genuine and false, as well as communal and personal, forms of recollection that became constitutive of and defined the parameters in which, the memory of the Famine migrants was shaped.[26]

In 1998 the island's official memorial was placed beside the Monument to the Physicians, a stone structure with narrow corridors leading through the earth towards a wall of glass.[27] Designed by Lucienne Cornet and the Émile Gilbert and Associates architect firm, the sensitively non-specifically titled *The Memorial* is dedicated to all the immigrants who died on the island. The glass wall overlooks the burial field with white crosses (Figure 5.2). On it are etched the names of the known dead buried there (from Douglas's records), with space left

Figure 5.2 View of West Cemetery, from *The Memorial*, 1998, Grosse Île, Quebec Canada. Lucienne Cornet and Émile Gilbert and Associates architect firm. © Parks Canada.

blank indicative of those whose names are missing. The monument's location counters its typology of enclosure with inherent visual revelation, overlaying the view of the outdoor cemetery with a textual litany of death.

Complexities associated with commemorating catastrophic death in material forms are reflected at Grosse Île in the range of memorial devices developed. At Grosse Île, though separately affecting, taken together these varied attempts to memorialize the horror of both 1832 and 1847 have translated into a series of symbolic representations of death that, on one level, transform a metaphorically contained site of ritual remembrance into a hyper-cemetery and tourist destination. References to the Famine dead of Grosse Île in Quebec were made on murals in Northern Ireland in the 1980s, which also featured Celtic crosses and white burial crosses.[28]

The contentious evolution of the Grosse Île Famine burial sites as memorial sites underlines the importance of place in historical representation and elucidates the relativity of meaning implied by acts of remembrance. The controversial processes of ownership over the past and its expression in memorial practice and monumental forms at both the Montreal and Grosse Île sites reflect multivocal perspectives defining the situation of diasporic experiences both within and without of competing nationalist, sectarian, ethnic and cultural agendas. Though a differently socially dissipated site of burial, the internal syntax of some of the overlapping formal elements at Grosse Île are comparably negotiated at cemeteries in Ireland containing Famine burial plots. This is evident, for example at the site selected for the first ever official National Famine Commemoration Day in 2009: Abbeystrowry Cemetery in Skibbereen, County Cork (Figure 5.3).

Entering the Cork cemetery through a small porch area, a stone panel on one side has text that describes the Famine ('1845–50') as 'Ireland's worst single disaster' and declares that Skibbereen, 'epicentre of this horror, suffered more than most'.[29] The text also reveals that about 9,000 Famine victims were buried without coffins in Famine burial pits within the graveyard, though figures are cited somewhat differently elsewhere.[30] In the front gravelled area of the cemetery is a row of six small blank stone slabs overlooked by a taller row of five slabs. The back row of standing stones visually recalls the format of war and institutions' cemeteries and has text running across it, outlining some of the Famine's effects on the area. The stones are situated in a paved area in which also lie three stone

Figure 5.3 Abbeystrowry Cemetery, Skibbereen, County Cork, Ireland. © Terri Kearney.

grave-like slabs, each with a cross deeply etched on its surface. This small area is marked by a simple white stone, which reads: 'In memory / of the victims of / the famine 1845–48 / whose coffinless bodies / were buried in this plot'. To the centre of the general cemetery is an older decoratively contrasting Famine memorial, erected in 1888 by a local blacksmith.[31] This upright, gate-like structure is made of white wrought iron with a harp form at its centre surrounded by floral tendrils.

As at Grosse Île, the range of commemorative elements at Abbeystrowry indicates both the deep-reaching effects of the Famine felt in the area and the cultural struggles over how best and by whom to convey the experiences in material form. These graveyard sites negotiate contentious aspects of their histories, from uncertainty over numbers of the dead buried to fractious debates on ownership of associated memorial processes. The raised consciousness of these places has much to do with local activism for commemoration, in the face of wider official indifference or wariness at various times. The range of monumental elements at Grosse île and

Abbeystrowry – the variety of textual emphases, the fluctuation between positive signifiers of death and religious resurrection and more ambiguous absences – constitute a mixed set of signs and symbols that negotiate the difficult task of materially uttering the ultimate outcome for so many Famine victims.

Unlike Grosse Île, as a functioning cemetery Abbeystrowry is a place of return for local people. Its signification thus operates outside of the hyper-cemetery concept – though sharing its visual signs – and emerges instead as a space for unintentional as well as planned Famine remembrance. Incorporated more subtly into the fabric of ongoing social and personal rituals at Skibbereen than Grosse Île could possibly be (due to its location and historic and touristic functions), Abbeystrowry sits closer to the expanded field of memorial practice Andreas Huyssen discusses in the context of urban memorial parks.[32]

Away from the conventions of enclosed cemeteries, populated with repeated signs and recognizable symbols, are other, differently cogent, places for remembering Famine death. Memorial parks and gardens of remembrance are distinguished as places to visit and leave which have potential for a broad set of visitor descriptors as they function as social, even aesthetic, spaces. Public gardens are typically appreciated in terms of integral landscaping and as places to sit or stay in for various durations and can promote social interaction as well as individual reflection. Gardens of remembrance, specifically, give rise to considerations of history in the context of daily life. One such garden dedicated to the Famine memory is in Carrick-on-Shannon, County Leitrim, in the north-western region of Ireland.

In the centre of the town a former workhouse building now houses St Patrick's Community Hospital, the only one of the three workhouses built in County Leitrim that remains standing. Its attic retains an empty whitewashed interior reminiscent of Famine-era dormitories,[33] and was opened as a memorial in September 2008. It contains a central aisle with raised sections on either side, where inmates sat or lay on straw. To the back of the hospital lies the Great Famine Commemoration Garden with a plaque to identify the area's former use (Figure 5.4). This was a graveyard area where hundreds of people were buried without markers. The workhouse graveyard was opened in 1849, when local graveyards were unable to cope with the number of deaths.[34] Thousands are thought to have died in County Leitrim during the Famine whose graves were never identified.[35]

Figure 5.4 Famine Garden of Remembrance, St Patrick's Hospital, Carrick-on-Shannon, County Leitrim, Ireland. Image provided by author.

As there is uncertainty over the exact numbers buried at the site due to incomplete records, remembering in generality is promoted. Without obvious representation employed to indicate a mass loss, the landscaped garden is characterized by the presence of native Irish trees, soft grass, seating and a fountain. As a garden of remembrance, it is a quiet, sheltered spot and promotes contemplation. A plaque on site reminds the visitor that this man-made beauty spot is also a site where the profound trauma of Famine burials was played out, and a stone cross and other elements indicates this aspect of the site's history. The distress and bustle that would have accompanied burial in Famine times is overridden by the present-day atmosphere of still reflection.

The garden has functions other than as a site of commemoration: not least as a contemporary place of retreat for hospital workers, patients and visitors in need of respite from their daily encounters with illness. As a place of remembrance, it shares with the cemeteries at Grosse Île and Abbeystrowry a direct history as a Famine burial site, but its hybrid status as both a garden and a burial ground subtly situates its commemorative function within day-to-day hospital life.[36]

This shadows a transition from the anticipated signs of cemeteries towards the unanticipated signs or surprise found at less formally denoted mass grave sites, which also contribute to the expanded field and forms of commemorative visual culture.

Framing Emptiness: Wilderness as Witness

In a discussion on visitor experiences at Auschwitz and Birkenau, Chris Keil focuses on differentiations between representation and presentation of the past and outlines how visits to death camps mediate the memory of the Holocaust.[37] He links Birkenau's vastness with a sense of emptiness and loss: 'Vacancy and loss is articulated not only by signs of absence, but by the absence of signs, by the apparent lack of interpretation, or presentation.'[38] Though this seems to imply the site is a monument, Keil notes 'the place cannot stand as a monument to itself without the mediation of a mimetic stratum'. The desire to create a monument of Birkenau has resulted in a structured intervention of processes of conservation and preservation to generate the appearance of an unmediated trace of the past. On the level of representation, Birkenau documents, according to Keil, 'the artful and conscious construction of illusion'.[39]

The provocation of emptiness and loss that Keil encountered at Birkenau – 'the imaginative demand for silence and absence'[40] – is emphatically iterated at non-cemetery-style Famine burial sites throughout Ireland. At variance with the neater conventions of symbolically endowed cemeteries, these now mostly rural burial sites have in common with Holocaust camps identities as history tourist destinations, though the evolutions of the sites are radically different, as indeed the histories alluded to are incomparable. The linkage, rather, revolves around a type of tourism practice, or way of visiting a place that the visitor does not live in, that Geoffrey M. White notes 'recreate[s] a social milieu in which the past is interactively represented, understood and evaluated in relation to multiple, and at times competing frames of history'.[41] Though his analysis relates specifically to group tours of sites of conflict in the context of what he terms the 'tourism memoryscape' of 'war tourism', White's emphasis on what Peter Hohenhaus refers as 'place authenticity' in fact relates just as much to what Keil terms mediation of place or the 'construction of illusion'. These interpretations of place help to consider the affective impact of even what

160

are latterly out-of-the-way Famine burial sites, that simultaneously hold abiding significances for local communities.

Infrequently visited when compared to the booming tourist industry of World War II concentration camps, and with each Famine burial site uniquely mediated, these lesser heralded burial grounds are nonetheless connected by the historical weight of subsequent tropes of dark tourism, here framed by rural tourism associations of wilderness. Wilderness as a concept is tied to modern socially produced perceptions of tourism, art and history. Central to each of these representational modes, that are also forms of visual culture, are ideas of the other. Concepts of both the other and the origin are of and from the wilderness also, rendering it a site of identity differentiations within a greater project of modernity.

Many rural tourism drives are directed at urban dwellers seeking confirmation of nature defined through either visiting spectacular viewpoints or, for the more adventurous, experiencing wilderness. In these actions, tourists become active agents of cultural differentiation at designated rural sites, with nature a sought-after experience of difference. Namely, this is difference to their day-to-day life, where the locations visited are consciously perceived as 'landscape', that is to suggest a representation of place. The concept of nature visually synthesized through the history in art also has dual purpose. The construction of the picturesque relies on the perception of nature as non-threatening, and Donald Crawford notes, '[...] to be discovered or noticed by us',[42] while the human as a Romantic body in nature is iterated most zealously in the encounter with the sublime power of uncontrollable elemental forces, often pictorially deployed as symbolic fate.

These representational paradigms can be simultaneously indicative, or even expressive, of social status. Justin Carville traces the connections of social relations to space in the evolution of a visual cultural form that merges tourism and art: late-nineteenth-century photography of rural landscapes by 'middle-class naturalists', reflected the fact that 'tourism was not just about the visual consumption of the natural world but also the representation of it'.[43] In representational practices broadly, which includes the writing of history, as with tourism and art, the notion of wilderness can be described as both symbolically appropriated, visually and socially, and itself a subject. Perhaps particularly for those living outside of these localities, framed encounters with history instigated by

Figure 5.5 Cherryfield Famine and Pauper Graveyard, Baunta Commons, Callan, County Kilkenny Ireland. Image provided by author.

visiting mass Famine and Pauper graveyards, such as at Cherryfield, Baunta Commons, Callan in County Kilkenny and Carrigastira, County Cork, resonate at the confluence of such systems of representation.

A well-signposted route from the main surrounding roads leads to the Cherryfield graveyard (Figure 5.5). Nearing the site, the road turns into a very narrow country lane, the final stretch of which can only be accessed by pedestrians. In summer, it is an attractive leafy walkway by a stream, with grass in the middle of the lane. After a few minutes' walk down this way, on the right a stile over a stone wall leads to the memorial graveyard. An entrance stone erected in 1986 by the Callan Heritage Society, indicates (in capital letters) the site is dedicated: '[i]n memory of / the uncounted victims / of famine and poverty /buried here, most of / whom died in Callan / Workhouse 1841–1922'. Jonny Geber notes that there was 'noticeably high incidence of poverty in Kilkenny' in pre-Famine accounts, with 'the poor in the outskirts of the town of Callan [...] said to inhabit cabins that were mere holes'.[44] In light of such stark impoverishment, it is worth noting Willie Nolan's iteration that it was at Callan in the autumn of 1849 that the 'politicization of the land question had its origins' – with the

Figure 5.6 Entrance Stone, Cherryfield Famine and Pauper Graveyard, Baunta Commons, Callan, County Kilkenny, Ireland. Image provided by author.

formation of a tenants' protection society which he outlines led to the foundation of the Tenant League in August 1850.[45]

At the Cherryfield Famine and Pauper Graveyard, two adjoining fields are surrounded by shrubs and trees and separated in part from each other by a high hedge. To the right on entering the first field is a stone memorial dedicated by Afri[46] (Figure 5.6). On the left, there are seats facing a stone altar structure in the middle of the field. Beyond the altar is a large wooden cross with a stone base. The second field has no structural elements within it. Both parts of the site are intrinsically designed by surrounding hedges and trees; the only break is a walkway between the two and the wall at the entrance side of the first field. A ditch runs along this wall, creating the impression that the fields are situated on raised ground.

Etched on the base of the dedication stone in capital letters is: 'To the memory of Callan's Great Famine victims whose suffering continues amongst the poor of Asia, Africa and Latin America today. Their memory challenges us to work for a more just and equitable world.'[47] Further text on the stone quotes the social scientist Dessalegn Rahmato, 1987: 'Famine is the /closing scene of a / drama whose / most important / and decisive

Figure 5.7 Swinford Workhouse and Famine Graveyard, Swinford, County Mayo, Ireland. Image provided by author.

acts / have been played / out behind closed doors.' To the left of this is a list: 'Ireland 1845 / Bangladesh 1974 / East Timor 1975 / Brazil 1979 / Ethiopia 1984/ Somalia 1992 / Angola 1994.'

The central image of the stone depicts a male crucified figure in a generalized representation of a peasant worker or labourer: a scythe comprises the arm of the cross and a shovel the shaft. The man's hat is suggestive of a much hotter, sunnier climate than Ireland's. These pictorial elements present a potentially universal figure (though also a transmuted Christian crucifixion icon), and along with the text quotation and list, situate the graveyard within a universal paradigm in which suffering is equated with implied sacrifice.

The stone also depicts a small etched portrait of Edmund Rice, with the dates 1844 and 1994 inscribed on either side. Rice (1762–1844) was the Callan-born founder of the Christian Brothers, an institution of religious brothers, who ran many schools throughout Ireland. Linking the site to a named local luminary, finds an echo at the similarly atmospheric Famine Graveyard to the back of Swinford Hospital (formerly a workhouse) in County Mayo, which is, more stridently, associated with the founder of the agrarian protest movement, the Land League, Michael Davitt (1846–1906) who was a local of nearby Straide (Figure 5.7). Alongside an image of and quotation from Davitt, the Swinford site images and quotes Mahatma Gandhi generating a comparable pattern of international and local affiliations, to that found at the Cherryfield graveyard.

Though these various elements recognize loss of life as a global experience and the development of the memorial aspects of the sites as locally contingent, the graveyards at both Cherryfield and Swinford are framed as sites of memory most forcefully, not by words, iconography and man-made structures, but by manipulation of their natural elements. Perhaps with more dramatic import at Cherryfield, due to its out-of-town location, space becomes place in this small section of land as indications of universal experience coincide with an intensely private practice of commemoration. The grass of the site is soft underfoot, while the wall of greenery generates a sense of shelter and potential for a quietly reflective encounter with the site. It is not located in a place that any other than locals, would happen upon by chance. However, as an area of great rural beauty the roads and laneways to it are likely to be popular among walkers and cyclists of nearby residences, as well as functioning as access points for agricultural workers and farm owners. The surrounding countryside is relatively flat and so the taller trees on its perimeter rustle with the near-constant breeze. As the graveyard is a considerable distance from main roads, not much traffic or machinery noise is likely to be heard.

The site is dominated by an effect of its natural elements that promote a feeling of interiority and even seclusion from the area beyonds its borders. The space, definitively segregated from the wider plain beyond it by a barrier of trees, shrubs and walls, echoes a sense of rural distinctions between manufactured territories and a broader description of the outdoors. These elements of separation encourage the visitor to sit, stand or walk in contemplation of the two small empty fields. These conditioning factors of the site are as Keil's 'artful and conscious construction of illusion'. This is the burial ground for an uncertain number of unknown people. It is maintained as a commemorative site by discreet ploys such as the lack of specific information provided and in particular by a subtle augmentation of its boundaries. At once in nature, the visitor to Cherryfield is also separated from it by the synthesis of an unresolved historical representation illuminated by competing frames of reference that employ local, national and international cues.

The heightened ground is the place where the dead were buried and their physical remains presumably still reside. Enveloping the visitor, Cherryfield as a memorial site promotes awareness of how individual presence is a catalytic cue to acknowledging such a collective absence. Underpinning this advocacy of location-based remembrance are the colliding imperatives of processes of representation (including commemorative culture) that meet in the suggestion of wilderness which permanently shadows the notion of outdoors. Framing emptiness to evoke absence at Cherryfield is accentuated by the consumption of a space shaped, primarily, by interventions in a rural site and, secondarily, by textual and imaged linkage to collective absences, across time and continents.

Related frames of reference are apparent at Carrigastira Famine Graveyard, but the overriding atmosphere is defined by a more overt engagement with natural elements appearing as wilderness. Though not, at time of writing, clearly signposted from the nearby town of Macroom the graveyard is strikingly visible from a minor road. At the roadside, an iron gateway indicates a path through a field towards a walled section, outlined by tall trees. The trees generate a dark and crowded scene and, viewed from the gateway, make an ominous image in the context of a sweep of low-lying fields. A stone slab at the roadside entrance has unattributed text:

> Our pen, our art won fame:
> Philosophers to Ireland came
> Alas came penal laws, tyrant's hand,
> Famine, plague stalked our land
> By yonder plot in mass we lay,
> Pilgrim, reflect and pray.
> May this land at peace and free
> Again serve God and humanity.

A Gaelic text is on another slab on the other side of the entrance. On entering the burial site, a chaotic scene of bushes, trees and undergrowth greets the visitor (Figure 5.8). A wooden sign nailed to a tree points out the direction of the 'Perimeter Walk'. This walk is a roughly mapped route around the edges of the site, within the walls and outline of trees. To the left, an open-ended

Figure 5.8 Carragistira Graveyard, County Cork, Ireland. Image provided by author.

hut structure is visible, with a roofed altar area, with naive-style paintings on the interior depicting Famine images. A series of logs constitute seating in front of the hut. Away from this, in rockier terrain, a forlorn-looking wooden sign rises from the ground behind a stone with the words 'Mass Grave' crudely painted on it. The man-made structures on the site have a makeshift aspect to them: the hut and signs appear to have been installed at minimum expense, nor has much been spent, or required, on their upkeep. Trees and bushes throughout seem ad hoc, and birds noticeably rustle among the dense greenery around and overhead.

As a site insistently marked off from its wider context, a densely variant area of plants, trees and some flowering shrubs, the initial sense of untamed nature is intensified by an awareness of enclosure. It is a struggle to walk the complete site; parts of it are so overgrown that full access is impossible. This frustrating inability to cover the ground by walking encourages visitor contemplation of the site, as the wildness of the undergrowth seems to physically foreground both the significance of the site's history and why its details remain undisclosed.

At both Cherryfield and Carrigastira the transformation of space into place occurs through mediation of the sites mainly as designed forms of wilderness. Though Cherryfield contains field sites, the natural aspect is arguably as much tamed nature as wilderness, in the formal mode of gardens of remembrance. As Carrigastira appears a more prescriptively wild burial site, the real graveyard seems simultaneously transformed into a representation, or an image, of itself, shadowed by its man-made interventions. Ideas of witness are distinguished at these differentiated sites of designed wilderness in ways that reference the concepts of tourism and art as social and cultural practices that represent the past, as well as the present and, as such, are implicit in patterns of the formations of both social memory and so-called collective identity.

Jonathan Bordo stresses that preferences for wilderness are caught up in European interests in locating sources, or origins of national and cultural identities that rely on ideas of absence, of what is missing or what cannot be reached or found. He writes: '*Ness* transforms the wild from errant, arid, a void, to transgressive, exultant, a condition of pure presence or absence. Wilderness as a linguistic locator manifests or instantiates the condition of wilderness.'[48] Pictures and picturing perpetuate this concept of wilderness or what Bordo emphasizes as *the* wilderness.

To differentiate how a picture can act as, or become, a witness, he cites the example of Van Eyck's *Arnolfini Wedding Portrait*, 1434: '[w]hat seems to look out so transparently, looks at. A representation collapses into a sign.'[49] He suggests therefore that the painting is a witness to events it images, as opposed to surviving as a mere representation of something outside of itself. Bordo further argues that a picture's role as witness in modernity is connected to ideas of modern trauma:

> Trauma colloquially understood as 'an event without a witness' finds in *the* wilderness a symbolic scaffolding, which actualizes landscape as a mise-en-scène for obliteration and the memoryless in contrast with classical representation where landscape is a mise-en-scène for history and historical narratives [...][50]

And also:

> With modernity, there is no wilderness without a picture [...] *The* wilderness might thus be construed as a monument without a witness, a trace that denies its discernibility as a sign.[51]

While for Bordo pictures are central to comprehending the idea of witness in relation to both trauma and the wilderness, Keil's analysis of two death camps teases out distinctions between what is considered reality and its representation, often used to distinguish between various sites of dark history. However, as representations are also real, and reality is always represented, the death camps Keil accounts are unstoppably, if differentiated, mediated sites. In that form of social sense, such sites are markers of both the event they, by name, have place authenticity with, and of the history of cultural memory that renders them destinations today.

If, as Bordo suggests, the wilderness is unrepresentable, it is, like trauma, then only present as a representation alluding to past experiences that remain not fully disclosed. The ultimate witness that Agamben discusses as the one who is no longer able to speak, who is absent,[52] might then be understood to hold in common with '*the* wilderness' both eternal absence and radically incommunicable experience.

As sites of mourning and destinations for heritage tourism, mass Famine burial sites might so considered to appropriate *the* wilderness, as a cue to reflection upon the absent witnesses, now subjects, of history.

Comparatively, Cherryfield has a calmer, airier sensibility, while Carrigastira is defined by a more claustrophobic ambience. As open-air sites, Cherryfield, Swinford and Carrigastira commemorate collective human loss by soliciting the solitude of personal contemplation. Cherryfield and Carrigastira are difficult-to-find locations – with no car parks, interpretative centres or guides – and so accessing these graveyards requires a substantial commitment to destination on the part of the non-local visitor. By dint of that, each burial site is subtly indicated by evocatively understated interventions, thus respectfully granting absence the space in which to make its presence felt.

By different means, the physicality of these three sites among many others across the island frames emptiness and encounters with the past as occurring through sensory experiences of place, which in turn facilitates a visitor's commemoration of a catastrophic loss of life. These graveyards are critically connected by the implication that the representation of Famine death is dramatically dependent on a participatory theatre of mourning that can also affiliate local contexts with national and international narratives of remembrances. These are most influentially formed, to affect, within a staging of what today can be selectively perceived when signified by the visitor's presence as *the* wilderness; places that were once busy with life and death.

Photographing Absence: Unmarked Burial Sites

A medium that can only image what is, or once was, present – as Barthes's much-quoted observation goes: '[e]very photograph is a certificate of presences'[53] – photography is also a means to defy any person's inevitable absence. The practice of photography is argued as a weapon of depiction[54] that seeks to destroy death as the end of life.[55] Documentary photography as a particular way of creating and then reading images, or a distinct genre, has been critiqued for its potential as a practice of complacent 'confirmation'.[56] Perhaps it is as Walter Benjamin conjectured in his 1931 text on photography: 'Won't inscription become the most important part of photography?'[57]

While photography of Famine experiences was virtually non-existent, there were photographs taken in Ireland during Famine times. Liam Kelly writes that the process of daguerreotype was so cumbersome that photography was not a practical journalistic tool, rendering it more accessible as a way of recording upper-class life and iconic portraits.[58] While Carville notes that with the emergence of photography in Ireland in 1839 reflected that 'Anglo-Irish landowners who dominated photographic culture on the island up to the late 1850s embraced the same aesthetic interests in photography as their contemporaries in England',[59] he finds that '[w]ithin Irish visual culture the Famine is most conspicuous through its photographic absence; that is to say, its lack of depiction in the mechanical form of the photographic image'.[60]

However, Carville argues, looking at the 'cultural uses of photography' in the immediate aftermath of the Famine suggests it can be traced in the form rather than the content of photographs, as indicated by preferences for the more picturesque – and 'aesthetically palatable' – ruins of Celtic heritage, for example, and also by the appropriation of post-Famine eviction images within nationalist cultural memory.[61] And so, the photographic post-Famine landscape can be conceived as 'emerging within the shadow of the Famine, which cast its residual gloom across the Irish landscape before and after its most calamitous years of 1845 – 52'.[62] Further to this, Carville elucidates that not only was the picturesque landscape constructed through some nineteenth-century painted representations, but by the landscaping of the landlord's demesne itself, which became through land clearance 'manicured and cleansed of the unsightly appearance of the peasant's cottage'.[63]

In marked contradistinction to such construction of place as picturesque representation of land-ownership, encounters with concepts of *the* wilderness suggested by both visiting such as Cherryfield and Carrigastira, give rise to purposefully unresolved confrontations between the past and the present and, between reality and representation. As well as demarcated Famine burial grounds, a large number of unacknowledged burial sites remain part of the Irish landscape. Though many are unknown quantities in every sense, existing as 'unanticipated signs', the location of such unmarked Famine graves is often known locally, with some more formally remembered in archives and through practices of visual representation, such as documentary photography and art practices.[64]

Given Carville's account of the post-Famine landscape of Ireland, what is the representational significance of picturing mass Famine graves in photographs of largely unmarked burial sites for the commemoration of a grievous history? Given the fleeting power of readily available documentary photographic media imaging human suffering in the twenty-first century, what type of cultural memory is promoted by the visual culture of twentieth-century landscape photography of nineteenth-century Famine burial sites? And where and by what means are these images as landscapes inscribed, to appropriate Benjamin's use of the term, to make social sense?

Writing on landscape photographs of sites of former Holocaust death camps, Ulrich Baer suggests: 'The framing of such sites in terms of landscape art forces us to recognize the disappearance of the event as part of its inherent and original dimension and possibly motivates us to halt this disappearance.'[65] The photographs he discusses are images of clearances in the landscape. Their titles are the indicative markers which reveal the former content of the now empty sites and link them to a memory of atrocity that, as time goes by, moves further outside of a viewer's frame of reference. In relation to commemorative cultures of the Famine, the impact of land as empty and of time passing on the history commemorated are also pertinent.

Reliant primarily on folk memory, many unmarked Famine burial sites are liable to be forgotten in a generation, as many have probably already been. Cormac Ó Gráda writes on famine histories worldwide that '[o]ral history and folk memory may plug some of the gaps left by the lack of standard documentary sources'.[66] Reasons why Famine burial sites may be forgotten are varied, with a survivalist desire to disassociate from a history of penury a possible contributing factor, or, arguably, so-called survivor guilt influencing psychological distancing, but such forgetfulness may also have origins in associations during the Famine with contagion spreading from corpses.[67] Even so, the voluntary, largely unpaid role of local historians and interested residents throughout Ireland in keeping regional Famine histories alive is vast and underrated as a national historic resource, to which numerous private folk-villages, rural museums and living-rooms cluttered with workhouse documents and artefacts testify.

In a more formal mode, narrative testimonies within the NFC recount dramatic stories of burial and non-burial. That men were too weak from starvation to carry bodies over distances is cited as one reason why many were not buried in a graveyard or had no gravestone. There are accounts of entire families left to die at roadsides and in ditches, their unburied corpses later eaten by vermin. Each testimony is introduced with the name of the speaker or writer and their place of origin. In some cases, a date of birth provides a temporal context for the narrator's relationship to the Famine.[68]

In this archival context, the NFC's collection of photographs of marked and unmarked burial sites that forms part of its wider collection of 80,000 images preserved on film negative, glass plates and transparencies presents a tantalizing, and partial, visual record of some lesser-known Famine burial sites. The photographic archive was begun in earnest in the 1940s by Kevin Danaher (Caoimhín Ó Danachair) who was first employed as a collector in 1939.[69] The Commission's founding director, Séamus Ó Duilearga, 'bought a Rolleiflex camera for the Commission at a bargain price' on a trip to Germany in 1936.[70] Danaher initially began making an archive of photographs of informants whose oral testimony he was recording, but expanded on this to compile and catalogue his 'extensive photographic documentation of traditional life',[71] despite the fact that, as a report in 1946 noted, the Commission had 'only one small general-purpose camera, somewhat out of date, and one 16-mm camera'.[72]

Since then, a number of other interested folklore researchers have contributed images, many of which depict burial sites showing ditches and fields either in panoramic views of the countryside, with houses visible, or in close-up shots, with focal points such as stones or trees. Captions indicate the locality and type of burial site imaged. Chiefly, the photographs of unmarked sites depict a rural sensibility close to the visual values of Cherryfield and Carrigastira burial sites. From the lines of stone walls and tilled land to the detail of bark on a tree stump, these images replicate the search for a formal visual focus that attends photographic documentary conventions. The photographs mark the places imaged as both aesthetic forms and memory sites associated with likely agonizing death, in wayside spots. More than the sum of the place names on the captions, the images create a document of random burial bred by widespread distress.

One example was taken by Danaher in 1946, *Grave of Famine Victims, Kerry* and is archived under the Graves and Tombs collection (Figure 5.9). Shot in black and white, the image is a close-up of part of a ditch between two fields, with a stone wall running across the background. The vantage point of the photographer, and the viewer, is that of looking

Figure 5.9 *Famine Graves, Kerry.* Graves and Tombs, 1946, Caoimhín Ó Danachair. Nitrate film negative, black and white, 60 x 40 mm. © National Folklore Collection, University College Dublin.

down into and along the grassy textured ditch, alongside a field interspersed with some small stones. At a slightly off-kilter angle, the frontal and central diagonal of the ditch, emphasizes its emptiness, to create an unsettling image. Ditches feature in other images in the NFC and utilized as unmarked grave locations implies a history of desperate burial, as ditches usually demarcated field or land divisions in lieu of walls or hedges: appearing as spaces between two places.

Another common type of location used for Famine burials where formal gravesites were inaccessible is referenced in another image in the NFC: *View of Gort na Cille graveyard. Unbaptised children and famine victims reputedly buried here* Kilcrohane, Bantry, County Cork, 1977, by historian Séamas Mac Philib[73] (Figure 5.10). Mac Philib's image is also in black and white but takes a wider scenic view than Danaher's. In the foreground is a field marked with stones jutting up at various angles, possibly as markers of burial. In the background are hazy mountains across a splendid bay view, behind some houses and a large briary-looking overgrowth. The title of the photograph alludes to a history of burial in Ireland that predates the Famine (and continued after it) when unbaptized children and individuals considered on society's margins, such as the mentally ill, as well as those who committed suicide, were commonly buried outside of cemeteries. These usually unconsecrated sites were known as *cillíní* (*cillin* is Irish for little cell or church) though the term is most commonly used in reference to unconsecrated children's burial grounds. These were sometimes sites that had previous ritual significance, such as ring forts or the sites of earlier religious structures.[74] During Famine times, some of these sites became amalgamated with places of hurried Famine burials.

These, and other, extraordinary images in the NFC point to both the cultural resonance of landscape photography, with its 'inscription' in the fullest sense, and the not yet fully mined rich resource of folk memory, or vernacular history. Such locations as imaged in the collection, like the oral testimonies gathered, are reliant on local knowledge, albeit non-archaeological, as the Mac Philib's use of the word 'reputed' appears to acknowledge. While the pictorial idiom of a Romantic Irish landscape presented in fine arts and tourism campaigns, particularly through the twentieth century, may frame viewpoints on such images, the captions and context of viewing mitigate usefully against potential limits of the aestheticizing of place. Instead, the cultural inscriptions direct the viewer of the images to a form of secondary witnessing, within a landscape already made familiar by tropes of art and tourism, and seemingly coexistent with its agrarian utility.

Observing that photographs as historical documents are often considered secondary to text, Kelly points out that not only do images not

Figure 5.10 *View of Gort na Cille Graveyard. Unbaptised children and famine victims reputedly buried here. Kilcrohane, Bantry, County Cork,* 1977, Séamas Mac Philib. Acetate negative, black and white, 60 x 60 mm. © National Folklore Collection, University College Dublin.

exist for long in isolation from each other, they do not exist separately from textual sources. Suggesting that images (including art images) should be considered, not as a final confirming part of a history that prettifies the story already told, Kelly asserts images as objects with documentary weight and equivalence to textual sources.[75] Added to this, the dichotomy of photographic imaging – the picture (itself an object) and what it references, directly or indirectly – has been central to both the history of photography and critical debates surrounding its representative significance.[76]

The NFC photographs of burial sites bear comparison with Baer's analysis of the desire to make absence appear in a photographic language that might oscillate between documentary and art: with the mediation of these places, through practices of representation, both located and imaged.

As photographs rely in the first instance on what a photographer sees – literally, historically, culturally and economically – and what a lens can reflect (technically and selectively), the attempt to recognize lesser-known sites of Famine burial through the production of photographic images treads a tricky balance between seeing the contemporary landscape of Ireland and stating the catastrophic losses definitive of its modern history. In Baer's analysis, the viewer's pivotal status in the process of visualization attendant to photography is underlined: 'The tension – between the landscape's invitation to the viewer's projection and photography's inalterable pastness – finds a parallel in the difficulties of representing historical trauma.'[77] This indicates how deeply entrenched in the telling of history are conceptual gaps between reality and representation; experience and documentation; presence and absence.

Regarding the photographs of the former locations of Holocaust death camps, the empty spaces, Baer writes: 'In casting the finality of the photographic image within the experience of place, these images extend the sense of being addressed or called upon that seems no longer self-evident for many.'[78] Like Kelly, Baer advocates a type of representation that reconstitutes the gap between what is seen as (tangible) evidence and what it is possible to know. This extends Bordo's thesis on comprehending landscape, of which *the* wilderness is one persuasive concept, as a form of secondary witnessing. And so, photographs that visually document unheralded burial sites present, by historical proxy, images of absence.

Loss, Representation, History

Famine burial sites are indicators of the undignified death from starvation-related conditions and diseases, the hasty and mass burials these conditions precipitated, and are highly disturbing outcomes of the Famine to contemplate. The absences created by such horrific loss of life can seem thwarted by the tranquility and bleak beauty of many of the graveyards. Once marked as such, these places become representations of a history that is both local and national. In a reversal of Bordo's assessment of Van Eyck's painting, the sign collapses into a representation and then oscillates between these positions of cultural significance.

The formal groomed cemeteries of Grosse Île and Abbeystrowry are overtly symbolical sites while remaining effective as signposted settings for public mourning. The seclusion that characterizes the non-cemetery form of graveyards at Cherryfield and Carrigastira is at once a sign of history and a representation of a commemorative appropriation of emptiness, constructed through experiences of wilderness.

Photographs of less delineated grave locations and unmarked burial sites image locations of loss, without any need to dig beneath the surface to count the dead witnesses. Photography's own discourse and its ripples through worlds of journalism bear out how imaging a situation, as the greater project of history attempts to do retrospectively, can both endorse and disrupt notions of what is anticipated as truth. The spirit of Judith Butler's example of the power of photographic images of Vietnam during the Vietnam War, which she argues 'disrupted the visual field and the entire sense of public identity that was built upon that field', with the result of significantly transforming public opinion in the First World,[79] can since be found in forms of citizen journalism, fed through social media such as Twitter. In this context and as archived images, the photographs in the NFC collection are documents of times and people that are now inaccessible. In the same account, these photographs are solid reminders that Famine burial sites are not simply tourist sites: as sites of memory, the images function as witnesses in a breach between locational and general material memory of Famine death and burial.

Reading this range of commemorative forms overwriting Famine burial sites suggests that the conceptual gap between reality and representation can be usefully denotive. The 'darkness' of the selected sites discussed here is carried past the limits of specific locational darkness (reality) and light (representation) into a wider realm of cultural memory, forging a type of witnessing to an enormous loss of life. Famine burial sites – whether memorialized, visited, photographed, talked about or forgotten – have a central importance in the ongoing conception of a harrowing aspect of a grievous history, and its visual cultural forms critically tip the balance of historical power between concepts of significant trace and symbolic representation.

6

Beautiful Places: Commemorative Tourism and Grievous History

Walking after the Famine: Place and Reciprocal Memory

Over the night of 30 March 1849 and the following morning, a group reported to have numbered in the hundreds[1] walked from Louisburgh to Delphi in County Mayo and back, on a round journey of at least 20 miles.[2] The group, described by Ciarán Ó Murchadha as 'smallholders and their families' had gathered at Louisburgh from the surrounding areas to seek status as paupers so they might receive entitlement to outdoor relief.[3] At Louisburgh, the group was purportedly told by two commissioners, relieving officers, that they would have to apply instead to a board of guardians meeting at Delphi Lodge the following morning where they would be inspected at 7am. On meeting the board at Delphi at midday, they were refused the right to assistance or relief and so had little option but to return home to Louisburgh and beyond. On the journey home as many as 20 people may have died, and more later on as a result of the cold conditions encountered by the walkers, many of whom were already in varying weakened states of starvation and related ill health.[4]

Figure 6.1 *Doolough Memorial*, County Mayo, Ireland. Image provided by author.

Two weeks later, a letter published in the *Mayo Constitution* outlines that two more bodies were found on the mountain passes, with the post mortem concluding that they had died 'from starvation and cold'. The letter-writer notes seven were at that time dead; some found 28 miles from Delphi and that nine or ten had not yet returned home.[5]

Today, by a rural road in Doolough Valley, County Mayo, overlooking the lake of the same name, is a roadside memorial commemorating these eventful two days (Figure 6.1). Doolough is an Anglicized version of *Loch Dubh*, Gaelic for Black Lake, and the valley reflects the mountainous and desolate beauty to be found across now lightly populated parts of the Mayo landscape. The memorial is in the form of a cross, made from local sandstone. The rough, worn-looking shape alludes to the form of a Celtic cross. Etched in capital letters on a stone plaque on one side of the base is the following text:

> To commemorate
> The hungry poor
> Who walked here in 1849
> And walk the third world today

Freedom for South Africa 1994.
How can men feel themselves
Honoured by the humiliation
of their fellow beings
Mahatma Gandhi in South Africa

Charlie Connelly describes another memorial in the same valley he encountered when retracing the Doolough walk: '[A] simple stone cross engraved with the words "Doolough Tragedy 1849, erected to the memory of those who died in the famine 1845–49", around which passers-by had placed stones, slowly forming a cairn that will one day swallow up the monument itself.'[6]

The two monuments relate to the same event and each, while keen to promote a particular memory associated with that place, affords local history a geographically wider and present-day resonance. The first, more formal monument conveys its interest in Irishness in the conventions of its form. The wording of the text positions the sorrowful episode as symptomatic of a wider grievous history associated with Doolough in a context of comparable universal plight and, importantly, resistance. The second memorial described (though it pre-dates the first one) is less concerned with international affiliations. Instead it expands the local tragedy to that of all who died during the Famine. A cross, it also appeals to a Christian symbolism, while the growing pile of stones renders the memorial an active shrine of remembrance that addresses the temporal and often local nature of remembrance. As walkers intervene in the memorial of others who passed by before them, adding to the pile of stones, each acknowledges the events and greater history associated with the site as worth noting.

The events at Doolough are further commemorated through an organized form of active commemorative tourism: one that determinedly enacts a sense of collectivity in the interests of raising awareness of global injustice. A fundraising event takes place every springtime in the form of a sponsored walk through the Doolough Valley between Delphi and Louisburgh in aid of alternate causes, the first of which was organized by Afri in 1988.[7] The event and location are renowned for the attendees, who have included Archbishop Desmond Tutu, Kim Phúc, Vedran Smailovic, children from Chernobyl and refugees from Zaire.[8] Drawing attention to the limited functions of static memorials, at the time of its inauguration, little commemorating the Famine nationally, the annual event brings to the fore an opportunity for the construction of affiliations in the present day, with one in particular becoming a repeated feature of reciprocity within the cultural memory of the Famine.

In 1997, the chief of the Choctaw Nation was present at the commemorative event, and members of the Choctaw people regularly attend the annual walk. In 1992, a group of Irish men and women, raising $710,000, undertook a sponsored walk of 500 miles from Mississippi to Oklahoma, along a route known as part of the Trail of Tears, named in memory of the Native Americans who were forced by the US Government to migrate along that way beginning in 1831. According to Connelly, 15,000 Choctaw people left their native lands in Alabama, Mississippi and Louisiana, and more than 2,500 of those never arrived.[9]

The reciprocal linkage in sponsored walks relates to a direct historic link between the Famine and the Choctaw people. Two years before the fateful episode associated with Doolough, an article in the *Arkansas Intelligencer* on 8 May 1847 states that the Choctaw raised funds for the Irish Famine. The money was administered in Ireland and the contribution was described by the Society of Friends as 'the voice of benevolence from the western wilderness of the western hemisphere'.[10] The details of the Choctaw connection are recounted variously, with the amount collected by the Choctaw Indians usually stated at $170.[11]

The link between the two nations is often cited in relation to the annual Doolough walks and in Midleton, County Cork, in honour of this extraordinary gesture of generosity, a sculpture by Cork-based artist Alex Pentak was unveiled in 2017. Taking the form of nine 20-feet-high stainless steel eagle feathers in a bowl-like formation, it is situated in the scenic tranquility of Bailick Park. The work is entitled *Kindred Spirits*, suggesting collective correlation between the Irish and Choctaw nations.[12] The implication of a parallel between two very different collectively inscribed experiences is not uncommon in seeking to recount injustice. For example, even at the time of the Famine, visitors to Ireland made comparisons between the plight of the poorer classes in Ireland and the situation of slaves in America.[13]

Popular confusion and academic contradiction over elements of the events at Doolough point, in the first instance, to a lack of balanced record-keeping during the Famine (such as negligent handling of public safety). It also highlights a meaningful role for commemorative alliancess in the production of history and, specifically, through this example of reciprocal appropriation, in the synthesis of nationhood. William Logan and Keir Reeves write that 'memory distortion and the fabrication of myths [...] occurs commonly in postcolonial situations where the creation of a national identity is necessary to achieve political and cultural cohesion'.[14] Nations, and a range of collective identities, as imagined communities of Benedict Anderson's formulation,[15] are rehearsed in the competing variations on the narrative history of the original events at Doolough, in versions of the nineteenth-century Choctaw aid and annually in the collective commemorative events.

Drawing on Anderson's work, David Rieff suggests that 'collective historical remembrance falls between history and memory, in a sense using both instrumentally without being a great respecter of either'.[16] On the construction of heritage, which can be argued to be a manifestation or expression of so-called collective remembrance, David Brett posits an integral link between tourism and heritage.[17] Brett further notes that 'the heritage experience' is an extension of a division of consciousness 'into time rather than space, by offering us a "sight-seeing" into our own or others' presumed pasts'.[18] This division of consciousness is doubly performed, in overtly manipulated spectacles over history, where commemorations of local and national stories of the past become universal instances of commemoration through events designed to raise consciousness of present-day injustice, as practiced at the annual Doolough walk. Arguably, then, assigning the terrible events in 1849 Doolough a proactive function in the present, the use of historical account is pragmatic and directed towards the future. This future is not just for a national application, but can be directed towards stating a universal relevance of remembering the Irish Famine by drawing attention to dispossession elsewhere. The alignment of Gandhi's words on the formal monument with the memorialization of the Famine accentuates an emphasis on cultural memory's potential as core to societal betterment beyond introspective national concerns.

Reflecting on his Doolough walk, Connelly writes:

> I felt a definite contentment that the nameless victims of the
> Doolough cruelty had not vanished into the wispy caverns of

obscurity but had drawn together oppressed people across the world, people from wildly different cultures and centuries who had suffered themselves and were determined that these things should not be forgotten; that some basic human good should come out of it all.[19]

His point needs some qualification, as there are named victims known of the events associated with Doolough as well as uncertainty surrounding those not yet named as dying as a result of that journey. Over-identification between diverse experiences can elide significant differences, as exist between the Famine-era walk to Delphi and the Choctaw Trail of Tears. To avoid undermining the specificity of each situation of suffering, the transition between geographically rooted history and different global contexts is enacted along the Doolough route by the production of a reciprocal form of commemoration, annually re-inscribed.

In this formulation of memorial practice, traversing that beautiful place in memory of this dark episode and in the invisible footsteps of hundreds of desperate people, local history becomes outward oriented action, as commemorative reciprocity occurs between individuals and collective identities; across places; and over time. In this context, uncertainty over some statistical facts of the historic episode fosters alliances beyond historical equations and the gesture of walking is exposed to its fullest potential as a globally engaged, active, present- and future-oriented commemoration.

Commemorative actions such as following heritage trails, visiting memorial parks, stopping at roadside monuments, workhouse sites and even the more unexpected discoveries of relief structures across the landscape of Ireland reflect on aspects of the type of remembrance performed in a memorial walk such as at Doolough, whether in the formality of the annual walk, or as a passing visitor. Each of these types of walking or traveling the land promote performances of cultural identity, both different and differential, through the 'sight-seeing into the past' of Brett's description. In what ways do the sites linked to various forms of what might be collectively described as commemorative tourism function as tourist destinations and places of return for local communities, and at the same time, forge connections to Famine and wider historical narratives, some of nationhood, other relating to grievous histories more generally?

The channeling of visitor experiences might be usefully considered in the light of what Homi Bhabha has termed pedagogical and performative nations, which he relates, respectively, to the 'masterdiscourse' and the everyday lived edges of nationhood.[20] He further notes that within this paradigm 'hybrid sites of meaning open up a cleavage in the language of culture which suggests that the similarity of the symbol as it plays across cultural sites must not obscure the fact that the repetition of the sign is, in each specific social practice, both different and differential'.[21] While he writes of migratory cultures and related social signs of collective identity, from rehearsed master narratives to cultural practices, that are manifestly specific to places and times, inter-cultural dynamics can find expression too through touristic preferences and practices. Given the ever-widening dynamics of an increasingly commonplace experience of travel and tourism, in Emma Willis's terms the world opened up for viewing, interchanges between pedagogical representations of the past at heritage trails and collective identities performed through socially-prescribed engagement with these places make them sites that, in part, write the nation, and arguably more besides, through temporally defined experiences of place.

Heritage Trails and the Search for History

> The land is still there, in all its natural beauty and fertility. The sparkling Shannon, teeming with fish, still flows by their doors, and might bear to them, as the Hudson and Thames bear to the people of New York and of London, fleets of ships laden with wealth.
>
> Correspondent, *Illustrated London News*, introductory article, 'Condition of Ireland: Illustrations of the New Poor-Law', 15 December 1849

The quote from the *ILN* refers to County Clare and emphasizes the cruel irony of both the natural beauty of the land and waterways of Famine Ireland and their potential to replenish impoverishment. The promotion of active tourism in remembrance of the Famine occurs variously at locations throughout Ireland to redeem these observations. Alongside the production of reciprocal memory as a function of commemoration, some emphases within Famine-related heritage trails focus on contextualized narratives, others on original and replicated artefacts or condensed timelines to distinguish their differing memorial and touristic agendas. Some sites are structured as elements of a wider local heritage projects, as exemplified by the Skibbereen Trail in County Cork, and others are privately funded enterprises, such as the Doagh Famine Village on the Inishowen Peninsula, County Donegal. Some sites are integral to sited leisure functions as is the Celia Griffin Memorial Park in Galway city and others are situated at roadsides contributive to the landscape of route travel through Ireland as is the *An Gorta Mór* Famine memorial between Lahinch and Ennistymon in County Clare. The purpose of the trails and travel-related formats of these sites reflect on differentiated metaphorical enactments of nation as collective identity, and of history as nonetheless individually comprehended.

Discussing the Myall Creek Memorial in Australia, Bronwyn Batten writes that visitors to the site routinely experience a personal pilgrimage to the past and their national identity.[22] She advises of the pitfalls of using a specific historic episode to symbolize numerous events that have historical similarity: 'How thorough (and truthful) a history can be told when we seek to generalise the events to broadly explain a darker period of history.'[23] In her analysis, the problematic simplification of facts for the purpose of representative clarity can be heightened in overt efforts to make a local memorial site symbolic of an aspect of national history.

At the Famine representations in the Cork, Donegal, Galway and Clare sites looked at here, the transient visitor performs a function of re-inscribing cultural identity in their negotiation of each site's pedagogical presentation of narratives centred on historical experiences, linked to cultural memory. In the act of walking and engaging with each trail's content and layout, contrasting concepts of historical writing emerge, with the struggle to avoid oversimplifying the Famine as a discrete history addressed differently at each of these selected sites.

In June 2015, *Skibbereen: The Famine Story*, a walking trial app and book, was launched, updating the previously established trail map and leaflet, *The Skibbereen Trail – An Historical Walking Tour*.[24] The well-illustrated book focuses on contemporary reports of people and places of the area during the Famine. The walking trail comprises a number of sites with direct links to the Famine, starting at the Courthouse, directing the walker up and down a number of streets, around the edge of the town and

Figure 6.2   Trail Map, Skibbereen, County Cork, Ireland. © Terri Kearney.

culminating at Abbeystrowry Cemetery on the outskirts of the town (Figure 6.2).

Some of the buildings remain standing today, with official trail plaques to indicate their number on the trail and the significance of the building, while others no longer survive. Some sites are fully accessible and can be, literally, touched or walked through while others can only be viewed from a distance, due to private ownership. Many of the buildings highlighted on the trail have had other local functions: a mill was a temporary soup kitchen; a hotel saw a visiting British lord throwing loaves of bread out the windows to a starving crowd outside; a car park was formerly the site of an auxiliary workhouse.

Included on the trail are sites of mass demonstration and political activity. One point passes the site of a mass rally, or 'monster meeting' as they were known, said to have been attended by at least 75,000 people on 22 June 1843. These meetings were held by Daniel O'Connell to articulate his reasons for seeking repeal of the 1803 Act of Union with England.[25] The trail also passes the site of a mass protest rally in which road workers, employed on the Public Works Relief Scheme, demonstrated over delays in their pay and low wages and were confronted by armed soldiers in a four-hour-long stand-off. At another point on the trail, attention is drawn to the home of Jerry Crowley, who after the Famine co-founded the Phoenix National and Literary Society, which later grew into the Fenian Movement, linking the Famine to revolutionary politics and a spirit of Republicanism.[26]

Politically oriented points on the trail indicate a strong interest in positioning the Famine in terms of social unrest and political change. Before the trail's final stopping point, it passes the site of another auxiliary workhouse where fever patients were kept, and the street of Bridgetown, notable for accounts provided by James Mahony (some of whose work is discussed in Chapter 1) in the *ILN*.

On walking the trail, the memory of these shards of the past is intricately caught up in a web of social conditions, reactionary politics and suffering attendant on mass dispossession. The Skibbereen trail presents a metaphorical enactment of history embedded in ongoing experiences of time and place. In its resistance to separating local Famine history from wider histories, the trail content suggests a locally inspired Famine narrative that is nonetheless an open-ended trigger for coalitions of collective identity conjured in the present and, most significantly perhaps, one performed by an active construction of history on the part of each visitor travelling the trail route.

These concerns are differently negotiated at the Doagh Famine Village. Set up by Pat Doherty in 1997, it is a multifunction seasonal site: in the summer, a general tourist site and, in the month before Christmas, a family-oriented Lapland.[27] In its summer tourist guise, the initial reception area of the impressively sized site is made up of a village street, off which are a lecture room, museum and exhibition areas and a café housed in small cottages. The main trail contains a series of artificially constructed buildings and remnants of dwellings, each individually presented in varying scales, from life size to miniature. A map leaflet provided on site states:

> This outdoor museum tells the story of life in this area in the 1970s going back to the Famine in the 1840s [...] The Centre is designed not to divide on religious grounds but to show a view of past Irish history where there were no winners.

Figure 6.3 Eviction Scene, looking out from Time Tunnel, Doagh Famine Village, Inishowen Peninsula, County Donegal, Ireland. © Pat Doherty.

An introductory guided tour is offered, which takes the form of a short talk in the lecture room, followed by a guide-led walk around the main Famine section of the trail, a roofed walkway called the 'Time Change Tunnel Taking you from 1900s back to 1800s'. A number of staged Famine-related scenarios, including a burial scene made up of costumed mannequins, are interspersed between text panels hanging from the ceiling which link Famine facts with statistics on more recent poverty across the globe. On the roadway after the tunnel are life-size mock-ups of a *Scalp*, *Scalpeen* and an *Eviction Scene*. At Doagh, a scalpeen refers to homes set up by evictees in the shells of the cottages from which they had been evicted; it shares with the common understanding of scalp a sense of temporary habitation and rough cover from the elements.

The *Eviction Scene* comprises a cottage in front of which is stationed a swing ball structure, ready to demolish the dwelling (Figure 6.3). There are fully costumed mannequins in the roles of a family of evictees and a landlord's agent carrying out the eviction order. Beside the staged eviction on a small overgrown hill is a *Mass Rock*, complete with life-size mannequins among the greenery, staged to suggest attendance at a secret Mass. These were large stones where people met to celebrate Mass, when the public practice of the Catholic faith was prohibited.[28] Opposite the eviction scene is a miniature *Landlord's Mansion*, including small toy animals and trees to indicate estate grounds.

The placement of all these elements to directly establish counterpoints between the dwelling types plays on the power of contrast in depiction. The *Mass Rock* generates a looser affiliation between Famine evictees and the broad suppression of Catholic religious beliefs that became part of the colonial project in Ireland. The blanket correlation of the rock to the *Eviction Scene*, the *Scalp* and *Scalpeen*, and indeed their comparative realism, further counters the stately luxury described in the artifice of the miniature *Landlord's Mansion*. Though the time tunnel arguably simplifies a tourist's potential to somehow visit the past, the juxtapositions of the various structures configure a dramatically condensed lineage of history. As counterparts in a larger story, these elements of societal contrast indicate that such differences were predicated on a common project: colonialism.

The map leaflet implies parity between Ireland's past and the more recent experiences of others outside of Ireland:

> By the end of your tour of our Visitor's Centre, you may be offended, saddened, or maybe feel that something like this should never have happened. Maybe now is a good time to stop and think.
> Ireland today is among the richest nations of the world. Today famine is rife in Sudan, Biafra, and Ethiopia. Television screens bring their problems to our attention, but do we bother to do anything about it? These places are our Irelands – we are their landlords.

The centre opened when such concepts of Ireland as a nation wealthy enough to extend significant foreign aid were commonplace. Even so, the blatant structure of the time tunnel can be read as a self-conscious collapsing of historical, or monumental, time in an acknowledgement of the pageantry of historical representation. This awareness is echoed by the latter part of the site, which includes continuously updated representations of a changing Irish economic situation, notably with a streetscape featuring a house-like building with a sign saying: Anglo Irish Bank.[29]

Two more recent memorial sites, in Galway and Clare, present an alternate approach to more monumental time-frames presented variously at Skibbereen and Doagh, and also, facilitate the more incidental, as well as

Figure 6.4 Celia Griffin Memorial Park, Galway, Ireland. Image provided by author.

intended, tourist of history. Though diversely configured, each site is centred on memorializing the fate of a young local child. These memorial sites signify not only the story of the named child they reference, but their narrative function as a cue to contemplate the larger disaster of the Famine.

In Galway city, the Celia Griffin Memorial Park is dedicated to the memory of a young girl's death in a convent in the city during the Famine (Figure 6.4). A large entrance stone near the roadside entrance, includes excerpts from the inquest held in March 1847 in Galway, into the death of the six-year old girl from starvation-related illness, under the title inscribed in capital letters: 'Galway, Saturday, March 13, 1847 / Starvation – Inquest':

> An inquest was held on Thursday last, before Michael Perrin, Esq., D.C., at the Presentation Convent, on view of the body of Celia Griffin, a girl about six years of age, from the village of Corindulla, near Ross, in this county. It appeared in evidence that the poor creature had been reduced to extreme poverty and that the family to whom she belonged, eight in number, were in the same pitiful condition. She had been recommended to the Ladies of the

Presentation, by Rev. George Usher, as a fit object for relief, and accordingly she and her two sisters received a daily breakfast at that excellent Institute. They met Mr Usher on the Rahoon road about a fortnight ago, but Famine had so preyed upon her feeble constitution, that, on the morning of Wednesday, she was unable to taste food of any description – so that on the post mortem examination made by Doctor Staunton, there was not a particle found in her stomach.

She with her father, mother, brothers, and sisters, came to Galway about six weeks ago, in the hope of obtaining some charitable relief, and during that period have been begging in the streets, and about the country. The parents of the deceased formerly resided on the estate of Thomas Martin, Esq, MP. When Doctor Staunton was called on he found deceased in a state of inanition, except an occasional convulsive action of the muscles, and her body might be said to be literally skin and bone – with all the appearance of starvation. She was so exhausted, as not to be able to use the food supplied to her. The Jury found that her death was caused for want of the common necessaries of life, before she received relief at the Presentation Convent.

Beneath this text is a dedication: 'This park is named in memory of Celia Griffin and all the children who died in the Great Famine.' Not the site of her death or burial, the park is integrated into both its locality along a spectacular breezy coastal walk and a heritage trail through the city that reflects on wider Famine and historic experiences there. Situated between the Claddagh and Salthill Promenade, the scenic coastal park at Grattan Beach is a popular walking route for locals and hosts panoramic views of the Atlantic Ocean, as well as a view to the hills of County Clare across Galway Bay.

The site's development as a memorial park was promoted by a local man, Mark Kennedy and since its dedication in July 2012, includes a Famine Ship Memorial, referencing some 100 ships which departed from Galway Bay during the Famine years.[30] Demarcated by three tall standing stones, the central rough limestone memorial stone draws attention the lighthouse at Mutton Island, while the two sculpted standing stone elements either side list the names of 50 ships. The park has latterly been developed as a culmination point for memorial walks through the town. The dual emphasis on an individual's story, in the emotive recounting of the thereby emblematic starvation to death of a young girl, and the scale of collective experiences of emigration, suggested by the ship's names and reference to the local lighthouse, are compounded by the scenic quality of the location experienced when visiting the park.

On the road between Lahinch and Ennistymon in County Clare is the Famine memorial, *An Gorta Mór*, dedicated in 1995. Situated between the local deserted workhouse and the site of a mass grave, the memorial was supported by the AOH (Board of Erin and Board of America) and Clare County Council. The sculptural work by artist Alan Ryan Hall consists of two large limestone door structures (each 3 metres high) with ornate metal hinges indicated.[31] Against one, the metal figure of a small boy presses urgently (Figure 6.5); the other has a disembodied cast female head – the boy's mother – and a pair of clenched fists protruding from it. Beneath the human elements is the text:

> Gentlemen,
>
> There is a little boy named Michael Rice of Lahinch aged about 4 years. He is an orphan, his father having died last year and his mother has expired on last Wednesday night, who is now about being buried without a coffin!! Unless ye make some provision for such. The child in question is now at the Workhouse Gate expecting to be admitted, if not it will starve.
>
> Robs S. Constable

The memorial depicts a story revealed in the archives of local workhouse records from Ennistymon Library in which, on 25 February 1848: a young boy was left outside the workhouse door and the text above hand-written in a note pinned to his shirt.[32]

The memorial's spatial, material and iconographic elements echo a language of graveyards: the graveled surrounds encase a stone tiled area and gilt lettering on the smooth limestone of the upright elements speak of conventions of cemeteries and headstones, as much as of monuments. The head and hands of the boy's mother are reminiscent of statues prevalent on tombs memorializing individuals of wealth or renowned disposition. The pauper woman is immortalized in these iconographic and sculptural gestures with the memorial thus countering historic claims to imaging, re-dressing the social imbalance of who might have their portrait on their grave.

Figure 6.5 *An Gorta Mór*, Detail, 1995, Alan Ryan Hall. Road between Lahinch and Ennistymon, County Clare, Ireland. Image provided by author.

The quoted note, as with the presented inquest text at the Celia Griffin Memorial Park, evokes the poignancy of a specific found story, and is also notable for its stated lack of closure. Visitors to the site are not told what became of Michael Rice, but the fate of him and his parents did not bode well from such impoverishment. A short distance from the main sculptural elements is a small stone slab with a brief explanation of its historical context. The choice of figurative protagonists – a dead woman and orphaned child – are emotive signifiers, disclosing the language of vulnerability common in figurations of Famine and their story presented as emblematic scenario.

While *An Gorta Mór* is a clearly delineated site of memorial of the lives of others who have gone before, its position at along a main road also allows for the possibility of unexpected or unplanned visits. By broadening the scope to remembering the Famine dead to unintended, casual, observers, such as drivers passing by who pull over to investigate, this roadside location accentuates the contingently social nature of aspects of outdoor publicly sited memorials.

To function as sites of Famine memory, the Skibbereen trail, the Doagh centre, the Celia Griffin Memorial Park and the Ennistymon/Lahinch memorial are reliant upon a visitor's active engagement with differing historical representations. As a tourist of history across these sites, a visitor is presented with the understanding that a search for history is a search for cultural identity: these places accommodate a knowing look at Famine histories in which an undisturbed past will not and cannot be found.

On the Skibbereen trail, this is declared by repeated layering of Famine experiences into a wider historical fabric of a modern nation and the varied visibility and accessibility of trail points in the lived in environment of a town. At Doagh, blatant manipulations of scale, emphatically artificial presentations and an agenda to update material information on display underscores an awareness of the temporality of tourist performance in searches for modern history formulated around a national story in the context of a tourism business. While at Ennistymon/Lahinch the focus is on a specific experience, at Galway, the site draws on both experiences of an individual and the generation of a wider diaspora. These sites, as well as the Doolough site, produce, in the present, recurrently reordered senses of the past accorded by a modernity shaped by dispossession. By spatially and temporally provoking contemplations on hunger, destitution and emigration, these places expose the contingent nature of historiography.

Engaging with these sites, as part of a tourism of travel, is nonetheless a commemorative practice in which pilgrimages to the past iterate that the passing of time is a mode of addressing the present and future also, as is attendant to the cultural complexity of recalling grievous history for contemporary consumption.

The Shadow of Workhouses and Relief Works

> [...] we turn back to the coast and note that the shore ahead, that of Ceathrú and Chnoic, is or was serviced by a road, while that of Iaráirne's land is not. The road, a wide, untarred and unwalled track, comes over the ridge of the hill that hides the Lodge to the north-west, crosses broad crags, the more recent 'striping' of which has interrupted its course with a couple of walls, then turns eastwards along the coast in the lee of the storm beach, and ends abruptly against the boundary wall. It was a famine relief work of the late nineteenth century, and like most such projects what little utility it had (for the transport of seaweed and wrack from these low-cliffed and accessible shores) was to the benefit of the larger landholders and not to that of the hungry wretches who laboured on it for their daily dish of boiled maize.[33]
>
> Human swinery has here reached its acme, happily: 30,000 paupers in this union, population supposed to be about 60,000. Workhouse proper, I suppose, cannot hold above 3,000 or 4,000 of them, subsidiary workhouses, and outdoor relief the others. Abomination of desolation; what can you make of it! Outdoor quasi-work: 300 or 400 hulks of fellows tumbling about with shares, picks and barrows, 'levelling' the end of their workhouse hill; at first glance you would think them all working; look nearer, in each shovel there is some ounce or two of mould, and it is all make-believe; 500 or 600 boys and lads pretending to break stones. Can it be a charity to keep men alive on these terms? In face of all the twaddle of the earth, shoot a man rather than train him (with heavy expense to his neighbours) to be a deceptive human swine.
>
> Thomas Carlyle, from *Reminiscences of my Irish journey in 1849*, published, London, 1882[34]

In the first passage quoted above, Tim Robinson describes a walk on Inis Mór, the largest Aran island off the coast of County Galway, with reference to a type of relief programme operating throughout Ireland at the time of the Famine. The second passage is from Thomas Carlyle, a Scottish-born historian, essayist and social critic who travelled Ireland in the summer of 1849, specifically to see firsthand the effects of the Famine, having witnessed, as John Crowley suggests, 'hordes of starving and destitute Irish descending on English cities'.[35] The scene on which Carlyle commented was relief works at Westport Workhouse, County Mayo.

The remnants of relief works, in particular roads and walls, built during this period are at best barely marked with many yet unknown or unclear in place authenticity. There are few plaques or markers of where these roads and walls begin or end, stand or were laid down. Tourist guidebooks cite examples and websites for trails, and tours mention in passing that this or that structure was built during the Famine. In many places, it is locals who can distinguish sites of relief works, and Robinson's text alludes to this kind of locally held knowledge. His description of the road brings into focus how today the varied usefulness of the works in terms of infrastructure development can evoke, where known or retold, the despair of a past era. Carlyle's views, as discussed by Crowley, are those of an imperialist, bitterly opposed to the Poor Law, underpinned by an attitude of anger toward landlords and Russell's Liberal government.

Implicitly under-acknowledged traces of Famine experience, relief works have profound potential as commemorative culture and extend discussions on formalized sites of history, and their intervening relationship to cultural memory, beyond the parameters of museums, heritage sites, tourist trails, memorial parks and monuments. These walls, roads, piers, buildings and even follies are persistent presences, many as unacknowledged sites of history, in what are now both urban and rural areas across the landscape of Ireland and warrant exploration in the context of wider relief schemes, particularly the workhouse system.

The imperatives that prevailed over the instigation of outdoor relief works as one official measure of addressing the increasingly dire situation of a distressed population were caught up with colonial perspectives that had already cast Irish people in a relative disposition to the British mainland, supposedly lacking both modernization and the desire for betterment, as discussed in the Introduction and in Chapter 1. The Relief Commissioners to Ireland set about attempting to coordinate food aid around the country in conjunction with local workhouses and manual labour programmes, or relief works, through amendments to the Poor Law.[36] With far-reaching ramifications, Charles Trevelyan, as the Government official with responsibility for relief measures in Ireland from mid-1846, saw work as the key to bettering what he perceived as the collectively flawed Irish character and as the main route to addressing the crises presented by the precipitation of the effects of Famine, which were in turn due to lack of effective redress. He wrote in a letter, dated 3 February 1846, to Sir Randolph Routh, Chairman of the Relief Commission:

> the greatest improvement of all which could take place in Ireland would be to teach the people to depend upon themselves for developing the resources of their country, instead of having recourse to the assistance of the government on every occasion.[37]

Trevelyan's attitude to the Irish at this time, and his proposition as to what course of action might solve the problems facing the Irish, was contiguous with a view shared by others and apparent in the press of the day, which widely depicted the Irish as lazy and unwilling to work, a generally 'indolent' society in Carlyle's terms.[38]

While, under Robert Peel, the British government had instigated the Poor Law (Ireland) Act of 1838 to provide relief, under John Russell's premiership Trevelyan brought in a less lenient system in the Poor Employment Act of 1846. This had two core effects: firstly, the notion of earning relief was paramount, and secondly the localized funding of relief meant that the pressure on incapable local authorities and relief committees was intense. A temporary relief commission had been set up in November 1845 to provide relief supplementary to that provided by the Poor Law (Ireland) Act of 1838.[39]

The emphasis on work was considerable in both indoor and outdoor relief. In workhouses, labour was promoted as a means for inmates to earn their keep and generally encourage good character. For men, this usually meant grinding corn by turning enormous capstan mills, breaking stones or working on workhouse land, while women did needlework, cleaning, general household chores and took care of the infirm inmates.[40] Though admission to workhouses was strictly by family, on entering a workhouse women, men, girls, boys and infants were all separated, which effectively broke up family units internally.[41] Sleeping conditions were basic and cramped even when not over-crowded. Added to this, the diet of Indian meal had poor nutritional value as it was often inadequately cooked and compounded inmates' vulnerability to illness, rendering the labour programmes difficult to undertake, at best.

Of the 130 workhouses built throughout Ireland between the 1830s and 1840s, 19 were built in Connaught, 36 in Leinster, 32 in Munster and 43 in Ulster.[42] Many unions took loans from the British Government to build the workhouses and the repayments were difficult during the economic crisis of the Famine, leading to administrative problems, which resulted in even more basic conditions. Contemporary written accounts – within either local or national histories – often outline the rampant nature of illness in the workhouses, with matrons, clerks and physicians often succumbing to death along with inmates.[43]

Few workhouses remain structurally intact to a significant degree and there are no direct fully conserved or recreated workhouse dormitories, dining halls or infirmaries in the country, from Famine times.[44] Today, some remain in part as adapted sites and a consequence of life going on after the Famine as these sites became utilized for different purposes, many as hospitals. Other workhouse buildings remain dilapidated on the landscape and others are simply ground areas remembered as the place where thousands sought shelter and many died and were buried. Many of these sites can merely accommodate wall plaques to remind visitors of the histories and former function of these places.[45]

In some cases, the association of what was later stigmatized as 'the poorhouse' was viewed as symbolic of colonial oppression which led to politically motivated destruction of workhouses and their contents in the early twentieth century. While soup kitchens were typically short-lived building adaptations in the first place, workhouses took years to build and employed thousands in the building process. Though some illustrations were produced of the soup kitchens during the Famine, today representations of Famine workhouse experiences are largely under-developed though clearly have potential as powerfully emotive sites of history and it was in part the inadequacies and failures of the workhouse system that predicated the scale of outdoor relief.

One workhouse museum that incorporates a focus on the Famine is at The Workhouse, Figart, Dunfanaghy in County Donegal, opened in 1995. It was a functioning workhouse from 1845 to 1922, and its engrossing exhibition strategy centres on a narrative developed around one local

Figure 6.6 Vignette of Wee Hannah, The Workhouse, Figart, Dunfanaghy, County Donegal, Ireland. © Moses Alcorn.

woman, Wee Hannah, whose story is also told a booklet sold on site. Vignettes throughout the small restored part of the workhouse utilize audio to account her life-story from her childhood in Famine times to her adulthood, inclusive of her workhouse experiences (Figure 6.6).

In contrast to this filled space, and as at the conserved area in St Patrick's Hospital in Carrick-on-Shannon (discussed in Chapter 5), at Donaghmore Agriculture and Workhouse Museum, Rathdowney, county Laois, a relative absence of figuration seems symbolically employed to indicate the erosion of individual dignity and large-scale loss of life. At the uniquely atmospheric and expansive Donaghmore site, a range of representative strategies are utilized in the exhibition area and the greater building functions both as a memorial to Famine-time destitution and as an agricultural museum. The Famine aspect of the site is powerfully evocative, with exhibition displays about selected inmates and access to the overwhelmingly large site spans both external aspects, including a burial ground to the rear, and an internal, series of echoing empty rooms[46] (Figure 6.7).

Though at the start of the summer of 1846 many workhouses were only half-full, by winter of that year most in Connaught and Munster were over-

Figure 6.7 Donaghmore Agriculture and Workhouse Museum, Interior Detail, Rathdowney, County Laois, Ireland. Image provided by author. By permission of Donaghmore Agriculture and Workhouse Museum.

populated by hundreds, while Commissioners turned away hundreds more seeking shelter.[47] By the end of 1849 the capacity of occupancy in workhouses was for over 250,000 inmates at any given time.[48] Statistics on population decline from 1846 to 1851 show that Connaught and Munster were significantly affected by annual rates of excess mortality and general population decline and further suggest that proportionate to each local population, there were fewer Famine-related deaths in provinces with more workhouses.[49]

From summer 1846, outdoor relief was received only when the local workhouse was full and Stuart McLean draws attention to the fact that by August 1846 there were 650 local committees in Ireland, the majority of which were in the south and west,[50] compensating for the national distribution of workhouses. The committees were initially responsible for issuing tickets to work on local labour relief projects, but this responsibility was later assigned to the Board of Works, which was considered less partial.[51]

Mary Daly writes that by summer 1846, approximately 100,000 were employed on relief works across Ireland organized by the Board of Works, and 30,000 on schemes controlled by grand juries.[52] According to John O'Connor, the number on the rolls of the public works programme was 285,817 in November 1846,[53] and Peter Gray cites a peak of 714,390 in March 1847, noting that each labourer was 'seeking to support a family of four or five on meagre wages'.[54]

The work was hard and many of the resulting structures had little long-term purpose or obvious community gain beyond immediate remuneration in the form of food and board. Projects outside the workhouse were developed with task-related pay. What began as work for men eventually also became the work of women and children as escalating destitution rendered many desperate for a means to earn enough to buy food. Added to this, the malnourished state of the workers meant many could not work at all or, when they did, could not work well. Gray argues that the work must have augmented excess mortality rates: he points out that 'heavy labour in the harsh winter conditions of 1846–47 placed extreme stresses on the bodies of the malnourished, who began to die in large numbers on the works in early 1847'.[55]

While largely impoverished sections of society sought work permits to labour on the relief projects, it was then and is since generally considered that relief works were widely insufficient, as the workhouse relief had also been, and a wholly inadequate response to the widespread and dire nature of the escalating calamity of the Famine. As signs of Famine experiences, relief structures represent in their scale and geographical reach crossovers between individual suffering and the wretchedness of many. As man-made elements of the landscape with varying utility and visibility, many relief structures seem objects out of place, with some presenting an aesthetic out of time. The traces of relief work projects receive differentiated levels of formal acknowledgement throughout Ireland, but all present occasions to consider how the Famine can be commemorated outside designated sites, as memory that is happened upon, by chance, or even unnoticed in daily life.

Considering relief structures as hybrid sites of meaning is not to suggest an epitome or representation of all Famine relief works: the variety of types and purposes of structures built during the Famine, and the range of contemporary contexts in which they survive, wholly or in part, are multifarious. While some linkage can be argued between structures as generally appearing incongruous to their context, others are so physically integrated into the lexicon of Irish stone works that they are rendered invisible, while materially present, if only in part. These modes of cultural reading aside, each relief structure remains indexical of the specific experiences of past individuals and communities at particular locations. Though differently realized and accounted, these sites denote the weight of a mammoth representational task: as the most tangible traces of labour undertaken by so many to support so many, the places where stone was broken and re-utilized survive as provocations for reflection on history and memory and the fascinating gaps in understanding that lie in between.

A long wall runs along the border of counties Tipperary and Waterford through the Knockmealdown Mountains and over the ridge of the main mountain (Figure 6.8). In local hotels and on numerous walkers' blogs, the wall is described as a Famine relief work. Today, what is left of it stands as a visually striking element in a landscape of gentle hills, popular with hillwalkers and tourists.[56] In Famine times, this hilly terrain was a perceptibly harsh landscape that would presumably have provided little sustenance to those living around it without hard farming labour, though it was noted for its turf supplies. There are recorded Famine relief projects in

Figure 6.8 County Border Wall, Knockmealdown Mountains County Border Wall, Counties Tipperary and Waterford, Ireland. Image provided by author.

Figure 6.9 Fermoy Famine Wall, County Cork, Ireland. Image provided by author.

the area including a road to Cahir and the upgrading of the Vee Road that runs through the mountains and walls along it.[57] The road is popular with tourists, cyclists and hillwalkers for its spectacular vee-turn.

To the eye of today's hillwalker, the area presents an experience of great natural beauty. The difference between the location as it was read in Famine times and today's leisure and touristic view of rural Ireland is brought into sharp focus by the presence of the county border wall undulating in rhythm with the land's contours. The wall poses a problem of interpretation. There are many similar-looking stone walls around Ireland, but most of them clearly define a field or separate land ownership. This mountain wall has little obvious function, as county regions in Ireland do not, in the main, have physical borders, and so remains as a structure that seems, on reflection, both out of place and out of time, whether a so-called Famine wall or not.

On the hill entering Fermoy town, County Cork, from a main national road, a high wall separates the busy road from a line of houses and a pedestrian pathway, with the two levels inter-accessible by steps at intervals (Figure 6.9). It is no more than 300 m in length and reaches a sloped end at the base of the hill. Constructed as a Famine relief work, the wall stands as a local testament to an era that saw mass death in the town. Solidly built, it is tidy in form and visually striking, and now has an abrupt beginning and end. In its town context, this compact Famine wall has continued utility as a marker of space keeping pedestrians and cars apart.

The range of relief works include those uncertainly identified as such and others clearly asserted as the product of Famine labour programmes, as respectively accounted in the two examples here. Others are overlaid by intervening histories such as a road on the rugged windswept Beara Peninsula on the south-western Atlantic seaboard of Ireland (Figure 6.10). What is today called Healy's Pass, in memory of local politician Tim Healy from the early Free State era, who oversaw the road's development in the early twentieth century, is reported to have been first cut out as a Famine relief work in 1847.[58] The road links the County Cork and County Kerry sides of the peninsula and is packaged as a looped drive within 'The Wild Atlantic Way', a government tourism project. Formally launched in early 2014, 'The Wild Atlantic Way' promotes the areas and activities of nine counties along the western coast of Ireland from north to south described as: '2,500 km of the world's most diverse and spectacular coastline'.[59]

The roadway's current definition by way of its description in the leisure industry of tourism as a breathlessly dramatic driving route, both overlays and claims the slower and older reputed history as a Famine relief project: The Wild Atlantic Way website suggests it is one of the most famous 'famine roads'.[60] Relief structures are thus susceptible to overwriting by historical processes, often reflected in the naming of locations as cultural identity relentlessly refocuses on the present or recent past. In this way, many sites and remnants of relief structures remaining hidden in plain sight, and though variously veiled by intervening cultural memorial practices still cast shadows of the past across the landscape.

Contemplation of such relief structures recognizes that the past, future and present exist in a constantly changeable relation between lived experience and utilitarian considerations. The steps on the Fermoy wall, for example, are not practical as access points, for the road to which they lead is a very busy route through the town. Parts of the county wall as still stand in the Knockmealdown mountains may or may not have been

Figure 6.10   Healy's Pass, Beara, County Cork, Ireland. © Fáilte Ireland.

Famine era structures, but proximity to the Vee-road lend a borrowed authenticity, while the wall's primary use is as a visual guide to hillwalkers. Robinson's account of relief works on Inish Mór similarly suggests they have no obvious function in working life, but as cultural signs can also contribute to part of a wider historical practice suggestive of formations of collective identity, while retaining local specificity. These readings reflect Bhabha's observations on the difference and differentials of signs in practice. To ascribe to each sign, such as a site of Famine relief work, its local and named specificities renders cultural significations of a sign, any sign, as collectively relevant and thereby distinguished.

Considering such structures and sites of history as palimpsests, demarcated in Famine times, but also as places that pre- and post-date the Famine, might also be considered in terms proposed by Hannah Arendt to take account of the present day and look to the future in the production of social meaning. She proposed that the fissure between remembrance and anticipation is both temporal and spatially outlined, but only in a conceptual realm.[61] Stretching struggle as metaphor, Arendt borrowed from Franz Kafka on what he had perceived as the fight between the past and the future.

Kafka outlined his vision as a situation in time where the past pushes him into the future, as the future drives him back into the past. His desire was to rise above it and let the two forces directly fight each other, and so he focused on a linear conception of time. Arendt redefined Kafka's struggle as one that resembles a parallelogram of forces (both temporal and spatial) in which the subject is necessary as agent, for the parallelogram resides only in the mind's eye. For Arendt, this gap in time is an aspect of life to be endlessly renegotiated and recreated:

> This small non-time-space in the very heart of time, unlike the world and the culture into which we are born, can only be indicated, but cannot be inherited and handed down from the past; each new generation, indeed every new human being as he inserts himself between an infinite past and an infinite future, must discover and ploddingly pave it anew.[62]

While Arendt's thesis is more directive of what might be described as a 'monumental time', where chronology is progressive and for examples, often formulated into epochs through various institutional forms of which academic history-writing is one, and an individual's and any given society's efforts to comprehend their place in history is another, her way of thinking about historical time may bear relevance to how a walker or tourist might contemplate the generally understated presence of a Famine relief structure.

These intermittently, and often unexpectedly, found sites of history generate counterpoints between the past and the future, where it is possible to envision a conceptual space that takes account of the three states – past, future and present. Such stumbling across largely unheralded sites of history enunciates the discovery of and 'ploddingly paves anew' historical understanding as an active mode of remembrance. In effect, this can temporarily transform pockets of the beauteously compelling Irish landscape into ethereal shape-shifting sites of cultural memory.

Forged through Famine labour projects as indexical to hunger, hardship and social competition for survival, relief structures can be considered through a comparable tug-of-war paradigm. In this conceptual space, as a way of sensing the past, arises the gap of Arendt's discussion: the anticipation, in the present, of places open for sightseeing, as a prepared-for and planned personal experience, pushes against seeing the, at times, unexpectedly encountered traces of what happened here before now.

Contemplation on Arendt's 'non-time-space in the very heart of time' reveals the potential of unanticipated remembrance; here, a road, a wall or a ruin of such, that seems out of place, and in some cases misplaced in time too, triggers a means of addressing the past that effectively links that place in time by the singularity of the structure as encountered. Reading sites of history to implicate each relief structure or the traces of one as a hybrid sign (in Bhabha's terms) in practice; making each equally poignantly inscrutable when measured on the reductive scales of monumental history.

These vulnerable and often obscure structural remains of labour works lie in sharp spatial contrast to the vast scale and delineation of sites encompassing workhouses, fever sheds and burial grounds. Workhouses, today large unwieldy shells of institutionalization that darkened the edges of many towns, and their subtler counterpoints on the landscape in the traces of the outdoor relief programmes that attended the failure of the workhouse system, are heavily burdened sites of history. Locations of these sites echo with the sad and sorry lot of 'the human swinery' that passed through; the 'hungry wretches who labored'.

Landscapes of Remembrance

Across Ireland are landscapes of remarkable beauty: national and international tourists specifically seek out Ireland's coastal counties for stunning ocean and sea views and its hinterland for verdant fields and forests, wandering waterways and diverse mountain ranges enticing all levels of walks, hikes, cycles and drives. The very description of the Romantic spectacle associated with western seaboard counties in particular – windswept, rugged, harsh terrains – contributed to their unfolding as sites of intense Famine suffering, and later rendered them a locus for early twentieth-century cultural idealism in depictions of 'The West' across image and text media, as evident in a range of art, illustrative and heritage practices discussed in earlier chapters. Since then, these places have become settings for the memorialization of Famine experiences, some explicitly and others arbitrarily so, and even a cue for correlations between different grievous historical experiences.

Perceptions of place and accounts of cultural relativities – usually decided through a complex of geopolitical interests – are central to sites of Famine remembrance reliant on active tourism, in the form of ritual walking, following heritage trails, taking the air in a memorial park, stopping at roadsides monuments, at old workhouse sites, or coming across unexpected sites of history in the landscape. Formally adapting or signposting places as zones of remembrance, and visitor interaction through these various forms of journey as means to memorialize the past, promotes these sites as threshold forms of commemoration that are at once reflexive of personal experiences and affiliations with collective, often national, identity on the part of the visitor.

The sites associated with Skibbereen, Doagh, Clare and Galway differently address a tangle of historical perceptions by presenting alternate emphases in routes, representations and choreographed dissipations of time. At Doolough, these concerns achieve a looser, more flexible appropriation of memory where the range of commemorative forms advocate active remembrance, stirred at a particular place to open local historic experiences to symbolic appropriation. This renders the area's geographical aspect, in part, a function of its temporal capabilities in a type of reciprocal memory that knowingly acknowledges history's indeterminacy and cultural coalition as valuable mechanisms for making visible, in terms of collective awareness, histories and ongoing situations of dispossession.

As relief schemes produced a trading of food and shelter for labour, workhouses stand as extraordinary memorial objects. Where activated as sites of memory, often on the perimeter landscapes of towns and cities, their extensive institutional scale indicates the vastness of historical suffering and lingering socio-economic connotations associated with these places. As a substantially underestimated aspect of cultural memory, relief structures produced in Famine times, like disused and memorialized workhouse sites, are also incommensurable with everyday practicality and so constitute an inadvertent type of commemorative form: rarely promoted as tourist sites, it is an interested visitor that seeks them out or investigates their presence after coming across one.

Still physically incumbent on landscapes that in many instances had no ongoing utility for them, the material remnants of both workhouses and the fruits of the labour of works programmes evocatively point to experiences of dispossession. At some times ruins, and in places perhaps misidentified, these overwritten sites of history remind of the impossibility of finite disclosure by any particular commemorative form and bear witness to Batten's caution on the undermining effect of overgeneralizing representations. Relief structures in particular are highly susceptible to remaining hidden as potential Famine sites of memory: buried by history, many are yet unknown across Ireland.

The beautiful places discussed in this chapter promote active tourism as a journey to be re-travelled that locates historical understanding as a comprehension to be re-made. A visitor's cultural distance from the past is suggested to be in need of ongoing revision: an individual's performance of Famine memorialization produces an awareness of the contingencies between history, place and memory, which at the same time, echoes the critical links between voice, index and sign. These elements of active tourist practice can appear as aesthetically present, that is visible and singularly readable, at a confluence of time and place in the form of experiential heritage enacted across the landscape.

Conclusion
Imaging the Great Irish Famine

A small wooden cross is on display in the atrium of Mount St Anne's Retreat and Conference Centre, Killenard, County Laois. There is an inscription on paper pasted onto the back of the cross and signed by Thomas Willis (Figure C.1). It reads:

> During the frightful plague, which devastated a large proportion of Ireland in the years 1846–47 – that monstrous and unChristian machine a '*sliding coffin*' was from necessity used in Bantry Union for the conveyance of the Victims. To one common grave – The material of this cross, the symbol of our Redemption, is a portion of one of the machines, which enclosed the remains of several hundreds of our countrymen during their passage from the wretched huts or waysides where they died, to the pit, into which their remains were thrown. T. W.

Another piece of paper has the text: 'This Cross was given to me about the year 1870 by Thos Willis MD then residing at Rathmines, Maynooth 3rd June 1885, John O'Rourke.'

Dr Thomas Willis was a Dublin-based physician and apothecary noted for his promotion of the health of the working classes and was a founding member of the Irish St Vincent de Paul charity in 1844.[1] Willis is reported to have made three similar crosses out of the base of a hinged coffin, one of which he kept while another was given to a 'Mr. A.M. Sullivan'.[2] Canon John O'Rourke wrote the second text and also added a metal figure of Jesus to the front of the cross. O'Rourke later donated this cross to the Presentation Sisters in Maynooth, County Kildare, Ireland, when he was

Figure C.1 Famine Era Coffin Cross, Detail. Text purportedly written by Dr Thomas Willis. Image provided by author. By permission of Presentation Sisters, St Anne's Retreat and Conference Centre, Killenard, Portarlington, County Laois, Ireland.

Parish Priest in the area. The cross now hangs in the retreat and conference centre run by the Sisters in County Laois.

Willis was appointed one of two Poor Law Inspectors for Bantry, County Cork, in 1847 after serving as a Guardian for the Bantry Workhouse.[3] James Martin writes that Willis later served unions in Kanturk, County Cork, and in Cavan.[4] In Bantry, Willis witnessed the severe inadequacies of relief systems. While Bantry workhouse was, in 1847, meant to accommodate 600,[5] its minutes of 5 May 1849 note an aspiration to reduce the number of inmates, of the workhouse and auxiliaries, to 1,800 by the following week.[6] John O'Connor notes that lack of funds meant the inmates had but one meal a day, as noted in the minutes of the Board of Guardians on 2 March 1847, and further quotes minutes of 25 May 1847: 'The filth of the wards [...] is past endurance.'[7] During Willis's time as Guardian, the workhouse had building extensions and auxiliary sites opened intended to accommodate 976 inmates,[8] but remained unable to cope with the scale of the catastrophe then unfolding.

Willis's coffin cross was part of a touring exhibition project by the NMI in 1997. The making of the cross forged a remnant of deprivation into a revered object. As such, the cross has a dual denoted purpose: a rare artefact of Famine death, it is also a symbolic object for the living with a specific resonance of implied martyrdom. The cross's significance oscillates between the horrors it was party to and the quiet contemplative moments it promotes today. And so, this small wooden object, overwritten by interventions and provenance, sits at a crossroads between conventional searches for historical authenticity and the commemorative potential of visual culture.

Figure C.2 Dorothy Cross, *Endarken*, 2000. Video Still, DVD, 1 minute. Image provided by artist and Kerlin Gallery. © Dorothy Cross.

Artist Dorothy Cross's video work *Endarken*, 2000, was shot on location in Connemara, County Galway, in the west of Ireland.[9] (Figure C.2) In the one-minute loop, a cottage ruin, locally thought to have emptied during the Famine, is shown with trees growing through where the roof had been. The high grass and reeds surrounding it sway frenziedly in the speeded-up time of filming the green landscape under a grey misting sky. In the centre of the image a small black dot, as Gill Perry phrases it, 'expands like a pupil to cover the entire frame', to repeatedly obliterate the outdoor image.[10]

Connotative of a filmic dot at the start and end of early animation films, the black dot promises a revelation in cinematic language, only to confound that expectation and the desire to see or read the cottage fully. The dot's clean artificial circumference contrasts rudely with the softer, atmospherically active scene of the crumbling cottage in the process of being reclaimed by the land it was built on. Ultimately, the deserted living space appears in Cross's work as not fully open for interpretation: the structure is simply there, going in and out of vision and superseded by a recurring blind spot in cultural manipulation, visualized by the intermittent black dot.

Ralph Rugoff emphasizes the unnaturalness of images: 'artifice and potential treachery are inherent in the field of visual representation, leaving us perpetually vulnerable to misreading (and inaccurately classifying) the surfaces and events we perceive.'[11] Elucidating the reductive potential of both representation generally and nostalgic notions of Irish collective identity, Cross's repeated masking of a cottage scene indicates that there are other ways of looking at the past, rather than insisting that anyone might retrieve, unmediated, the fabric of another era. Willis' Coffin Cross similarly points to the shadowing of historical experiences by interceding cultural histories, inclusive in its form and current location of religious indication. Even cursory representational themes that can be derived from both these objects relate to the harshest outcomes of famine as a social form of political violence: the cottage elucidates the desolation of dispossession; the reported coffin remnant figures stark negotiations of death.

Viewing an artefact, such as the Coffin Cross, or an artwork, like *Endarken*, and reading their text, in the broadest sense, either through direct observation or here in reported account, is a performed memorialization of dispossession. Mieke Bal writes: 'framing adds baggage to the staged image because it is *performed*. Framing, in fact, is a form of performance.'[12] The significances of either the Coffin Cross or *Endarken*, for example, are framed by an individual's experience of them, social awareness of their performative function and positioning in a wider context of commemorative culture, in this case pertaining to a grievous history.

The framing that occurs through writing is proffered to emulate the possibilities of framing that occurs, much more persuasively, in direct experience of cultural forms, such as visiting exhibitions, memorials, museums, browsing a life-story from the past online, following heritage trails, touring the landscape marked by absences at sites of burial and by past presences at sites of relief works programmes. These can all happen by chance, like noticing an object of history at a retreat and conference centre, or a representative proxy in a contemporary art exhibition. Cumulatively, as presented here, the imaging of the Great Irish Famine reflects upon a broad, complicated and interactive spectrum of ideologies, cultural histories, political interpretations, colonial and post-colonial identity relations, heritage preferences and the ensuing making of social sense of the past in the present.

Representation as Dispossession

Readings of commemorative forms of visual culture as proxies for historical understanding promote a personal dispossession of sorts in which a secondary witnessing of the past takes place in the present day. As a cultural tourist may be argued to desire discovery of a understanding of the lives of those who have lived before them, any viewer may be, momentarily, dispossessed of their contemporary self as they contemplate the experiences of another, an other, by way of such objects of historical proxy.

Judith Butler and Athena Athanasiou propose to reclaim dispossession, typically the denotation of marginalized, downtrodden and disadvantaged humanity, as a concept of potential political resistance. This centres on political responsiveness as a form of engaged dispossession:

> The predicament of being moved by what one sees, feels and comes to know is always one in which one finds oneself transported elsewhere, into another scene, or into a social world in which one is not the centre. And this form of dispossession is constituted as a form of responsiveness that gives rise to action and resistance, to appearing together with others, in an effort to demand the end of injustice.[13]

In her earlier work, Butler calls for a rethinking of self and other in a network of relationality and, cogently, a dual notion of performance in speech through processes of naming: 'language acts upon us before we act and continues acting on us, as we act'.[14] These ideas promote an understanding that the vulnerability of each human, and their body's welfare, is defined by states of interdependence – namely, dependence on others. Furthermore, concepts of individuality are altered in light of social interconnectedness, as Butler outlines universal reliance on infrastructures for livable lives. And so, when infrastructures fail, human vulnerability comes to the fore.[15]

The failure of infrastructures on which people depend and the preconditioned precariousness of many indicate who suffers hunger during any famine, as was the case in the mid-nineteenth-century Irish Famine. This reflects on the politics of food that predicated and then exacerbated the catastrophic outcomes of crop failures in 1840s Ireland. The Famine period, or as Christine Kinealy has termed it 'seven years of food shortages',[16] altered the demographic profile of an entire landmass in less than eight years and influenced in divergent manners the evolution of a national identity in Ireland and throughout diasporic communities. Thomas Bartlett indicates the Famine and its aftermath as a trigger for sustained population decline that stretched into the late twentieth century.

> In just thirty years the population of Ireland had fallen by approximately one-third, with nearly 3 million people missing from the record [. . .] by 1921 some 8 million people who had been born in Ireland were living elsewhere, mostly in the United States'.[17]

Some historians and cultural analysts argue that the shadow of the Famine lingers on as an inadequately addressed aspect in the forging of a modern republic.[18] Individuals' experiences of hunger are shaped in the collective formation of famine as a socially constructed occurrence. How might such a terrible and particular history of systematic dispossession relate to a twenty-first-century viewer's momentary dispossession of self in contemplation of the vulnerable lives of others, by way of commemorative forms of visual culture?

If imaging of historical suffering and its contingent spectatorship are, to borrow from Butler, speech acts in which the subjects and viewers of representation are differentially acted upon, then such recognition might underline the interconnectedness of the lives of others with the life of the viewing self, even with taking into account separations wrought by temporal and geographical considerations. Critically, the viewer is not *the same as*, to coin Jill Bennett's emphasis of the phrase, but relational in the making and memorializing of vulnerabilities that define grievous history and ongoing experiences of vulnerability.

Reflecting on the ways in which visual culture has imaged vulnerable lives is evident in an extended case study of depictions of the mid-nineteenth-century Irish Famine across a range of commemorative media and practices from the time of the Famine to the early twenty-first century. The effects of societal dispossession looked at here – including hunger, migration, burial, relief programmes – relate to experiences of that particular grievous history. The commemorative visual cultural forms that account for representations of these outcomes have included Famine-era illustration and art, later models of public sculpture, museums, temporary exhibition projects, heritage centres and trails, memorial gardens and parks, empty buildings such as cottages and workhouses in varying states of preservation and disrepair along with formalized cemeteries and lesser known sites of graves and relief work projects. The historians, curators, illustrators, artists, heritage workers and local interest groups who have transformed these images, objects and historic places into sites of memory have negotiated complex challenges raised by this history, its uneven documentary sources and its seismic demographic and cultural impacts.

Visual Culture and Secondary Witnessing

No cultural form stands in isolation: rather, intricate webs of relations form pictures of the past. These are framed relentlessly in the present and also cumulatively overwritten by intervening histories. Conceiving identity as a product of history implies that processes of identification constantly alter as part of those interpretative processes that, as Guy Beiner puts it, craft the past. Over time, our relation to those who have lived before us, the others of history, changes. History writing is also informed by shifting cultural forms, and, with it, perceptions of otherness are modified.

The range of cultural forms that act as triggers to imaging the Great Irish Famine indicate a wider opportunity to consider the significance of representations of other grievous histories. Historic experiences of defeat and atrocity are radically incommunicable without interventions by secondary witnessing, as has been widely suggested in scholarship on the cultural forms of historiographies of orchestrated holocausts, such in World War II. Both in the absence of comprehensive testimonies and in conjunction with what documentary sources there are, the after-images generated by prosthetic, vicarious or postmemory form the narratives of time and place that describe histories of dispossession. These continue to unfold through, to redirect Debbie Lisle's use of the term regarding war and tourism, 'entanglements' of experiences of dispossession and the spectatorship that regards its representations. For Lisle, entanglement emphasizes relational rather than causational connection, to allow a view of the 'more open and heterogeneous ground on which war and tourism intersect'.[19] By extension, such a relational consideration of cultural frames that link dispossession and spectatorship might foster alternate and multiple zones of empathically driven practices of representation.

In recent times, hunger outside of famine is perhaps a more significant manifestation of unequal global access to food. In 2016 David Rieff commented that 'chronic malnutrition and undernutrition are far more likely to persist than famine (with a few geographical exceptions)' and their widespread incidence 'condemns whole societies to abiding poverty'.[20] As more of the world's material wealth is increasingly owned by fewer and fewer people,[21] leaving 'the rest' an expanded descriptor on a sliding scale towards deficits of one kind or another, how cultural forms are utilized to bear witness to anyone truly dispossessed is of increasing consequence. These are indicated not only by the expanding use of citizen journalism and social media to recount experiences, of politically and economically forced migrations in particular, but also by the deepening of artistic and curatorial approaches to such conditions.

If we can, as Butler proposes, pioneer connections of vulnerability over connections of power, with an attendant ethical responsibility, the potential to radically reconsider the visualization of such relations gains significance within visual culture. There is little innocuous about commemorative culture, and poetics is not a front for indifference. In relation to literature, for example, Elaine Scarry cautions that to dismiss Romantic emphasis would be to deny its greater context:

> [W]hile the poet pretends or wishes that the inert external world had his or her capacity for sentient awareness, civilization works to make this so. What in the poet is recognizable as a fiction is in civilization unrecognizable because it has come true.[22]

The poetics that underline the appearance of the past, such as by way of a small wooden cross or a filmic representation of a derelict cottage, indicate the range of variables of historiographic processes that differentially convey a sense of what happened before. Reflecting upon the acts of framing that cultural workers have already undertaken to commemorate the Famine is to draw attention to how they watch over the others of history. To adapt Butler's and Athanasiou's phrase, they have generated possibilities of appearing together with these others.

Leaning towards 'reading', rather than 'analysing', sites of Famine memory is an embrace of the subjective, interpretative undertones that attend even the most ardent objective claims on history. This is to iterate that understandings of heritage, of history, of what happened before now, are temporally and geographically contingent, occurring in subjectively and socially defined senses of time and place. In such a context, encountering the frames of historical otherness will always be contingent upon readers of such commemorative cultural forms insisting on spectatorship as an engaged representative practice: to think and rethink through visual culture as a mode of promoting shared secondary witnessing to experiences of dispossession, past, present and unfolding.

Notes

Preface

1. The use of the phrase 'sites of memory' takes its cue from Pierre Nora's concept of a broadly inclusive approach to the places, artefacts, objects and experiences on which history-telling can be focused, evident across his work. Pierre Nora, *Realms of Memory: Rethinking the French Past. Volume I: Conflicts and Divisions* (New York, 1996).
2. Eavan Boland, *New Collected Poems* (Manchester, 2005), pp. 204–5.
3. The 1995 exhibition as called *Famines Yesterday and Today: The Irish Experience in a Global Context* and the book is J. Crowley, W.J. Smyth and M. Murphy (eds), *Atlas of the Great Irish Famine* (Cork, 2012).
4. This acknowledges Linfield's use of the term 'grievous history' to describe experiences of 'defeat and atrocity'. Susie Linfield, *The Cruel Radiance: Photography and Political Violence* (Chicago and London, 2009), p. xiv.
5. See Primo Levi, *If This is a Man* and *The Truce* (London, 1994) and Giorgio Agamben, *Remnants of Auschwitz* (New York, 2008) on the function of witness in relation to Holocaust experiences.
6. Quoted in Nancy Chen, '"Speaking Nearby": A Conversation with Trinh T. Minh-ha', *Visual Anthropology Review* viii/1 (1992), p. 87.

Introduction   The Great Irish Famine: Dispossession and Spectatorship

1. Difficult heritage is used here to indicate 'a past that is recognised as meaningful in the present but that is also contested and awkward for public reconciliation with a positive, self-affirming contemporary identity'. Sharon Macdonald, *Difficult Heritage: Negotiating the Nazi Past in Nuremberg and Beyond* (London and New York, 2009), p. 1. While Macdonald associates this specifically with sites relating to atrocity that are a source of shame for the particular group relating that history, the term has resonance along the

much-debated lines of the long and complex interrelations of Irish and British histories, particularly in their twentieth- and twenty-first-century iterations around modernity.

2. David Lloyd, 'The Political Economy of the Potato', *Nineteenth-Century Contexts* xxix/2–3 (2007), p. 316.

3. Tomás O Riordan, 'The Introduction of the Potato into Ireland', *History Ireland* ix (2001), pp. 27–31.

4. Thomas Kenneally, *Three Famines – Starvation and Politics* (New York, 2011), pp. 28–30.

5. John Feehan, 'The Potato: Root of the Famine', in John Crowley, William J. Smyth and Mike Murphy (eds), *Atlas of the Great Irish Famine* (Cork, 2012), pp. 28–37.

6. Ciarán Ó Murchadha, *The Great Famine: Ireland's Agony 1845–1852* (London and New York, 2011), pp. 4–7.

7. Stephen J. Campbell, *The Great Irish Famine: Words and Images from the Famine Museum Strokestown Park, County Roscommon* (Roscommon, 1994), p. 15.

8. Thomas Bartlett, *Ireland: A History* (Cambridge, 2010), p. 281.

9. Ó Murchadha, *The Great Famine*, pp. 4–7.

10. Christine Kinealy, *The Great Irish Famine – Impact, Ideology and Rebellion* (Basingstoke and New York, 2002), p. 18.

11. Kevin Whelan, 'Pre and Post-Famine Landscape Change', in C. Póirtéir (ed.), *The Great Irish Famine: The Thomas Davis Lecture Series* (Cork, 1995), p. 26.

12. James S. Donnelly Jnr, *The Great Irish Potato Famine* (Stroud, 2002), p. 8.

13. Christine Kinealy, *Apparitions of Death and Disease: The Great Hunger in Ireland* (Hamden, CT, 2014), p. 29.

14. John Kelly, *The Graves are Walking: A History of the Great Irish Famine* (London and New York, 2012), p. 2 and Ciarán Ó'Murchadha, *The Great Famine: Ireland's Agony 1845–1852* (London and New York, 2011), p. 135.

15. Lloyd, *Political Economy*, pp. 311–12.

16. Ibid., p. 313.

17. Ibid.

18. McLean also references Joep Leerssen's work. Stuart McLean, *The Event and its Terrors – Ireland, Famine, Memory* (Stanford, CA, 2004), p. 67.

19. Bartlett, *Ireland*, pp. 272–3.

20. Paschal Mahoney, *Grim Bastilles of Despair: The Poor Law Union Workhouses in Ireland* (Hamden, CT, 2016), p. 9.

21. John O'Connor, *The Workhouses of Ireland: The Fate of Ireland's Poor* (Dublin, 1995), p. 120.

22. Ibid., p. 126.

Notes to Pages 6–9

23. Laurence M. Geary, '"The Late Disastrous Epidemic": Medical Relief and the Great Famine', in C. Morash and R. Hayes (eds), *Fearful Realities – New Perspectives on the Famine* (Dublin, 1996), p. 56.
24. Kinealy, *The Great Irish Famine*, p. 41.
25. See Irene Whelan, 'The Stigma of Souperism', in Póirtéir (ed.), *The Great Irish Famine*, pp. 135–54.
26. Discussed in Kinealy, *The Great Irish Famine*, pp. 37–8.
27. Ó Murchadha, *The Great Famine*, pp. 50–1. Wood 'viewed the Famine as providential in design', and his response was shaped by such 'fundamental beliefs'. Peter Gray, 'British Relief Measures', in Crowley et al., *Atlas*, p. 83. Trevelyan was the most senior official who oversaw relief efforts: a 'reforming and conscientious public servant with strong religious convictions, he often privileged principles over common sense'. Enda Delaney, *The Curse of Reason: The Great Irish Famine* (Dublin, 2012), p. 4.
28. Christine Kinealy, 'The Operation of the Poor Law during the Famine', in Crowley et al., *Atlas*, p. 92.
29. Christine Kinealy, 'The Role of the Poor Law during the Famine', in Póirtéir, *The Great Irish Famine*, p. 4; Kinealy, 'Operation of the Poor Law', p. 92; 'Role of the Poor Law', pp. 104–22.
30. Kevin Whelan, 'Immoral Economy: Interpreting Erskine Nicol's *The Tenant*', in Boston College Museum of Art (ed.), *America's Eye: The Irish Art of Brian P. Burns* (Chestnut Hill, MA, 1996), p. 59.
31. Alvin Jackson, *Ireland 1798–1998* (Malden, MA, Oxford and Victoria, 1999), p. 75.
32. In practice this outrageously parsimonious decision was inoperative, and the government had to support numerous unions from 1847 through to 1849: private charity, transmitted through the British Relief Association, also helped to support impoverished areas. In May 1849 a measure was passed to permit the Poor Law Commission to transfer levies from the more prosperous east of the country to the devastated areas of the south and west; and in 1850 the Treasury advanced a loan of £300,000 to bail out the indebted unions. Ibid., pp. 75–6.
33. Peter Gray, *The Irish Famine* (London, 1995), p. 51.
34. Kinealy, *Apparitions*, pp. 28, 31.
35. Kinealy, *The Great Famine*, p. 36.
36. Ibid., p. 55.
37. L. Perry Curtis, Jr, *Notice to Quit: The Great Irish Famine Evictions* (Hamden, CT, 2015), p. 11.
38. There have also been TV documentary, mini-series and film works. These have summoned diverse approaches to the subject, ranging, for example from the notable four-part Radharc-produced documentary, *When Ireland Starved*, 1995 to the black comedy feature film set on an ill-fated developing site of a Famine theme park, *Wide Open Spaces*, 2009. BBC and RTE co-produced the TV mini-series *The Hanging Gale* in 1995, which is set in 1846.

223

Its narrative follows the experiences of four brothers and includes rare depictions of Famine-era eviction and the hard labour of relief work programmes. To date, the only feature film to examine the Famine in any depth is *Black 47*, 2018, directed by Lance Daly. This is a revenge film with western overtones in which the plot is driven by fallouts from and anti-social behaviour during the Famine. An impressive cinematic rendering of the period, the film includes a range of astutely observed Famine experiences with, notably, a number of characters speak Irish Gaelic throughout. These objects of study are better suited and deserving of full media-focused analyses than necessarily considered within a paradigm of artistic, material and spatial aspects of commemorative visual culture of the Famine, as is the focus here.

39. This selection is not intended to be read as comprehensive of material heritage sites relating to the Famine: rather, it indicates the breadth of images, objects and places articulated as sites of Famine memory. For example, I discuss deserted cottages in relation to representations of homelessness, workhouse sites in the context of narratives of history, and the visual culture of death before and during the Famine in more detail elsewhere. Respectively, Niamh Ann Kelly, 'The Irish Cottage in Famine Remembrance', in D.A. Valone (ed.), *Ireland's Great Hunger, Volume 2* (Lanham, MD, Boulder, CO, New York, Toronto and Plymouth, 2010); Niamh Ann Kelly, 'Narrating Sites of History: Workhouses and Famine Memory', in O. Frawley (ed.), *Memory Ireland Volume III: Cruxes in Irish Cultural Memory – The Famine and the Troubles* (Syracuse, NY, 2014); and Niamh Ann Kelly, *Ultimate Witnesses: The Visual Culture of Death, Burial and Mourning in Famine Ireland* (Hamden, CT, 2017).

40. Mieke Bal, *Travelling Concepts in the Humanities – A Rough Guide* (Toronto, Buffalo, NY and London, 2002), p. 4.

41. Jill Bennett, 'Aesthetics of Intermediality', *Art History* xxx/3 (2007), p. 443.

42. Ibid., p. 449.

43. Sharon Macdonald, *Memorylands: Heritage and Identity in Europe Today* (London and New York, 2013), p. 52.

44. Ibid., pp. 16, 17.

45. Ó Gráda:

> classic famine means something more than endemic hunger. Common symptoms in normal times include rising prices, food riots, an increase in crimes against property, a significant number of actual or imminent deaths from starvation, a rise in temporary migration, and frequently the fear and emergence of famine-induced infectious diseases.

> Cormac Ó Gráda, *Famine: A Short History* (Princeton, NJ and Oxford, 2009), pp. 6–7.

46. David Campbell, 'Geopolitics and Visuality: Sighting the Darfur Conflict', *Political Geography* xxvi (2007), pp. 379–80.

47. Elaine Scarry, *The Body in Pain* (New York/Oxford, 1985), p. 19.
48. Ibid., p. 165.
49. Ibid., pp. 166–7.
50. Susan Sontag, *Regarding the Pain of Others* (London, 2003), p. 42.
51. Scarry, *The Body*, p. 171.
52. Ibid., p. 306.
53. Margaret E. Crawford, 'Subsistence Crises and Famines in Ireland: A Nutritionist's View', in M.E. Crawford (ed.), *Famine: The Irish Experience, 900–1900* (Edinburgh, 1989), p. 198.
54. Aid agencies and relief workers often lament the lack of action prior to famine. For example, Astill noted: '[w]ith no pictures of Ethiopian-style famine to outrage western citizens, Congo's prospects look grim'. James Astill, 'The Hidden Disaster', in 'Famine in Africa', *Supplement, The Guardian, in association with Concern*, 30 November 2002.
55. Marianne Hirsch, 'Projected Memory: Holocaust Photographs in Personal and Public Fantasy', in M. Bal, J. Crewe and L. Spitzer (eds), *Acts of Memory: Cultural Recall in the Present* (Hanover, NH, 1999), p. 10.
56. Marita Sturken, 'Tourists of History: Souvenirs, Architecture and the Kitschification of Memory', in L. Plate and A. Smelik (eds), *Technologies of Memory in the Arts* (Basingstoke and New York, 2009), pp. 18–35.
57. Adriana Cavarero, *Horrorism: Naming Contemporary Violence* (New York, 2011).
58. For example, David Fitzpatrick, *Oceans of Consolation: Personal Accounts of Irish Migrations to Australia* (Cork, 1995).
59. Margaret Kelleher, 'The Female Gaze: Asenath Nicholson's Famine Narrative', in C. Morash and R. Hayes (eds), *Fearful Realities – New Perspectives on the Famine* (Dublin, 1996), p. 125.
60. Ibid., p. 128.
61. Maureen Murphy, *Compassionate Stranger: Asenath Nicholson and the Great Irish Famine* (Syracuse, NY, 2015), p. xxiv.
62. Kelleher, 'The Female Gaze', p. 123.
63. Françoise Vergès, 'A Museum without Objects', in I. Chambers, A. De Angelis, C. Ianniciello, M. Orabona and M. Quadraro (eds), *The Postcolonial Museum: The Arts of Memory and the Pressures of History* (Abingdon and New York, 2016), pp. 28–9.
64. William J. Smyth, '"Variations in Vulnerability"': Understanding Where and Why the People Died', in J. Crowley, W.J. Smyth and M. Murphy (eds), *Atlas of the Great Irish Famine* (Cork, 2012), p. 187.
65. Ibid.
66. Juliet Steyn, 'Vicissitudes of Representation: Remembering and Forgetting', in J. Kidd, S. Cairns, A. Drago, A. Ryall and M. Stearn (eds), *Challenging History in the Museum* (Abingdon and New York, 2016), p. 142.
67. See James Young, 'The Holocaust as Vicarious Past: Art Spiegelman's "Maus" and the Afterimages of History', *Critical Inquiry* xxiv/3 (1998), pp. 666–99;

Dora Apel, *Memory Effects: The Holocaust and the Art of Secondary Witnessing* (New Brunswick, NJ and London, 2002); and Alison Landsberg, *Prosthetic Memory – The Transformation of American Remembrance in the Age of Mass Culture* (New York, 2004).

68. Hirsch, 'Projected Memory', pp. 7–8.
69. James Young, *At Memory's Edge: After-Images of the Holocaust in Contemporary Art and Architecture* (New Haven, CT and London, 2000), p. 2.
70. Ibid., p. 11.
71. Campbell, 'Geopolitics', p. 357.
72. Campbell draws on Poole's work. Ibid., p. 361.
73. Jenny Kidd, 'Introduction: Challenging History in the Museum', in Kiddet et al., *Challenging History*, p. 4.
74. All of the quotations from the Dáil debates and reports are taken from the Web Archives: Dáil Éireann, Vol. 456, No 5, 5 October 1995. oireachtas debates.oireachtas.ic/debates. Accessed 5 November 2017.
75. Ibid.
76. Ibid.
77. Ibid.
78. Ibid.
79. Ibid.
80. Ibid.
81. Ibid.
82. Ibid.
83. In 1997, UK Prime Minister Tony Blair acknowledged the historical failure of the London government in the 1840s. Kinealy, *The Great Famine*, p. 1. The message of reconciliation was read in the name of the British government by Irish actor Gabriel Byrne at a concert in County Cork. Kathy Marks, 'Blair Issues Apology for Irish Potato Famine', *Independent*, 2 June 1997.
84. Mary Daly, 'Historians and the Famine: A Beleaguered Species?', *Irish Historical Studies* xxx/120 (1997), p. 597.
85. O'Doherty (1939–2011) was born in Derry, Northern Ireland and was an architect and sculptor. He had a studio in Dublin and completed many public sculptures in Ireland and other countries. For more on his Enniskillen memorial, see Emily Mark-FitzGerald, *Commemorating the Irish Famine: Memory and the Monument* (Liverpool, 2013), pp. 158–61.
86. Dáil, Vol. 456.
87. The term Celtic Tiger was first coined by Kevin Gardiner, a UK economist, in a report for the American investment bankers, Morgan Stanley, who likened Ireland's economic boom in the 1990s to those of so-called Asian tiger economies. Eoin Burke-Kennedy, 'Inventor of "Celtic Tiger" phrase bails out of bank job', *Irish Times*, 21 March 2014.
88. Source: Dáil Éireann, Vol. 477, No 1, 26 March 1997. oireachtasdebates.oi reachtas.ie/debates. Accessed 5 November 2017. All currency is in Irish pounds (*punt*), the national currency of the time.

89. Counties that received grants for graveyard renovations were: Antrim, Clare, Cork, Donegal, Fermanagh, Kerry, Kildare, Leitrim, Longford, Meath, Monaghan, Tipperary, Waterford and Wexford (Dáil Éireann).
90. The annual commemoration revolves between the four provinces in Ireland, with ceremonial events also taking place outside of Ireland.
91. Peter Gray, 'Memory and the Great Irish Famine', in P. Gray and K. Oliver (eds), *The Memory of Catastrophe* (Manchester and New York, 2004), p. 45. Gray's discussion draws on Ó Gráda's related comments and notes the significance of Irish President Mary Robinson as the inaugurating patron of the Strokestown Park National Famine Museum. Ibid., pp. 52–6.
92. Roy F. Foster, *The Irish Story: Telling Tales and Making it Up in Ireland* (London, 2001), p. 34.
93. Ibid., pp. 29–31. Inspired by American and French revolutionary politics, the 1798 Rebellion, though widespread across a number of counties, was in effect relatively short, very bloody and defeated. Some 30,000 are believed to have died as a result of the rising. Alvin Jackson, *Ireland 1798–1998* (Malden, MA, Oxford and Victoria, 1999), p. 20. The National 1798 Centre is in Enniscorthy, County Wexford, near Vinegar Hill – where a significant and subsequently symbolic battle took place. Though the rebellion was quickly crushed by the British, it remains emblematically potent for concepts of Irish nationalism.
94. Famine Commemoration Committee, Department of the Taoiseach and European Community Humanitarian Office, *Ireland's Famine: Commemoration and Awareness* (Dublin, 1997), p. 38.
95. Luke Gibbons, 'Doing Justice to the Past', in T. Hayden (ed.), *Irish Hunger – Personal Reflections of the Famine* (Boulder, CO, 1998), p. 260.
96. Ibid., pp. 260–1.
97. Kinealy, *The Great Famine*, p. 2.
98. Quoted in Katy Deepwell, *Dialogues: Women Artists from Ireland* (London, 2005), p. 141.
99. Alanna O'Kelly, *Winter Lecture* (Irish Museum of Modern Art, 4 December 2001). Audio courtesy of Irish Museum of Modern Art (IMMA).
100. Karen Wells, 'Melancholic Memorialisation: The Ethical Demands of Grievable Lives', in G. Rose and D.P. Tolia-Kelly (eds), *Visuality/Materiality: Images, Objects and Practices* (Farnham and Burlington, VT, 2012), p. 155.
101. Ibid.
102. Thomas W. Laqueur, 'Introduction', *Representations (Grounds for Remembering)* 69/Special Issue (2000), p. 8.
103. Ibid.
104. Judith Butler, *Precarious Life: The Powers of Mourning and Violence* (London and New York, 2004), p. 35.
105. Ibid., p. 29.
106. Ibid., p. 34.
107. Ibid., p. 44. Butler draws on G.W.F. Hegel and Emmanuel Lévinas throughout her discussion.

108. Greg Ringer, *Destinations – Cultural Landscapes of Tourism* (London and New York, 2005), p. 9.
109. Theorists emphasize tourism's roots in conventions of pilgrimage. Ibid., pp. 3–4.
110. Ibid., p. 5.
111. While urban tourism has increased, McCain and Ray note heritage or cultural tourism, as a subset of rural or eco-tourism, as an area of pronounced growth. Legacy travellers give motivations for travel, in order of importance, as: visiting historic sites, wilderness and undisturbed nature, mountains, and visiting friends and relatives. Gary McCain and Nina M. Ray, 'Legacy Tourism: The Search for Personal Meaning in Heritage Travel', *Tourism Management* xxiv (2003), pp. 713–17.
112. Mimi Sheller and John Urry, 'Places to Play, Place in Play', in M. Sheller and J. Urry, *Tourism Mobilities: Places to Play, Place in Play* (London and New York, 2004), p. 6.
113. Ringer, *Destinations*, p. 2.
114. Thomas Blom, 'Morbid Tourism – A Postmodern Market Niche with an Example from Althrop', *Norwegian Journal of Geography* liv/1 (2000), pp. 29–36.
115. Emma Willis, *Theatricality, Dark Tourism and Ethical Spectatorship: Absent Others* (Basingstoke/New York, 2014), p. 215.
116. John Lennon and Malcolm Foley, *Dark Tourism: The Attraction of Death and Disaster* (London and New York, 2000), p. 5
117. Their examples: the Berlin Wall and Checkpoint Charlie. Ibid., pp. 19–20.
118. Ibid., p. 11.
119. Philip R. Stone, 'A Dark Tourism Spectrum: Towards a Typology of Death and Macabre Related Tourist Sites, Attractions and Exhibitions', *Tourism* liv/2 (2006), p. 151.
120. Peter Hohenhaus, 'Commemorating and Commodifying the Rwandan Genocide', in L. White and E. Frew (eds), *Dark Tourism and Place Identity: Managing and Interpreting Dark Places* (London and New York, 2013), p. 149.
121. Ibid., p. 153.
122. Leanne White and Elspeth Frew, 'Exploring Dark Tourism and Place Identity', in White and Frew, *Dark Tourism* (London and New York, 2013), p. 4.

1 Figuration and the Site of Famine

1. Quoted in Margaret E. Crawford, 'Subsistence Crises and Famines in Ireland: A Nutritionist's View', in M.E. Crawford (ed.), *Famine: The Irish Experience, 900–1900* (Edinburgh, 1989), pp. 200–1. A regular correspondent for the *Cork Southern Reporter*, Donovan undertook remarkable work for the sick and dying during the Famine, and also published medical observations on

starvation in *The Lancet*. Michael Foley, *Death in Every Paragraph* (Hamden, CT, 2015), p. 27. Foynes notes his work in relation to aided emigration. Peter Foynes, *The Great Famine in Skibbereen and District* (Skibbereen, 2004), pp. 54–5.

2. Crawford, 'Subsistence Crises', p. 198.

3. Ibid., p. 205. The conditions include: scurvy caused by lack of vitamin C; the eye disease xerophthalmia caused by inadequate vitamin A levels; and pellagra caused by insufficient vitamin B.

4. Laurence M. Geary, 'Medical Relief and the Great Famine', in J. Crowley, W.J. Smyth and M. Murphy (eds), *Atlas of the Great Irish Famine* (Cork, 2012), p. 199.

5. As described on the 'Disease Epidemics' panel at the Johnstown museum.

6. 'Potatoes, which grew prolifically even in poor or rocky soil, provided over 50 per cent of the population with an adequate and healthy diet.' Christine Kinealy, *The Great Irish Famine – Impact, Ideology and Rebellion* (Basingstoke and New York, 2002), p. 18. A lack of balance in food types and poor food preparation caused most illness. Crawford, 'Subsistence Crises', p. 198.

7. Cathal Póirtéir, *Famine Echoes* (Dublin, 1995). Póirtéir's book incorporates text collated by Commission researchers from 1935 onwards. The NFC's website states its collection has 'more than 1.5 million pages of material and many thousands of hours of recordings'. www.ucd.ie/irishfolklore/en/. Accessed 26 February 2017.

8. Niall Ó Ciosáin, 'Approaching a Folklore Archive: The Irish Folklore Commission and the Memory of the Great Famine', *Folklore* cxv (2004), p. 222. He describes the process in 1945, when the NFC conducted a survey and collection of folklore relating to the Famine:

> It circulated a short questionnaire to its full-time and part-time collectors, and accumulated about 3,500 pages of testimony in both English and Irish [...] On the one hand, the Folklore commission and its archive was established precisely as a repository of national memory, manifest in the oral tradition, and can itself be considered a form of institutionalized public memory. On the other hand, the work of the Commission in practice conceived of memory as personal recollection [...] None of the informants had lived through the Famine, and moreover were not solely reliant on oral tradition for their knowledge of it.

Niall Ó Ciosáin, 'Famine Memory and the Popular Representation of Scarcity', in I. McBride (ed.), *History and Memory in Modern Ireland* (Cambridge, 2001), pp. 96–7.

9. Mícheál Briody, *The Irish Folklore Commission: 1935–1970: History, Ideology, Methodology* (Helsinki, 2008), p. 20.

10. Séamas Mac Philib, 'Obituaries: Kevin Danaher (Caoimhín Ó Danachair)', *The Journal of the Royal Society of Antiquaries of Ireland* cxxxii (2002), p. 153.

11. Cormac Ó Gráda, *Black '47 and Beyond: The Great Irish Famine in History, Economy and Memory* (Princeton, NJ, 1999), p. 223.
12. Ibid., p. 195.
13. Guy Beiner, 'Recycling the Dustbin of Irish History: The Radical Challenge of "Folk Memory"', *History Ireland* xiv/1 (2006), p. 46.
14. Ibid., p. 47.
15. Quoted in Póirtéir, *Famine*, p. 90.
16. Crawford, 'Subsistence Crises', p. 202. She further quotes Donovan: 'the total insensibility of the sufferers to every other feeling except that of supplying their own wants'. Ibid.
17. Hitherto known as an artist, *Hunger* was McQueen's first general release film. Sands was sentenced to 14 years' imprisonment for carrying arms. Protest actions by prisoners, known as the Dirty Protests (or Blanket and No Wash Protests), were instigated in efforts to be recognized as political prisoners. Prisoners on protest refused to wear clothes provided by the prison and had to be washed by force; smeared their prison cells with excrement and directed urine from their cells onto prison corridors. Prior to this, a number of women were reported ordered off hunger strike at Armagh women's prison.
18. Bartlett describes 'The Troubles' as a 'rather anodyne term commonly applied to the murderous ethno-religious conflict that was seemingly intractable in the north [of Ireland] from the late 1960s'. Thomas Bartlett, *Ireland: A History* (Cambridge, 2010), p. 469.
19. Barbara Pollack, 'Film: Body and Soul', *Art in America*, March 2009, pp. 75–6.
20. Gary Crowdus, 'The Human Body as Political Weapon: An Interview with Steve McQueen', *Cineaste*, Spring 2009, p. 24.
21. Ibid., p. 23.
22. Pollack, 'Film', p. 76.
23. The film's cumulative immersive quality is undoubtedly underpinned by McQueen's practice as an artist.
24. Kieron Corless, '*Hunger*: Interviews', *Sight and Sound* (November 2008), p. 26.
25. The priest is a composite representation of priests associated with the conflict.
26. As justification for his willingness to hunger strike to death, even against external Republican advice, Sands recounts a childhood incident on a cross-country run. He put an injured foal out of its misery by drowning and in doing what he deemed necessary, became a leader to the other boys.
27. John Lynch, 'Hunger: Passion of the Militant', *Nordic Journal of English Studies* xiii/2 (2014), p. 187. Lynch discusses the philosophy of Martin Heidegger in relation to this.
28. Wilson notes that upsurges of violence, in 1976, 1981 and 1985, in particular, all gained international publicity and were followed by a decline in tourism, though later in the 1980s this was less evident, which may in part reflect on 'terrorism in the North' ceasing to be 'as newsworthy as it once was [...] in the international press'. David Wilson, 'Tourism, Public Policy and the Image

of Northern Ireland since the Troubles', in B. O'Connor and M. Cronin (eds), *Tourism in Ireland: A Critical Analysis* (Cork, 1993), p. 144.

29. Crowdus, 'The Human Body', p. 22.
30. Pollack, 'Film', p. 87.
31. This has reverberations regarding the Broadcast Ban imposed from 1988 to 1994 on 11 loyalist and republican organizations, including Sinn Fein.
32. Sculptural figurations of the Famine are more common outside Ireland than within. Emily Mark-FitzGerald, *Commemorating the Irish Famine: Memory and the Monument* (Liverpool, 2013), p. 119. Even so, such figurations are widely reproduced tropes.
33. Stuart McLean, *The Event and its Terrors – Ireland, Famine, Memory* (Stanford, CA, 2004), p. 67.
34. David Hume cited the Irish temperament as the reason for Ireland's supposed 'failure' to embrace the Reformation. Ibid., p. 60. Friedrich Engels wrote that the 'whole character of the [English] working class assimilates a great part of the Irish characteristics', and so the English lowered their level of 'civilization' as a result of Irish immigration. Ibid., p. 52. Thomas Robert Malthus noted, 'the massed bodies of the Irish poor are figured as a site of procreative excess at once threatening and necessary to the well-being of British society'. Ibid., p. 65. Malthus was an economist who visited Ireland in 1817, touring the south. His ideas are often referred to as 'Malthusian' and referenced in relation to the 'lassez-faire' approach to Irish economics from the British perspective.
35. The Penal Laws (Laws for the Suppression of Popery) were in force in Ireland from 1691 until the Catholic Emancipation of 1829 and banned the practice of Catholic religion.
36. David A. Valone, 'Economic Identity and the Irish Peasantry on the Eve of the Great Hunger', in D.A. Valone and J.M. Bradbury (eds), *Anglo-Irish Identities, 1671–1845* (Lewisburg, PA, 2008), p. 288.
37. L. Perry Curtis, Jr, *Notice to Quit: The Great Irish Famine Evictions.* (Hamden, CT, 2015), p. 12.
38. Ibid., p. 13.
39. Paschal Mahoney, *Grim Bastilles of Despair: The Poor Law Union Workhouses in Ireland* (Hamden, CT, 2016), p. 9.
40. Justin Carville, 'Resisting Vision: Photography, Anthropology and the Production of Race in Ireland', in C. Breathnach and C. Lawless (eds), *Visual, Material and Print Culture in Nineteenth-Century Ireland* (Dublin and Portland, OR, 2010), p. 160.
41. Cork-born, Macdonald achieved moderate academic recognition after moving to London in the early 1840s. He exhibited at the British Institute in 1847 and 1849–51, and at the Royal Hibernian Academy in Dublin in 1842–4. As a child, he had etchings printed in a local publication, *The Tribute*. His father was an artist and caricaturist. Peter Murray (compiler), *Catalogue of The Crawford Municipal Art Gallery* (Cork, 1992), p. 178.

42. This was a token of gratitude for help Woodham-Smith received in researching her Famine-based novel *The Great Hunger*, 1962. Department of Irish Folklore, *Folk Tradition in Irish Art: An Exhibition of Paintings from the Collection of the Department of Irish Folklore, University College Dublin* (Dublin, 1993), p. 49.

43. 'It has to be said that pictures of such scenes of starvation would not have been easy sellers. Artists also wished to avoid direct political statements critical of the British government.' Anne Crookshank and the Knight of Glin, *Ireland's Painters 1600–1940* (Yale, 2002), p. 249. In the 1840s, Frederick Goodall led a group of English artists to Ireland, including Francis William Topham, Mark Anthony and Alfred Fripp, who depicted social conditions in Ireland, but as Curtis notes, 'their homely scenes of domesticity were rendered harmless by sentimentalization', presumably catering for marketable images. Curtis, *Notice to Quit*, p. 31. Also travelling throughout Ireland and making images at this time was the Dublin-born George Victor du Noyer (1817–69), who, from 1845, worked for the Geological Survey of Great Britain and Ireland and produced maps of Wexford, Waterford, Cork and Kerry for the survey. Petra Coffey, 'George Victor du Noyer 1817–1869, Artist, Geologist and Antiquary', *The Journal of the Royal Society of Antiquaries of Ireland* 123 (1993), p. 114. The Irish antiquarian George Petrie (1789–1866) had given du Noyer drawing lessons as a child, and throughout his working life, du Noyer observed Irish life in small drawings in a series of notebooks. Ibid., 103, 115.

44. Niamh O'Sullivan, *In the Lion's Den – Daniel Macdonald, Ireland and Empire* (Hamden, CT, 2016), pp. 73, 77.

45. Visitors to Ireland in the late eighteenth century noted the 'predominant hues in an Irish gathering were blue, black, brown and "dark snuff"', while others noted 'shades also of red, purple, olive, yellow, peach and pink'. Mairead Dunlevy, *Dress in Ireland: A History* (Cork, 1999), p. 137. Colours were achieved from home dyes typically derived from native plants.

46. Ibid., p. 140.

47. Ibid., p. 162.

48. Tom Dunne, 'The Dark Side of the Irish Landscape: Depictions of the Rural Poor, 1760–1850', in Crawford Art Gallery and Gandon Editions (eds), *Whipping the Herring: Survival and Celebration in Nineteenth Century Irish Art* (Cork, 2006), p. 122.

49. 'The pretty little girl is a clear reference to Gainsborough's most famous "fancy" picture, *Cottage Girl with Dog and Pitcher* (1785, NGI): the brown pitcher is at her feet, the dog over beside her mother.' Ibid.

50. O'Sullivan, *In the Lion's Den*, p. 30.

51. Donald W. Crawford, 'Comparing Natural and Artistic Beauty', in S. Kemal and I. Gaskell (eds), *Landscape, Natural Beauty and the Arts* (Cambridge, 1993), pp. 183–98.

52. 'The spectator might well believe that what was being portrayed was a stage scene rather than a contemporary historical event.' Sighle Bhreathnach-Lynch, 'Framing the Irish: Victorian Paintings of the Irish Peasant', *Journal of Victorian Culture* ii/2 (1997), p. 257.

53. Elaine Scarry, *The Body in Pain* (New York and Oxford, 1985), p. 286.

54. Dunne, 'The Dark Side', p. 122.

55. Prior to the Famine, women's opportunity to work in the domestic textile industry declined with the advent of centralized clothing factories in the north of Ireland. Margaret MacCurtain, 'The Real Molly Macree', in A.M. Dalsimer (ed.), *Visualizing Ireland: National Identity and the Pictorial Tradition* (Boston, MA, and London, 1993), pp. 14–15. This left cottage and tenant dwellers dependent on the working man of each household.

56. Watts stayed with his friend the poet Aubrey de Vere, in County Limerick. Mark-Fitzgerald notes this work as one of four thematically related canvases of early Victorian social realism in art. Mark-Fitzgerald, *Commemorating*, p. 22.

57. Simon Poe, 'The Cult of Beauty: The Aesthetic Movement 1860–1900, Exhibition Review', *The British Art Journal* xii/1 (2011), p. 79.

58. Colin Trodd, 'Before History Painting: Enclosed Experience and the Emergent Body in the Work of G.F. Watts', *Visual Culture in Britain* vi/1 (2005), p. 44.

59. Quoted in ibid., p. 43. Watts's writings on art and society suggest contradictory imperatives behind his pictorial decisions, from early critique on colonial attitudes and strictures on religious politics to later sympathy for British colonialism. David Stewart, 'Deconstruction or Reconstruction? The Victorian Paintings of George Frederic Watts', *Southeast College Art Conference Review* xii/3 (1993), pp. 181–6.

60. Lewis Johnson, 'Pre-Raphaelitism, Personification, Portraiture', in M. Pointon (ed.), *Pre-Raphaelites Re-viewed* (Manchester and New York, 1989), p. 150.

61. Ibid., p. 149.

62. Mahony co-established the Cork Art Union in 1841, after a period of European travel. He exhibited paintings throughout his life. Julian Campbell, 'The Artist as Witness: James Mahony', in Crowley et al., *Atlas*, p. 473. An associate of the Royal Hibernian Academy (RHA), Mahony painted panoramic scenes of Spain, France and Italy on his travels there. Mark-Fitzgerald discusses the variously straining relationship between Mahony's written and visual accounts. Mark-Fitzgerald, *Commemorating*, pp. 44–8. His watercolours of Queen Victoria's and Prince Albert's visits to the 1853 Industrial Exhibition in Dublin comprised 'a complicated symbolic apparatus that reinforces the overriding message of the exhibitions'. Nancy Netzer, 'Picturing an Exhibition: James Mahony's Watercolours of the Irish Industrial Exhibition of 1853', in A.M. Dalsimer (ed.), *Visualizing Ireland:*

National Identity and the Pictorial Tradition (Boston, MA and London, 1993), pp. 90–1.

63. While some historians attribute this series to Mahony, the Heritage Researcher at *ILN* archives informed this writer (email correspondence, October 2015) that no record exists of the author and/or illustrator for this 1849–50 series of reports from County Clare, other than references to the correspondent as male.

64. Quoted in Peter Gray, *The Irish Famine* (London, 1995), p. 53.

65. Niamh O'Sullivan, *The Tombs of a Departed Race: Illustrations of Ireland's Great Hunger* (Hamden, CT, 2014), pp. 40–4.

66. The circulation of ILN was 60,000 by the end of 1842, the year of its first edition and by 1848 reached a height of 80,000 with coverage of the French Revolution. www.iln.co.uk/heritage. Accessed 10 October 2016. Peter Gray notes that *Punch*, for example, had less circulation, but significant political influence in conjunction with the *ILN* and *The Times*:

> Its [*Punch*'s] circulation, at around 30,000, was below that of many other journals and was largely concentrated in London, but it reached many metropolitan opinion-formers who set the tone of British middle-class attitudes as expressed nationally. It was read by politicians, and several cabinet ministers commented on its pronouncements in their private diaries. Most importantly, *Punch* existed as part of a network of similarly- oriented journals. Its authors were keen to take their line on public affairs largely from *The Times*, by far the most influential newspaper of the day. Indeed one contributor, Gilbert a Beckett, was simultaneously a leader writer for both *The Times* and *The Illustrated London News*. The power of these three papers taken together was considerable – each complemented the other by focusing on a different aspect of middle-class taste.

Peter Gray, '*Punch* and the Irish Famine', *History Ireland* i/2 (1993), p. 29.

67. Quoted in Noel Kissane, *The Irish Famine: A Documentary History* (Dublin, 1995), p. 115.

68. The writer positioned responsibility for the condition of Ireland with inadequacies of the Poor Laws. His desire was to 'make the conditions of Ireland [...] more effectually known by selecting a single Union for remark, than by parading before our readers a great multitude of statistical facts'.

69. Kelleher describes more recent images of famine sufferers as necessarily helpless victims in the face of consequently empowered 'alleviators'. Margaret Kelleher, *The Feminization of Famine – Expressions of the Inexpressible?* (Cork, 1997), p. 27.

70. Susan Sontag, *Regarding the Pain of Others* (London, 2003), p. 70. This refers to Sebastiâo Salgado's photographic focus on the powerlessness of the powerless.

71. L. Perry Curtis, Jr, *Apes and Angels: The Irishman in Victorian Caricature* (rev. edn) (Washington, DC, 1997).

> Such symbolic substitutions [theriomorphism] became increasingly misanthropic and politically charged during the nineteenth century, when rapid urbanization and rampant profit seeking created a huge reservoir of poor, slum-dwelling workers, who were often characterized by respectable observers as disease-spreading 'scum' of sewer rats. (Ibid., p. xii.).

This gave rise to a desire to distinguish Irish immigrants from others on Britain's mainland though dehumanizing representations.

72. Gray, *'Punch'*, p. 31. Though Gray suggests that such images and references did not necessarily reflect dominant public opinion, he acknowledges their content gathered politicized momentum during the Famine years.
73. McLean, *The Event*, p. 137.
74. As Curtis's study implies, when migrations bring fears of contamination sympathetic views dissipate.
75. O'Sullivan, *The Tombs*, p. 24. O'Sullivan notes the impact of prevailing artistic trends and improving technologies of reproduction at this time the legibility of images circulated in newspapers. Ibid., pp. 11–24. This ILN article contains several since iconic images including the figurative sketches *Searching for Potatoes in a Stubble Field* and *Scalp of Brian Connor, Near Kilrush Union House*.
76. Children between the ages of one and five, old people, pregnant and lactating women are the most vulnerable to illnesses and death from famine. Crawford, *Subsistence Crises*, p. 201.
77. Paula Murphy, 'Madonna and Maiden, Mistress and Mother: Woman as Symbol of Ireland and Spirit of the Nation', in J. Steward (ed.), *When Time began to Rant and Rage, Figurative Painting from Twentieth Century Ireland* (London and Berkeley, CA, 1998), p. 98.
78. For example, W.B. Yeats wrote a play *Cathleen Ní Houlihan* in 1902 on the theme of heroism and Irish nationalism.
79. Though developed from a genre of love poems, the *aisling* was a highly political poem, famously developed by Aogán Ó'Rathaille (c.1675–1729).
80. For more on this see Moroney's discussion in a review of the exhibition 'Images of Erin in the Age of Parnell', 20 October 2000 – 31 March 2001, National Library of Ireland, Dublin. Mic Moroney, 'Images of Erin', *Irish Times*, 18 November 2000.
81. Marina Warner, *Monuments and Maidens: The Allegory of the Female Form* (London, Sydney, Auckland and Bergvlei, 1996), p. 332.
82. Bryan S. Turner, *The Body and Society* (London, 1996), p. 6.
83. Kelleher, *The Feminization*, pp. 7–8. The female as a narrative device in famine literature points to '[d]eep ambivalences [that] exist within the female figure; this doubleness can be glimpsed in many famine texts and is

acknowledged by some of the more reflective writers. The mother gives life but also death [...]'. Ibid., p. 229.

84. *A'Beathú* was made for the 23rd São Paulo Biennale, Brazil in 1996. O'Kelly (1955-) was born in Gorey, County Wexford, and has also represented Ireland at Documenta 8, Kassel, Germany, in 1987. A member of Aosdána, her work is in public collections, including the Crawford Art Gallery and IMMA. (Established by the Irish Arts Council in 1981, Aosdána, honours 'outstanding contribution to the creative arts in Ireland'. aosdana.arstcouncil. ie. Accessed 10 October 2016. Limited to 250 living artists, its prestigious membership is by peer nomination and election.)

85. Murphy, 'Madonna and Maiden', p. 100.

86. Quoted in Katy Deepwell, *Dialogues: Women Artists from Ireland* (London, 2005), p. 146.

87. *Ómós*, 1994–5, was a performance based on a folk story of a girl begging without speaking, as she runs after a carriage between Leenane and Westport in County Mayo. See: Niamh Ann Kelly, 'Transgressing Time: Imagining an Exhibition of Works by Alanna O'Kelly and Phil Collins', in M. Bal and M.A. Hernández-Navarro (eds), *Art and Visibility in Migratory Culture – Conflict, Resistance, and Agency* (Amsterdam and New York, 2011), pp. 161–74.

88. Alanna O'Kelly and Jean Fisher, *Alanna O'Kelly: 23rd São Paulo Biennal* (Dublin, 1996), p. 5.

89. Deepwell, *Dialogues*, p. 146.

90. Discussed in Murphy, 'Madonna and Maiden', p. 100.

91. Deepwell, *Dialogues*, p. 146.

92. The title refers to a poem *The Deserted Village* by the eighteenth-century Irish writer Oliver Goldsmith.

93. Catherine Marshall, *Monuments and Memorials of the Great Famine* (Hamden, CT, 2014), p. 18.

94. Catherine Marshall, 'History and Memorials: Fine Art and the Great Famine in Ireland', in C. Breathnach and C. Lawless (eds), *Visual, Material and Print Culture in Nineteenth-Century Ireland* (Dublin and Portland, OR, 2010), p. 27.

95. Deepwell, *Dialogues*, p. 140.

96. Alanna O'Kelly, *Winter Lecture* (Irish Museum of Modern Art, 4 December 2001). Audio courtesy of IMMA.

97. Sontag, *Regarding the Pain*, p. 23. Sontag was referring to Salgado's work. Writing on Salgado's images of the Sahel, Fred Richtin summons an argument against the expectation of horror:

> Would we prefer instead more of the journalistic shorthand that makes these Africans different from us in their victimization – bereft, with swollen bellies, covered in flies, surrendering to their circumstances? How can people view those all-too-common portrayals without finding them both superficial and dehumanizing? [...] The conventional and more easily digestible vocabulary of

disaster imagery – the poor doubly marginalized as flotsam – is not his [Salgado's].

In Sebastiâo Salgado, *Sahel, the End of the Road* (Berkeley, CA, Los Angeles and London, 2004), p. 4.

98. St Stephen's Green is a 22-acre leisure park. Enclosed for grazing since 1664, it was opened to the public in its present form and use in 1880.

99. The United Irish Society, better known as the Society of the United Irishmen, was an organization founded in both Dublin and Belfast with the aim of parliamentary reform and Catholic emancipation. Alvin Jackson, *Ireland 1798–1998* (Malden, MA, Oxford and Victoria, 1999), pp. 12–13. The society's advocacy led to the Rebellion of 1798, at the end of which Wolfe Tone was captured. He committed suicide in custody, at what is now called Collins Barracks, the site of the National Museum of Ireland's Decorative Arts and History Collection Exhibitions.

100. Delaney (1930–2009) was born in Claremorris, County Mayo. His use of the lost-wax method of bronze casting was learnt from working in foundries across Europe. Peter Murray, 'Refiguring Delaney', *Irish Arts Review* xxii/4 (2004), pp. 80–5. This contributed to the style of figuration for which he was renowned. A member of the RHA and Aosdána, his work has been widely exhibited and collected nationally and internationally.

101. This ladle is typical of Famine-era soup kitchen spoons. When the fountain operates, water flows down it.

102. The dog was stolen. According to the *Evening Herald*, 10 February 1969, it was a protest by art students who thought the well-fed looking animal distracted from the formal significance and political importance of the emaciated humans. Judith Hill, *Irish Public Sculpture* (Dublin, 1998), pp. 202, 274. The dog was later replaced by Delaney. Róisín Kennedy, 'Searching for the Vital Form', in Royal Hibernian Academy (ed.), *Edward Delaney – Bronzes from the Sixties* (Dublin, 2004), p. 13.

103. It is thought to have been blown up by the Ulster Volunteer Force (UVF). Murray, 'Refiguring', p. 84. This was possibly in revenge for the bombing of Nelson's Pillar in Dublin in 1966, which is thought to have been carried out by the Irish Republican Army (IRA).

104. Thomas Davis was a poet and writer and co-founder of the newspaper *The Nation*, which was the main outlet for the Young Ireland Movement, 'concerned with defining Irish identity and propagating a form of cultural nationalism'. Fintan Cullen (ed.), *Sources in Irish Art – A Reader* (Cork, 2000), p. 65.

105. Kennedy, 'Searching', p. 11.

106. Hill, *Irish Public Sculpture*, p. 202.

107. Hill suggests this sculptural attribute contributes to the 'essential vigour' of the figures of Tone and Davis. Ibid., p. 202.

108. Gillespie (1953-) was born in Dublin, studied art in England and lives in Ireland. He has public sculptures across Europe and the USA, as well as in Ireland and Canada.

109. The nearby Custom House (1791) was designed by James Gandon in 1781. It gained national historic resonance during the Irish Civil War, 1921–2, when the IRA burnt out its interior. The area is also significant as the site of the 1913 workers' 'lockout', during which food ships from Manchester and Liverpool workers docked nearby to distribute provisions.

110. Roger Kohn, *Rowan Gillespie: Looking for Orion* (Dublin, 2007), pp. 91–5.

111. Ciara Ferguson, 'Horror and Hope', *Sunday Independent*, 1 June 1997.

112. Kohn, *Rowan Gillespie*, p. 91.

113. Independent.ie, 'Rowan's Found a Niche', 24 May 2009, https://www.independent.ie/entertainment/books/rowans-found-a-niche-26538489.html. Accessed 9 February 2016.

114. The park was built by Aidan Flatley with landscape design by Jonathan Kearns. Funded by the Irish Park Foundation through a system of donors, the park was also funded by the Canadian and Irish official bodies.

115. Mark-Fitzgerald, *Commemorating*, p. 273.

116. http://irelandparkfoundation.com/. Accessed 6 September 2017.

117. In 2011, Clones was the site of the annual National Famine Commemoration ceremony. A memorial plaque at the site includes the text: 'Erected in memory of all the people from Clones Union who died because of the Great Famine 1845–1850; Also those who died in the workhouse 1845–1921; The meek shall inherit the earth'. Daly notes that the population of County Monaghan fell by 29.2 per cent between 1841 and 1851, which she comments was 'only fractionally below the percentage fall in County Mayo'. Mary Daly, 'Historians and the Famine: A Beleaguered Species?', *Irish Historical Studies* xxx/120 (1997), p. 597. Mulholland (1944-) was born in County Armagh, studied art in Belfast and is a member of the RHA and Aosdána, with works in public places in metal and stone.

118. Discussed in telephone conversation with the artist, November 2017. See also: Mark-Fitzgerald, *Commemorating*, pp. 123–4.

119. Pre-Famine Irish burial customs were typically defined by locally various adaptations of an extended period of mourning which included a celebration of the life of the dead, in social ritual practices known as waking the dead. These highly organized and often personally costly events, typically lasted over two nights and included a variety of activities, from hospitality, games and storytelling and allowed mourners time to travel to pay their respects to the family of the deceased. The NFC has many accounts of wakes, which were greatly thwarted by the Famine, though revived in limited forms in places afterwards. For more on the complexity and significance of these rich cultural forms associated with Irish mortuary traditions see: Gearóid O Crualaóich, 'The Merry Wake', in J.S. Donnelly and K.A. Miller (ed.), *Irish Popular Culture 1650–1850* Dublin, 1998); Patricia Lysaght, 'Hospitality at Wakes and Funerals

in Ireland from the Seventeenth to the Nineteenth Century: Some Evidence from the Written Record', *Folklore* 114 (2003), pp. 403–26; and Seán Ó Súilleabháin, *Irish Folk Custom and Belief* (Dublin, 1967). For further discussion on related Famine-era visual culture see: Niamh Ann Kelly, *Ultimate Witnesses: The Visual Culture of Death, Burial and Mourning in Famine Ireland* (Hamden, CT, 2017).

120. Myles Campbell, 'Carolyn Mulholland', in A. Carpenter and P. Murphy (eds), *Art and Architecture of Ireland Volume III – Sculpture 1600–2000* (Dublin, 2015), p. 249.

121. Bill Rolston, 'Political Murals in Northern Ireland', *Museum International* lvi/3 (2004), p. 41.

122. Ibid., p. 42. The 1916 Rising, also known as the Easter Rising, was an insurgency that took place over Easter week 1916 across Ireland. The main conflict site was Dublin city, where a key symbolic gesture took place as the proclamation of Ireland as a republic was read by one of the leaders of the uprising, Pádraig (Patrick) Pearse, outside the General Post Office on O'Connell Street. The leaders of the rising surrendered, were incarcerated, along with other rebel fighters, and were later executed, many in Kilmainham Gaol, Dublin. Their executions significantly increased public sympathy for their cause. The War of Independence ensued until an Anglo-Irish treaty was signed in London by Michael Collins in 1921 and Ireland as a Free State became effective in early 1922. Then followed a bitter civil war into 1923. Ireland was declared a republic in 1949, following the 1948 Republic of Ireland Act. 1916 centenary commemorations in Ireland have been contextualized within a larger government-supported programme termed the Decade of Commemorations (1912–22): 'The programme will be broad and inclusive, highlighting the economic and social conditions of the period, the shifts in cultural norms and the experience of the Irish abroad.' http://www.decadeofcentenaries.com/. Accessed 23 October 2017.

123. Mark-Fitzgerald, *Commemorating*, p. 53.

124. Rolston, 'Political Murals', p. 44.

2 Leaving the Famine: The Spectacle of Migration

1. Quoted in P.J. Meghen, 'Stephen de Vere's Voyage to Canada, 1847', *The Old Limerick Journal: Famine Edition* 32 (1995), p. 138.

2. James Donnelly Jnr, *The Great Irish Potato Famine* (Stroud, 2002), p. 180.

3. Jason King, 'Remembering and Forgetting the Famine Irish in Quebec: Genuine and False Memories, Communal Memory and Migration', *The Irish Review* 44 (2012), p. 32.

4. Ibid., p. 31.

5. Parks Canada – Grosse Île and the Irish Memorial National Historic Site of Canada website, www.pc.gc.ca/eng/lhn-nhs/qc/grosseile/index.aspx. Accessed 19 November 2016.

6. Mark McGowan, 'Famine, Facts and Fabrication: An Examination of Diaries from the Irish Famine Migration to Canada', *The Canadian Journal of Irish Studies* xxxiii/2 (2007), p. 49.
7. Mary Daly, 'Historians and the Famine: A Beleaguered Species?', *Irish Historical Studies* xxx/120 (1997), p. 598.
8. Marianna O'Gallagher, *Grosse Ile: Gateway to Canada 1832–1937* (Ste. Foy, 1984), p. 147.
9. Mary Lee Dunn, *Ballykilcline Rising: From Famine Ireland to Immigrant America* (Amherst, MA, 2008), p. 159.
10. Michael Quigley, 'Grosse Île: Canada's Famine Memorial', in A. Gribben (ed.), *The Great Famine and the Irish Diaspora in America* (Amherst, MA, 1999), p. 136.
11. Ibid., p. 138.
12. Ibid., p. 142.
13. A Medical Commission, established following an official enquiry into the quarantine station, further described the sick on the island in 'deplorable conditions' and found corpses lying in beds with the sick and dying on board the anchored ships. Quigley, 'Grosse Île', p. 139.
14. Noel Kissane, *The Irish Famine: A Documentary History* (Dublin, 1995), p. 164.
15. Colin McMahon, 'Montreal's Ship Fever Monument: An Irish Famine Memorial in the Making', *The Canadian Journal of Irish Studies* xxxiii/1 (2007), p. 48.
16. Quoted in ibid., p. 48.
17. Ibid., p. 48.
18. Ibid., p. 49.
19. Ibid., p. 50.
20. Jesse Feith, 'Coderre says Black Rock Memorial Plan is on Track', Montreal Gazette, 7 October 2017. https://www.pressreader.com/canada/montreal-gazette/20171007/281599535712121. Accessed 4 September 2017.
21. Jason King, *Irish Famine Archive* (2015), http://faminearchive.nuigalway.ie/. Accessed 14 June 2017.
22. Some landlords were initially lenient and generous, but for some, patience ran out as the situation dragged on and worsened and it became apparent that stopgaps, in the form of funding or rent alleviation, were not going to be enough to stem the tide of starvation or fill the depth of the widespread poverty. Such varied behavior is exemplified in documents accounted in: Mayo County Library, *The Famine in Mayo: A Portrait from Contemporary Sources, 1845–1850* (Castlebar, 2004).
23. William J. Smyth, '"Variations in Vulnerability": Understanding Where and Why the People Died', in J. Crowley, W.J. Smyth and M. Murphy (eds), Atlas of the Great Irish Famine (Cork, 2012), p. 187.
24. For further discussion on the cottage as a motif in representations of Famine homelessness see Niamh Ann Kelly, 'The Irish Cottage in Famine Remembrance', in D.A. Valone (ed.), *Ireland's Great Hunger, Volume 2* (Lanham, MD, Boulder, CO, New York, Toronto and Plymouth, 2010), pp. 140–60.

25. In 2017, the site had a substantial $5.3 million renovation over a twelve-month period. Marie Claire Digby, 'Irish Hunger Memorial in NYC reopens after €4.5 m renovation' *Irish Times*, 3 August 2017.

26. A ship's progress in 1847, considered to have been the worst and deadliest year of the Famine, is fictionalized to evocative effect in Joseph O'Connor's celebrated novel *Star of the Sea*, 2002.

27. Helen Litton, *The Irish Famine: An Illustrated History* (Dublin, 1994), p. 104.

28. O'Doherty also designed *The Great Hunger Memorial* in Westchester, New York, 2001. This is a bronze life-size figuration of a family group leaving a cottage, symbolically represented by two stone walls. Between the walls is an upturned keel, with potatoes transformed into skull shapes, indication of the failure of the potato crop and its consequence in death.

29. This is a source of debate among historians and the point on which accusations that the Irish Famine was a British-engineered genocide usually rest. Donnelly provides an account of these debates. Donnelly, *The Great Irish Potato Famine*, pp. 24–5. The controversy appears in popular culture, in the lyrics of Sinéad O'Connor's song 'Famine' in 1995: 'See Irish people were only allowed to eat potatoes /All of the other food, meat, fish, vegetables, /were shipped out of the country under armed guard / to England while the Irish people starved'. O'Connor et al., 1995. These lyrics are also discussed in David Lloyd, 'The Memory of Hunger', in D.E. Eng and D. Kazanjian (eds), *Loss: The Politics of Mourning* (Berkeley, CA, Los Angeles and London, 2003), pp. 205–28. Ted Greene notes the high extent of livestock and food exports leaving through Drogheda Port for Liverpool and other British ports, even during 1846–8, recounted in local newspaper reports, and in one example, the considerable contexts of 13 cargoes in one week are listed alongside an account of the financial struggles of the local workhouse. Ted Greene, *Drogheda: Its Place in Local History* (Julianstown, 2006), pp. 240–3.

30. Born in Dublin, Behan (1938-) is a member of Aosdána. Behan is also a member of the RHA and was a founder member of New Artists group in 1962 and the Project Arts Centre in Dublin in 1967. He has a number of public sculptures in Ireland, including the Liberty Tree in Carlow, commemorating the 1798 rebellion.

31. Between 1841 and 1851, the population of County Mayo fell by 29 per cent, from 388,887 to 247,830, with 114,057 attributed to deaths and emigration. Mayo County Library, *The Famine in Mayo*, p. v.

32. The mountain was a pilgrimage site in pre-Christian Ireland, with the tradition possibly 5,000 years old. There is evidence of a dry-stone oratory, dated AD 430–890, which could make it one of the oldest traces of a church in Ireland. A small visitors' centre was opened at the foot of the mountain in 2000. http://www.croagh-patrick.com/. Accessed 18 August 2017.

33. 17 March is St Patrick's Day, with large parades held annually in New York and many major cities worldwide where there is a significant Irish immigrant population, as well as Ireland, where it is an annual national holiday.

34. Guy Beiner, 'Commemorative Heritage and the Dialectic of Memory', in M. McCarthy (ed.), *Ireland's Heritages – Critical Perspective on Memory and Identity* (Farnham and Burlington, VT, 2005), p. 58.

35. Beiner contends that academic dismissal of popular commemorative events unhelpfully distances folk histories from academic history and ignores the need for more complex interdisciplinary study of heritage practices.

36. Colin Graham, '… "maybe that's just Blarney": Irish Culture and the Persistence of Authenticity', in C. Graham and R. Kirkland (eds), *Ireland and Cultural Theory: The Mechanics of Authenticity* (Basingstoke and London, 1999), p. 9. Graham proposes authenticity as a potentially useful means to consider varied aspects of Irish cultural studies, outlining three categories: Old, New and Ironic.

37. Pamela Gerrish Nunn, *Problem Pictures: Women and Men in Victorian Painting* (Menston, 1995), p. 125.

38. Nicol (1825–1904) also painted *The Emigrants/Irish Emigrants Waiting for a Train*, 1864, set in Ballinasloe train station, County Galway. Nicol was 21 years old when he first came to Ireland. It is likely that he did not witness the worst-affected areas in the rural west and south, but was aware of the Famine through contemporary print media. For more, see Brendan Rooney, 'Erskine Nicol R.S.A. A.R.A. 1825–1904', in N. Figgis and B. Rooney (eds), *Irish Paintings in the National Gallery of Ireland, Vol. I* (Dublin, 2001), pp. 14–17.

39. http://www.mcny.org/Collections/paint/Painting/pttcat32.htm. Accessed 10 January 2015. Waugh (1814–85) was noted for his panoramas. The museum's website also notes:

    > In 1860 there were 105,123 immigrants admitted at Castle Garden, of whom 47,330 were Irish, 37,899 German, and 11,361 English […] The ethnic prejudice faced by rural Irish entering this country is indicated in the trunk in the lower right labeled "Pat Murfy for Ameriky" and in the almost simian caricatures of the Irish farm boys attired in worn frock coats, peaked hats, and outmoded knee pants.

40. Barry Moreno, *Images of America: Castle Garden and Battery Park* (Charleston, SC, Chicago, Portsmouth and San Francisco, 2007), p. 7. Waugh was noted for his panoramas. Waugh's recognition of the new use of Castle Garden dates the painting after 1850, though it was painted as a homecoming image after a 'grand tour' to Italy, which ended in 1849.

41. Allen (1832–1914) was the first female honorary member of the Royal Hibernian Academy in 1878. She lived her adult life between Manchester and Dublin. This painting was exhibited in 1876, under the title *The Last Hour in the Old Country* at the Manchester City Gallery. Murphy remarks: 'Considering the antagonism between the British and Irish communities, this was a controversial subject for an Irish woman to show in Britain.' Derville Murphy, 'Margaret Allen, Social Commentator', *Irish Arts Review* xxvii/1

(2010), p. 90. Discussing subsequent works, Murphy makes the case for Allen as a nationalist artist and suggests that Elizabeth Butler was the next to follow in Allen's nationalistic terms with her 1890 work *Evicted*. Murphy draws attention to the lack of depth in Allen's backgrounds, citing the influence of photography on her work. Ibid.

42. Ibid.
43. http://jeaniejohnston.ie/ and www.dunbrody.com. Accessed 20 October 2017.
44. 'State to Part-Fund Famine Ship Replica', *Irish Times*, 29 March 2000. This historical information is from the Dunbrody website. The John F. Kennedy Trust is a charitable trust designed to promote the memory of the American President through a number of projects in the area, including the sponsorship of the *Dunbrody* ship. New Ross is considered to be the ancestral home of the Kennedy family and there is a large JFK Memorial Park just outside New Ross town. The onshore *Dunbrody* visitor centre received a €2.5 million investment from the JFK Trust in 2010. Elaine Furlong, 'Dunbrody May Not Sail Again – It's Not Worth It', *Irish Independent,* 17 February 2010. The Dunbrody Famine Ship Experience has expanded, on land, to include a restaurant and an Irish America Hall of Fame.
45. Guides on the *Dunbrody* Famine Ship Experience state that the characters and stories are drawn from historical evidence such as letters and diaries of Famine-era passengers on the *Dunbrody*.
46. Christopher Balme, 'Staging the Pacific: Framing Authenticity in Performances for Tourists at the Polynesian Cultural Center', *Theatre Journal* l/4 (1998), pp. 53–70. Balme's analysis is based on a visit to the centre in Hawaii.
47. Ibid., p. 67.
48. In the late 1990s the Irish government gave IEP 4.5 million to the Jeanie Johnston Project for the building of a replica, but by 2002 had given €13 million in total. It was valued in 2015 at €700,000. Olivia Kelly, 'Replica Famine Ship "Jeanie Johnston" Sinks in Value', *Irish Times*, 22 May 2015. The historical information is from the *Jeanie Johnston* website and a previously available on-board visitor leaflet. Tourism Ireland, *The Jeanie Johnston Walk-Around Guide* (n.d.).
49. Tourism Ireland, *The Jeanie*.
50. Nine separate representations are identified:
    (1) Ellen Mahony and her children;
    (2) Young Margaret Conway;
    (3) Margaret Ryal and Baby Nicholas;
    (4) Patrick Kearney;
    (5) James Stack and Family;
    (6) Margaret Prendergast;
    (7) Doctor Richard Biennerhassett;
    (8) Musician and Child; and
    (9) Captain James Attridge.

Women dominate as subjects in the emigrant tableau on the *Jeanie Johnston*, as pointed out in the text on 'Mary Prendergast', who followed her brother to the USA in 1854, though likely did not find him: 'No other emigrant group from Europe contained as many single women as the Irish. The women were predominantly young, like Mary, and many of them found jobs as domestic servants in the United States and Canada'. Ibid.

51. Emma Willis, *Theatricality, Dark Tourism and Ethical Spectatorship: Absent Others* (Basingstoke and New York, 2014), p. 219.
52. Ibid., p. 215.
53. Laurence M. Geary, '"The Noblest Offering That Nation Ever Made to Nation": American Philanthropy and the Great Famine in Ireland', *Éire-Ireland* xlviii/3–4 (2013), p. 126.
54. The Gaelic Revival is the term generally applied to a range of mid- to late nineteenth-century national movements that promoted Irish culture, language, history and folklore. These interests became strongly associated with wider calls for political independence for Ireland which culminated in the 1916 Rising. Key advocates included Pádraig (Patrick) Pearse, Douglas Hyde (later the First President of Ireland), Alice Milligan, Countess Constance Markievicz and Eoin O'Neill (founder of the Gaelic League in 1893, the key movement of the revival which prioritized and encouraged the importance of the Irish language), among many others. Archeological finds, such as the Tara Brooch in 1850 and the Ardagh Hoard in 1868, added fuel to the revivalist interest in pre-plantation material culture. Aspects of the revival movement expanded to formalize support for Gaelic games, with the founding of the Gaelic Athletic Association (1814); cultural revivals in literature, with Lady Gregory (1852–1932) and W.B. Yeats (1865–1939) setting up the Abbey Theatre (1904), for example; and stylistic influences in visual arts and crafts, exemplified by the establishment of the textile guild, Dun Emer (1903), and a stained glass studio, An Tur Gloine (1903). These cultural societies reflected on desires to define a national culture with particular respect for what were perceived as historical customs including Celtic and early Christian traditions.
55. Discussed in: Edward Said, 'Invention, Memory, and Place', in W.J.T. Mitchell (ed.), *Landscape and Power* (Chicago and London, 2002). Said acknowledges the work edited by Eric Hobsbawm and Terence Ranger, first edited in 1983. Eric Hobsbawm and Terence Ranger, (eds), *The Invention of Tradition* (Cambridge, UK, New York, Melbourne and Madrid, 2000).
56. Paul Gilroy, *The Black Atlantic: Modernity and Double Consciousness* (London and New York, 1993).
57. Ibid., p. 89.
58. Ibid., p. 218.
59. Ibid.
60. Fintan O'Toole, *The Ex-Isle of Erin* (Dublin, 1996), p. 114.
61. Ibid., p. 112.

62. The web content builds upon Trevor McClaughlin's two-volume account of emigrant experiences in an extraordinary register of all Irish female orphans who came to Sydney, Melbourne, Adelaide and Hobart between 1848–1851: *Barefoot and Pregnant? Irish Famine Orphans in Australia* Documents and Register (Victoria, 1991). The Famine Orphan Girl Database begun by McClaughlin is continuously updated, at time of writing, by the painstaking research work of Perry McIntyre, with support from descendants of the workhouse orphan girls.
63. www.irishfaminememorial.org/en/orphans/database/. Accessed 19 October 2017.
64. Graham, '"… maybe"', p. 11.
65. Ibid., p. 12.
66. Lloyd, 'The Memory', p. 225.

3   Sites of Memory and the Others of History

1. David Brett, 'Things in Their Places', *Visual Culture in Britain* x/2 (2009), p. 126.
2. Ibid., p. 135.
3. Tony Bennett, 'The Exhibitionary Complex', *New Formations* iv (1988), p. 76.
4. Brett, 'Things', p. 201.
5. Susan M. Pearce, 'Collecting Reconsidered', in S.M. Pearce (ed.), *Interpreting Objects and Collections* (London and New York, 1994), pp. 193–204. Pearce outlines sequences of fetishism and gradations of collecting as processes that differentiate between types of associative individual and group value systems.
6. Pierre Nora, *Realms of Memory: Rethinking the French Past. Volume I: Conflicts and Divisions* (New York, 1996), p. 13.
7. Luke Gibbons, 'The Global Cure? History, Therapy and the Celtic Tiger', in P. Kirby, L. Gibbons and M. Cronin (eds), *Reinventing Ireland: Culture, Society and the Global Economy* (London and Sterling, VA, 2002), p. 104.
8. Ibid., p. 105.
9. Barbara Kirshenblatt-Gimblett, *Destination Culture* (Berkeley, CA, Los Angeles and London, 1998), p. 144.
10. Ibid., pp. 166–7.
11. Paul Williams, *Memorial Museums: The Global Rush to Commemorate Atrocities* (Oxford and New York, 2007), p. 96.
12. Ibid., p. 97.
13. Juliet Steyn, 'Vicissitudes of Representation: Remembering and Forgetting', in J. Kidd, S. Cairns, A. Drago, A. Ryall and M. Stearn (eds), *Challenging History in the Museum* (Abingdon and New York, 2016), p. 143.
14. Jill Bennett, *Empathic Vision: Affect, Trauma, and Contemporary Art* (Stanford, CA, 2005), p. 99.

15. Ibid., p. 98.
16. Ibid., p. 69.
17. Ibid., p. 10.
18. Thomas W. Laqueur, 'Introduction', *Representations (Grounds for Remembering)* 69/Special Issue (2000), p. 7.
19. This permitted '(for the first time) outdoor relief from the rates for certain classes of paupers and for the able-bodied poor, if the workhouses were full, and required elected boards of guardians to relieve all those classed as destitute'. Peter Gray, 'British Relief Measures', in J. Crowley, W.J. Smyth and M. Murphy (eds), *Atlas of the Great Irish Famine* (Cork, 2012), p. 83. The categories of people to receive aid were: 1. destitute, helpless or impotent, 2. destitute, able-bodied persons not holding land and 3. able-bodied persons who held small portions of land. Peter Foynes, *The Great Famine in Skibbereen and District* (Skibbereen, 2004), p. 63.
20. Christine Kinealy, *Apparitions of Death and Disease: The Great Hunger in Ireland* (Hamden, CT, 2014), p. 31.
21. Christine Kinealy, 'The Operation of the Poor Law during the Famine', in Crowley et al., *Atlas*, p. 91.
22. Noel Kissane, *The Irish Famine: A Documentary History* (Dublin, 1995), p. 102.
23. Christine Kinealy, *The Great Irish Famine: Impact, Ideology and Rebellion* (Basingstoke and New York, 2002), pp. 61–89; Kissane, *The Irish Famine*, pp. 123–35.
24. James Donnelly Jnr, *The Great Irish Potato Famine* (Stroud, 2002), p. 83.
25. Kinealy, *The Great Irish Famine*, pp. 68–9.
26. Donnelly, *The Great Irish Potato Famine*, p. 80.
27. Kinealy, *The Great Irish Famine*, p. 68.
28. After they closed their soup kitchens, the Society of Friends continued to provide aid in the form of fishing and farming help, distributing tackle and seeds. Kinealy, *The Great Irish Famine*, p. 69. Unlike other religious groups providing aid, the Society showed little interest in what came to be termed souperism. Liam O'Flaherty's novel *Famine* depicts scenarios based on tensions between religious factions, voluntary committees and government agencies in the administration of relief; as fears of proselytizing could be a trigger for community upheaval. Liam O'Flaherty, *Famine* (Dublin, 1979), pp. 200–20. Such tensions resulted in the breakdown of many administering groups.
29. The recipe was developed by Alexis Soyer, a famous French chef at London's Reform Club. It was widely used in Government soup kitchens but was criticized by others, including the Society of Friends, as lacking in adequate nutritional value. Donnelly, *The Great Irish Potato Famine*, p. 83.
30. 'Teagasc is the agriculture and food development authority in Ireland. Its mission is to support science-based innovation in the agri-food sector and the

broader bioeconomy that will underpin profitability, competitiveness and sustainability.' www.teagasc.ie/. Accessed 30 August 2017.

31. For more detail on workhouse designs and on the differences between first-generation (1839–49) and second-generation (1850–3) workhouse layout designs see Paschal Mahoney, *Grim Bastilles of Despair: The Poor Law Union Workhouses in Ireland* (Hamden, CT, 2016), pp. 29, 42.

32. Jennifer Bonnell and Roger L. Simon, '"Difficult" Exhibitions and Intimate Encounters', *Museum and Society* v/2 (2007), p. 68.

33. Ibid., p. 76.

34. Ibid., p. 79.

35. Benda Hofmeyr, '"Isn't Art an Activity that Gives Things a Face?" Lévinas on the Power of Art', *Image and Narrative, Online Magazine of the Visual Narrative* (18: Thinking Pictures) viii/1 (2007), imageandnarrative.be/ thinking_pictures/hofmeyr.htm.

36. Hofmeyr cites Lévinas's example of 'the needy other – the orphan, the widow, the stranger'. Ibid.

37. Emmanuel Lévinas, 'Ethics of the Infinite', in R. Kearney, *States of Mind: Dialogues with Contemporary Thinkers on the European Mind* (Manchester, 1995), pp. 177–99.

38. Bonnell and Simon, '"Difficult"', p. 68.

39. Kirshenblatt-Gimblett, *Destination Culture*, pp. 17–78.

40. Eilean Hooper-Greenhill, *Museums and the Interpretation of Visual Culture* (London and New York, 2000), p. 25.

41. Ibid., p. 24.

42. Ibid., p. 13.

43. For a comprehensive account of the Strokestown site, its history, archive and evolution into a museum, see Ciaran Reilly, *Strokestown and the Great Irish Famine* (Dublin, 2014).

44. Callery's commitment was recognized in 2017, when he was awarded a European Union Prize for Cultural Heritage/Europa Nostra Award for dedicated service to heritage (through his work on the museum and archive at Strokestown House). Patsy McGarry, 'Famine Memorial, Jim Callery recognized by EU for History Role', *Irish Times*, 18 April 2017. The museum's first curator was Luke Dodd, succeeded by John O'Driscoll. The estate has an extensive archive, including much material on the Famine era in the locality.

45. Marese McDonagh, 'Strokestown House and Famine Museum to Begin Fresh Chapter', *Irish Times*, 5 October 2015. The article notes that the site receives up to 50,000 visitors a year, and, according the IHT that two-thirds of money spent visiting a heritage site are spent outside the property but in the local community.

46. http://www.strokestownpark.ie/. Accessed 9 May 2017.

47. The house was mostly built by Richard Cassels, the architect of Leinster House in Dublin and Russborough House in County Wicklow.

48. Ciarán Ó Murchadha, *The Great Famine: Ireland's Agony 1845–1852* (London and New York, 2011), p. 127.
49. Discussed in further detail in: Niamh Ann Kelly, 'Similarity and Difference: The Appearance of Suffering at the Strokestown Famine Museum', in A. Hoffman and E. Peeren (eds), *Representation Matters: (Re) Articulating Collective Identities in a Postcolonial World* (Amsterdam, 2010), pp. 133–54.
50. Text panels outline the respective uses of each stool. A Somali singer is quoted implying the African stool originated in Somalia.
51. Minh-ha as quoted in Nancy Chen, '"Speaking Nearby": A Conversation with Trinh T. Minh-ha', Visual Anthropology Review viii/1 (1992), p. 87. Murphy discussed anti-documentary impulses in relation to her film *Maeve* (1981). Her film *Ann Devlin* (1984) was shot at Strokestown estate. Desmond Bell, 'Interview with Filmmaker Pat Murphy', *Kinema*, Spring 2007.
52. Paula Findlen, 'The Two Cultures of Scholarship?', *The History of Science* 96/2 (2005), p. 236. Findlen describes microhistory as a genre of historical writing in terms of its emergence 'from the study of the same period that produced the sweeping narratives of scientific revolution', thus implying that 'a close reading of singular episodes producing unusually rich documentation, preferably of people whose voices might otherwise go unheard, revealed a different and more complex understanding of the past' as a means of resistance to hegemonic understandings of the late medieval and early modern periods. Ibid., p. 232.
53. Quoted in Reilly, *Strokestown*, pp. 183–4.
54. The Office of Public Works manages all state buildings and properties in Ireland. Its heritage remit consists of the National Monuments Services, Historic Properties Service and Visitors Service and it collects art for the state collection. www.opw.ie/en/nhp/. Accessed 17 November 2016.
55. The Young Irelanders were linked to the founding of *The Nation* newspaper by Charles Gavan Duffy, John Blake Dillon and Thomas Davis. The men, who were from three different provinces in Ireland, were eventually distinguished within the Repeal Association (which sought the repeal of the 1800 Act of Union between Great Britain and Ireland) from its leader, Daniel O'Connell. There is a monumental white marble statue of Smith O'Brien on a granite plinth on O'Connell Street in Dublin's city centre, designed by Michael Farrell and erected in 1870. It is significant as the first monument to a supporter of armed resistance to British rule to be erected in Dublin. Archive Consultancy for Dublin City Council, History of Monuments: O'Connell Street Area, Report (Dublin, 2003), pp. 9–12.
56. Alvin Jackson, *Ireland 1798–1998* (Malden, MA/Oxford and Victoria, 1999), p. 55.
57. Jackson notes a contemporary *Times* journalist's sneer at the 'cabbage-patch revolution'. Ibid., p. 56.
58. Niamh O'Sullivan, *The Tombs of a Departed Race: Illustrations of Ireland's Great Hunger* (Hamden, CT, 2014), p. 55.

Notes to Pages 111–114

59. Smith O'Brien's father is claimed to have descended from 'the High King Brian Boru, who defeated the Danes at the battle of Clontarf in 1014' (OPW leaflet).
60. Van Diemen's Land is the former name of the Australian state of Tasmania and from 1803 to 1853 it was a British penal colony. Some Irish were sent there for involvement with the Young Ireland Movement.
61. Hooper-Greenhill, *Museums*, p. 16.
62. Roy F. Foster, *The Irish Story: Telling Tales and Making it Up in Ireland* (London, 2001), p. 25.
63. The National Museum had nineteenth-century forerunners: the Museum of Irish Industry, the National History Museum and the Museum of Art and Science. All of which were 'bound up with the influential RDS (Royal Dublin Society)'. Marie Bourke, *The Story of Irish Museums 1970–2000: Culture, Identity and Education* (Cork, 2011), p. 172. The 1877 Science and Art Museum Act saw the establishment of the Dublin Museum of Science and Art, which in 1890 was housed in its own building on Kildare Street. The Natural History Museum continues to be separately housed on Merrion Square, and the Museum of Decorative Arts and History opened at Collins Barracks in 1997.
64. Douglas Newton, 'Old Wine in New Bottles, and the Reverse', in F.S. Kaplan (ed.), *Museums and the Making of 'Ourselves': The Role of Objects in National Identity* (London and New York, 1994), p. 288. Newton discusses the lasting effects of paradigms of conquest and display, citing ongoing instances of material and cultural theft to create collections, alongside legitimate imperatives, citing, as an illegitimate example, thefts by Iraqi forces from Kuwaiti museums prior to the Persian Gulf War. Ibid., pp. 270–1.
65. Iain Chambers, 'Afterword: After the Museum', in I. Chambers, A. De Angelis, C. Ianniciello, M. Orabona and M. Quadraro (eds), *The Postcolonial Museum: The Arts of Memory and the Pressures of History* (Abingdon and New York, 2016), p. 244.
66. Eilean Hooper-Greenhill, 'Interpretative Communities, Strategies and Repertoires', in S. Watson (ed.), *Museums and Their Communities* (New York and Abingdon, 2007), p. 90.
67. For example, a panel in the first exhibition area draws attention to the fact that the collection has only been developed in a programmatic way from 1949. The relationship between expectations of representation and reality is highlighted in another panel text, outlining the museum's mixing of visual sources to portray history:

> Life in rural Ireland has often been portrayed in a romantic way. Many artists portrayed the people of the countryside and the islands as heroic, innocent, and timeless, making their way of life seem pure and appealing. In our own time, tourist postcards and posters have promoted an idealised image of a peaceful and pleasant life lived on the small farms of Ireland. Popular films such as *Man of Aran* and *The Quiet Man* helped perpetuate the idea of an heroic or idyllic rural life

in Ireland. However, in reality the work was generally hard, the diet was often poor, and death from diseases like tuberculosis was common. Life was far from simple — people needed detailed knowledge and specific skills to survive. Yet, they could also enjoy the comforts of family and friends, and the traditional pleasures of storytelling and music. A range of artistic images is contrasted with photographs, which help to show the reality of Irish life — harsh for many, but relatively good for others.

Another panel describes the museum's distinction between the collections of Folklife and Folklore: the first concerns tangible aspects of life, the second intangible aspects.

68. https://www.museum.ie/Country-Life. Accessed 15 October 2017.
69. These are titled: *Romanticism and Reality*; *The Natural Environment*; *The Time*; *Trades and Crafts*; *Activities in the Home*; *Working on the Land and Water*; *Life in the Community*.
70. The Irish National Land League was founded by Michael Davitt in 1879, and its president was Charles Stewart Parnell.
71. Fenians is the term used for both the Fenian Brotherhood and the Irish Republican Brotherhood, which were fraternal organizations dedicated to Irish sovereignty that were founded in the mid-nineteenth century.
72. Mieke Bal, *Double Exposures: The Subject of Cultural Analysis* (New York and London, 1996), p. 299.
73. Kirshenblatt-Gimblett, *Destination Culture*, pp. 166–76.
74. Ibid., pp. 169–70.
75. William Logan and Keir Reeves, 'Introduction: Remembering Places of Pain and Shame', in W. Logan and K. Reeves (eds), *Places of Pain and Shame: Dealing with 'Difficult Heritage'* (Abingdon and New York, 2009), p. 13.
76. Trinh T. Minh-ha, 'The Totalizing Quest of Meaning', in N. Wheale (ed.), *The Postmodern Arts* (London and New York, 1995), pp. 258–78.
77. Jenny Kidd, 'Introduction: Challenging History in the Museum', in Kidd et al., *Challenging History*, p. 4.
78. Kirshenblatt-Gimblett, *Destination Culture*, p. 162.
79. Discussed in Henrietta Riegel, 'Into the Heart of Irony: Ethnographic Exhibitions and the Politics of Difference', in S. Macdonald and G. Fyfye (eds), *Theorizing Museums* (Oxford and Cambridge, MA, 2004), p. 88.
80. Quoted in Colm Tóibín and Diarmuid Ferriter, *The Irish Famine* (London, 2004), p. 21.
81. Christine Kinealy, 'The Great Irish Famine – A Dangerous Memory?' in A. Gribben (ed.), *The Great Famine and the Irish Diaspora in America* (Amherst, MA, 1999), pp. 239–53.
82. Quoted in Peter Gray, 'Memory and the Great Irish Famine', in P. Gray and K. Oliver (eds), *The Memory of Catastrophe* (Manchester and New York, 2004), p. 59.

83. See: Breandán Mac Suibhne, *Subjects Lacking Works? The Gray Zone of the Great Famine* (Hamden, CT, 2017) and Mac Suibhne, *The End of Outrage: Post-Famine Adjustment in Rural Ireland* (Oxford, 2017).
84. John L. Lahey, President of Quinnipiac University, quoted in introductory text on museum website. ighm.org. Accessed 13 August 2017.

4 After-Images: Temporary Commemorative Exhibitions on the Famine

1. All quotations and references for this proposal are taken from the Personal Research File of Catherine Marshall (2005).
2. The full text of Davis's essay, as it was originally published in *The Nation*, can be found in Fintan Cullen (ed.), *Sources in Irish Art – A Reader* (Cork, 2000), pp. 65–70.
3. Writers included Tom Paulin, Seamus Heaney, Seamus Deane, Richard Kearney, Declan Kiberd, Terence Brown, Marianne Elliot, Robert McCartney, Eanna Mulloy, Michael Farrell, Patrick J. McGrory, Terry Eagleton, Fredric Jameson and Edward Said.
4. For example, outside of Ireland, the University of Liverpool founded the Institute for Irish Studies (1988), and the University of Notre Dame, Indiana, set up the Keough-Naughton Institute of Irish Studies (1993); and, within Ireland, the National University of Ireland, Galway, established a Centre for Irish Studies (2002).
5. Other exhibitions include the 1995 Sculpture Society of Ireland and the West Cork Arts Centre Famine project; the Skibbereen Famine Workhouse Symposium, in which seven artists (Pauline Agnew, Agnes Devlin, Annette Hennessey, Carol Kavanagh, Lotte Pile, Alannah Robbins and Ad van Turnhout) created works in response to the site of the former local workhouse, with a set of postcards produced to remember the event; and in 1997, the National Museum of Ireland's touring commemorative exhibition was curated by Michael Kenny which highlighted a general paucity of Famine artefacts.
6. This usage of 'monumental time' borrows from Michael Herzfeld's use of the term as counter to social experiences of time, which he distinguishes as follows:

> Between social and monumental time lies a discursive chasm. Social time is the grist of everyday experience. It is above all the kind of time in which events cannot be predicted btu in which every effort can be made to influence them [...] Monumental time, by contrast is reductive and generic. [...] it reduces social experience to collective predictability. Its main focus is on the past – a past constituted by categories and stereotypes.

> Michael Herzfeld, *A Place in History – Social and Monumental Time in a Cretan Town* (New Jersey, 1991), p. 10.

This can be also related to Paul Ricoeur's conception of complex 'monumental time' as 'secreted' by 'monumental history, to use Nietzsche's expression' in his analysis of Virginia Woolf's 1925 novel, *Mrs Dalloway*. He writes: '[...] chronological time is but one audible expression [of monumental time]. To this monumental time belong the figures of authority and power that form the counterweight to the living times experienced by Clarissa and Septimus [...]'. Paul Ricoeur, *Time and Narrative, Volume 2* (Chicago and London, 1985), p. 106. He later discusses 'an insurmountable fissure [...] between the monumental time of the world and the mortal time of the soul' in which 'the temporal experiences' of characters in the book 'are ordered'. Ibid., p. 110. From this, monumental time can be extrapolated as both differentiated from and, to some extent, differentiating of experiences of biographical time.

7. James Young, *At Memory's Edge: After-Images of the Holocaust in Contemporary Art and Architecture* (New Haven, CT and London, 2000), pp. 3–4.

8. Stephen Bann, 'Art History & Museums', in M.A. Cheetham, M.A. Holly and K. Moxley (eds), *The Subjects of Art History: Historical Objects in Contemporary Perspective* (Cambridge, 1998), pp. 233, 237.

9. Svetlana Alpers, 'Is Art History?', in S. Kemal and I. Gaskell (eds), *Explanation and Value in the Arts* (Cambridge, 1993), p. 111.

10. Ibid., p. 123.

11. Ann Rigney, 'Plentitude, Scarcity and the Circulation of Cultural Memory', *Journal of European Studies* 35 /1 (2005), p. 15.

12. Ibid., p. 25.

13. Ibid., p. 24.

14. Silke Arnolde-de Simine, *Trauma, Empathy, Nostalgia* (Basingstoke and New York, 2013), pp. 40–1.

15. Quoted in Nancy Chen, '"Speaking Nearby": A Conversation with Trinh T. Minh-ha', *Visual Anthropology Review* viii/1 (1992), p. 87.

16. Cormac Ó Gráda, 'Making History in the 1940s and 1950s: The Saga of the Great Famine', *The Irish Review* xii (1992), pp. 87–107.

17. Ibid., p. 99.

18. National College of Art (Ireland) *Thomas Davis and the Young Ireland Movement Centenary: Exhibition of Pictures of Irish Historical Interest*, (Exhibition Catalogue) (Dublin 1946).

19. Including Cathal MacLúain, *Ocras 1850 (Hunger 1850)*; Michael O'Farrell, *Decorative Design (Evocative of 1846–47, Famine)*; Father Jack Hanlon, *The Eviction*; Geo. F. Campbell, *Evictions*; and Louis le Brocquy, *The Emigrant*.

20. Described as a 'journeyman artist', Davidson (1879–1954) earned her living through sales, commissions, teaching and writing, which Cahill suggests gave her a defining 'empathy with her subjects'. Katherine Cahill, 'In the Mainstream of Irish Naturalism: The Art of Lilian Lucy Davidson', *Irish Arts Review Yearbook* xv (1999), p. 36. Born in Wicklow, Davidson was well travelled, exhibited regularly at the Watercolour Society and the Royal Hibernian Academy and, though buried in a cemetery, her grave was unmarked. Ibid., p. 44.

21. Ibid. The appropriation of the west of Ireland as a motif for exploring Irishness was common in art of the early twentieth century, in the work of Sean Keating and Jack Yeats, for example. Kennedy, writing on the RHA exhibition of 1945, recalls how reviewer Stephen Rynne 'lamented the dominance of pictures relating to the west of Ireland. [...] and he pleaded with the authors of such works to "eschew Connemara, cancel reservations in Aran and have a think about the whole matter". S.B. Kennedy, *Irish Art and Modernism 1880–1950* (Belfast, 1991), p. 161.

22. Born in County Down, Woods (1893–1991) was a member of the Royal Ulster Academy, travelled and exhibited regularly and was governor of Belfast College of Art.

23. Lazybeds were a means of cultivating through a system of ridges and furrows, and at this time were developed with very narrow drainage and big banks, due to the scarcity of land among the densely populated rural areas. They are thought to have been a contributing factor to the speed at which the blight devastated the potato crops.

24. MacGonigal (1900–79) was Professor of Painting at the Metropolitan School of Art, member of the RHA and exhibited widely, nationally and internationally, during his life. Born in Dublin, he painted in the west of Ireland many times and Crofts notes his interest in the 'material culture of the Gaeltacht' in his 'series of western women painting of the late 1930s and early 1940s'. Susan Crofts, 'Maurice MacGonigal PRHA (1900–79) and his Western Paintings', *Irish Arts Review Yearbook* xiii (1997), p. 139. Brandt (1909–81) was born in Belfast and died in Dublin. A member of the Royal Hibernian Academy and an associate of the Royal College of Art, she was a professional portraitist, executed a number of public commissions and murals and was a member of the Board of the National Gallery of Ireland.

25. Ibid.

26. Cristín Leach, 'Muriel Brandt's 1916 Breadline', *Sunday Times (Ireland)*, 17 March 2016.

27. Kennedy, *Irish Art*, p. 115. Kennedy writes, 'It was, after all, an academy, and the business of academies is not to be innovative; yet it had failed, as Paul Henry earlier commented, to take *any* notice of the artistic revolution which began with impressionism in the late nineteenth century'. Ibid. See also Riann Coulter, 'Hibernian Salon des Refuses', *Irish Arts Review* xx/3 (2003), pp. 80–5.

28. Paul Ricoeur, *Time and Narrative, Volume 3* (Chicago, 1988), p. 188.

29. Ibid., Ricoeur's comments are discussed by Kelleher in her analysis of female representations in Famine literature, with individuations of famines through the portrayal of victims in literature as an effective strategy of depicting horror. Margaret Kelleher, *The Feminization of Famine: Expressions of the Inexpressible?* (Cork, 1997), pp. 13, 6.

30. 'Historians are interested in facts; critics in impressions and judgements [...] And perhaps most important, historians deal with the art of the past, and

critics with the art of the present.' Michael Ann Holly, 'Past Looking', in S. Melville and B. Readings (eds), *Vision and Textuality* (London, 2005), p. 68.

31. Ibid., pp. 83, 84.

32. Teagasc, Exhibition Press Release (1995).

33. 'In Kerry, the summer of 1846, with its freakish weather patterns, was remembered as "Bliain na tuile" ["the year of the flood"], in Clare the winter of 1846 was "Bliain an Board of Works", and in Donegal, 1848 was "Bliain na Scidíní" ["the year of the small potatoes"].' Niall Ó Ciosáin, 'Famine Memory and the Popular Representation of Scarcity', in I. McBride (ed.), *History and Memory in Modern Ireland* (Cambridge, 2001), p. 117.

34. The society was founded in 1989, 'to promote the writings of the novelist and to celebrate the beauty of Moore Hall and Lough Carra.' George Moore Society, *Famine* (Exhibition Catalogue) (Claremorris, 1995), p. 3. The society retains a significant portion of the art exhibited in 1995 in its Famine collection, which is intermittently exhibited.

35. Ibid.

36. Ibid., pp. 6–7.

37. Ibid., p. 7.

38. Ibid., p. 6.

39. Ibid., pp. 5–7.

40. Fallon noted that a number of the more famous male artists in the show did not live in or engage with the Dublin art scene. Dublin, he suggested, had a 'very provincial tendency to run after every "international" fashion – usually when it is played out virtually everywhere else'. Ibid., p. 6.

41. Graham (1943–) was born in Mullingar, Ireland. A member of Aosdána, his focus on neo-expressionism in the 1980s brought him much artistic and critical attention. This work was also exhibited in 'The Quick and the Dead', Dublin City Gallery: The Hugh Lane, 2009. Graham describes the initial title as indicative of 'the "certain" view at the time that the "victims" of the famine were responsible for their own death, misery and emigration' (email correspondence, November 2016).

42. O'Donoghue (1953–) was born in Manchester to Irish parents. This painting (102 x 153 cm) is one of a group based on his mother's birthplace, in Erris, County Mayo, which suffered sustained economic effects of the Famine. The title was an expression used by her to describe experiences of poverty. ighm. org. Accessed 5 February 2017.

43. Cathal Póirtéir, *Famine Echoes* (Dublin, 1995), pp. 88–9.

44. John Crowley, 'Exhibiting the Great Famine', in N. Buttimer, C. Rynne and H. Guerin (eds), *The Heritage of Ireland – Natural, Man-Made and Cultural Heritage. Conservation and Interpretation* (Cork, 2000), p. 400.

45. Reprinted in full in the Preface to this book, and also printed as a frontspiece of J. Crowley, W.J. Smyth and M. Murphy (eds), *Atlas of the Great Irish Famine* (Cork, 2012).

46. Crowley, 'Exhibiting', p. 400.

47. IMMA, *Representations of the Famine, Press Release* (1998).

48. IMMA, *Súil Eile: Selected Works from the IMMA Collection at Ballina Arts Centre, County Mayo, Press Release* (2007). The work was purchased by the IMMA in 1997. Thallabhawn is an anglicized version of *Tallamh Bhan*, meaning White Ground. Mweelrea is from *Cnoc Maol Réidh*, which translates as 'bald hill with smooth top'. The mound of stones and bones features in a documentary by Radharc (1995) where the narrator picks up a bone from the mound while discussing the Famine.

49. Catherine Marshall, *Monuments and Memorials of the Great Famine* (Hamden, CT, 2014), p. 19.

50. Fionna Barber, *Art in Ireland since 1910* (London, 2013), p. 240.

51. Elizabeth Thompson (1846–1933) was a successful English artist and exhibited regularly at the Royal Academy (RA) in London. She was renowned for her large battlescenes. Her title, Lady Butler, came from her marriage to a colonial officer Major Sir William Butler, which led to a number of works on Irish subjects. *Evicted* was exhibited at the 1890 RA exhibition. Department of Irish Folklore, *Folk Tradition in Irish Art: An Exhibition of Paintings from the Collection of the Department of Irish Folklore, University College Dublin* (Dublin, 1993), p. 21.

52. Cited in Cullen (ed.), *Sources in Irish Art*, p. 85.

53. Cited in: Anne Crookshank and the Knight of Glin, *Ireland's Painters 1600–1940* (Yale, 2002), p. 263.

54. Jacques Rancière, *The Politics of Aesthetics* (London, 2004), p. 39. Rancière accentuates the 'logic of stories' as deference to the Aristotelian hierarchical distinction between story and history, which he repeals. Ibid., pp. 37–9.

55. Ibid., p. 13.

56. Ibid.

57. Kevin Whelan, 'Between Filiation and Affiliation: The Politics of Postcolonial Memory', in C. Carroll and P. King (eds), *Ireland and Postcolonial Theory* (Cork, 2003), p. 98.

58. Guy Beiner, 'Recycling the Dustbin of Irish History: The Radical Challenge of 'Folk Memory'", *History Ireland* xiv/1 (2006).

59. Ibid., p. 47.

5   Grief, Graves and Signs of the Dead

1. Celtic high crosses, late eighth to twelfth centuries, demonstrate a hybrid of pagan and early Christian influence on the material culture and visual styles of Irish ecclesiastical art. The cruciform had a ring in the centre, surrounding the meeting point of shaft and arms. Usually didactic in pictorial content and colourfully painted in their original state, they served as a visual aid for the passing on through generations of Christian stories. For fuller introduction to the physical and symbolic complexities of the forms see: Peter Harbison, *Irish High Crosses with the Figure Sculptures Explained* (Drogheda, 1994); and

Hilary Richardson and John Scarry, *An Introduction to Irish High Crosses* (Cork 1990).

2. Stéphanie Toussaint and Alain Decrop, 'The Père-Lachaise Cemetery: Between Dark Tourism and Heterotopic Consumption', in L. White and E. Frew (eds), *Dark Tourism and Place Identity: Managing and Interpreting Dark Places* (New York, 2013), p. 15.

3. In this, Beiner refers to when contentious, often top-down, decision-making can have decisive influence over the final forms of remembrances of the past. Guy Beiner, 'Recycling the Dustbin of Irish History: The Radical Challenge of "Folk Memory"', *History Ireland* xiv/1 (2006), p. 46.

4. Colin Davis, 'Can the Dead Speak to Us? De Man, Lévinas and Agamben', *Culture, Theory and Critique* xlv/10 (2004), pp. 77–89.

5. Ibid., p. 80.

6. Ibid., pp. 88–9.

7. Recorded extents of increased excess mortality rates vary. Liam Kennedy, Paul S. Ell, E.M. Crawford and L.A. Clarkson, *Mapping the Great Irish Famine* (Dublin, 1999), pp. 37–8. 'The estimates necessarily hinge on assumptions about noncrisis birthrates and death rates, the decline in births during the famine and net emigration.' Cormac Ó Gráda, *Famine: A Short History* (Princeton, NJ and Oxford, 2009), p. 93.

8. Early in the novel, *Famine*, there is an affecting portrait of impending doom as a protagonist insists on spending money on a wake, in the face of a period of starvation. Liam O'Flaherty, *Famine* (Dublin 1979).

9. Cathal Póirtéir, *Famine Echoes* (Dublin, 1995), p. 8.

10. David Crane, *Empires of the Dead: How One Man's Vision Led to the Creation of WW1's War Graves* (London, 2013). Later known as the Imperial War Graves Commission and latterly as the Commonwealth War Graves Commission.

11. Counter to this convention of naming is that of 'the unknown soldier', common to many soldiers' graveyards and memorial sites. As a universal epithet for all unnamed dead soldiers, it is a persuasive reminder that the dead can be actively unnamed in remembrance.

12. The names were carved by stonemason, Brendan O'Riordan, and the project pioneered by locals, including historian, Martin Bob O'Dwyer. O'Dwyer also developed the local Cashel Folk Village, Cashel, County Tipperary in 1984, which includes a Famine Room derived around a Famine eviction scene vignette staged with mannequins.

13. Kennedy et al. point to the shift in population ratios between rural and urban, prior to and after the immediate effects of the blight: 90 per cent (close to 8,000,000) lived in the countryside in 1841, whereas 82 per cent (close to 5,000,000) did by 1871. Kennedy et al., *Mapping*, p. 27. In 1841, Cork had a higher population density than most of Connacht and Leinster. The surrounding border counties of Limerick, Tipperary and Waterford

were equally well populated at this time. Only Kerry to the west was comparatively sparsely populated. Ibid., p. 34. The Skibbereen Union, and the area known from 1850 as the Skull Union, were less well served in terms of relief (workhouse places and outdoor rations) than surrounding unions (ibid., pp. 127, 135), singling the area out for relatively worse destitution at a local level.

14. Interestingly, the NFC's focus, as instigated by Ireland's first president, Eamon de Valera, was on rural informants in the interview processes, which, while recording the valuable and insightful experiences of a reducing rural population, also, arguably, suited the ideological apparatus of a new nation implying that the more authentic voices of Ireland were to be found in the depleted demographic of rural places.

15. Toussaint and Decrop, 'The Père-Lachaise Cemetery', p. 14.

16. Mark McGowan, 'Famine, Facts and Fabrication: An Examination of Diaries from the Irish Famine Migration to Canada', *The Canadian Journal of Irish Studies* xxxiii/2 (2007), p. 49.

17. The cross was built at the instigation of the AOH, following on the 50-year marking of 1847 when members of the Irish community made a pilgrimage to Grosse Île. Michael Quigley, 'Grosse Île: Canada's Famine Memorial', in A. Gribben (ed.), *The Great Famine and the Irish Diaspora in America* (Amherst, MA, 1999), p. 150. Celtic cross forms are recurrent symbols of commemoration for many aspects of Irish history, including the Famine, and have been widely appropriated as signifying Irish national identity. In 1998, for example, in Kingston, Ontario, a Celtic cross was erected to the memory of the Famine.

18. McGowan, 'Famine', p. 48.

19. Quoted in Quigley, 'Grosse Île', p. 148. Douglas also wrote, 'It was with much difficulty that people could be found to make coffins, dig graves and bury the dead. As already observed, all our regular hospital servants were ill or exhausted by fatigue.' Quoted in Noel Kissane, *The Irish Famine: A Documentary History* (Dublin, 1995), p. 164.

20. Quigley, 'Grosse Île', pp. 148–9.

21. Mary Daly, 'Historians and the Famine: A Beleaguered Species?', *Irish Historical Studies*, xxx/120 (1997), p. 598.

22. O'Brien notes that some Irish women may have disappeared as identifiable statistics of survival, by way of marriage into French families, with their Irish names rendered socially invisible. Kathleen O'Brien, 'Famine Commemorations: Visual Dialogues, Visual Silences', in D.A. Valone and C. Kinealy (eds), *Ireland's Great Hunger: Silence, Memory and Commemoration* (Lanham, MD and Oxford, 2002), p. 288.

23. McGowan, 'Famine', p. 50.

24. Ibid., p. 53.

25. Jason King, 'Remembering and Forgetting the Famine Irish in Quebec: Genuine and False Memories, Communal Memory and Migration', *The Irish Review* xliv (2012), pp. 23–4.
26. Ibid., p. 35.
27. In 1998, the site was twinned with what is now the Irish National Famine Museum at Strokestown Park. More than 1,000 Famine emigrants arrived from Strokestown, and Douglas noted the squalor of one ship in particular, the *Virginius*. Quigley, 'Grosse Île', pp. 141–2. Of the 476 passengers who travelled on the *Virginius*, 268 died en route, on board the ship in quarantine or in the hospitals on land. Mary Lee Dunn, *Ballykilcline Rising: From Famine Ireland to Immigrant America* (Amherst, MA, 2008), p. 27.
28. O'Brien, 'Famine Commemorations,' pp. 279–80.
29. Full text on the stone reads, in capital letters:
    Ireland's worst single disaster, The Great Famine, 1845–1850, / resulted in the deaths of over a million of its people, / more than another million consigned to the emigrant ship. / Skibbereen, epicentre of this horror, suffered more than most/[. . .] and here, in the famine burial pits of this cemetery, / are placed the coffinless remains of c. 9,000 victims, / a chilling reminder of man's inhumanity to man. / Go ndéana dia trocaire orthu.
    The last part translates as: may God have mercy on them – a commonly used phrase when mentioning the dead in Ireland.
30. At the National Famine Commemoration Day ceremony, 2009, then Minister for Community, Rural and Gaeltacht Affairs, Éamon Ó Cuív, stated that between 8,000 and 10,000 were buried there.
31. A base plaque names the maker as Eugene McCarthy (Blacksmith) of Ilen Street, Skibbereen.
32. Andreas Huyssen, *Present Pasts: Urban Palimpsests and the Politics of Memory* (Stanford, CA, 2003), p. 96. Huyssen's account promotes the idea that memorials now exist in 'the expanded field', of Rosalind Krauss's description: 'preferred construction of memory sites in the expanded field [. . .] combine sculpture, landscaping, architecture, and design and their incorporation into an urban fabric'. Ibid., p. 109.
33. Carrick-on-Shannon and District Historical Society have overseen the attic retention as a memorial (carrickheritage.com). Accessed 16 September 2016. The garden was dedicated in July 1998 by President Mary McAleese and is maintained by the Rural Social Scheme administered by the Arigna Leader Programme. Donal O'Grady, 'Carrick Workhouse Attic Memorial Opened', *Leitrim Observer*, 12 September 2008.
34. Ibid.
35. Great Famine Garden of Remembrance: www.discoverireland.ie/. Accessed 8 February 2017.

36. Other sites such as the Famine Arboretum, Corkagh Park, Clondalkin, Dublin, share a related dual function as designated memorial sites and pleasure grounds, but bear no historical link to the Famine.
37. Chris Keil, 'Sightseeing in the Mansions of the Dead', *Social and Cultural Geography* vi/4 (2005), pp. 479–94. He writes that these are the subject of a taxonomy of visitor types whose behaviours differ: 'survivors, relatives, those with cultural, regional or historical interests, school visits and so on'. Ibid., p. 481.
38. Ibid., p. 489.
39. Ibid., p. 490.
40. Ibid., p. 491. Keil outlines how the Birkenau site was described as silent, in particular devoid of bird sounds, by some visitors, when on his visit there he heard many birds.
41. Geoffrey M. White, 'Is Paris Burning – Touring America's "Good War" in France', *History & Memory* xxvii/2 (2015), p. 76.
42. Donald W. Crawford, 'Comparing Natural and Artistic Beauty', in S. Kemal and I. Gaskell (eds), *Landscape, Natural Beauty and the Arts* (Cambridge, 1993), p. 188.
43. Justin Carville, 'Photography, Tourism and Natural History: Cultural Identity and the Visualisation of the Natural World', in M. Cronin and B. O'Connor (eds), *Irish Tourism: Image, Culture and Identity* (Clevedon/Buffalo, NY/ Toronto and Sydney, 2003), p. 235.
44. Jonny Geber, 'Burying the Famine Dead: Kilkenny Union Workhouse', in J. Crowley, W.J. Smyth and M. Murphy (eds), *Atlas of the Great Irish Famine* (Cork, 2012), p. 341. In his detailed book on the subject, Geber contextualises and accounts his archaeological dig on the site of the former Kilkenny Union Workhouse, now the location of the town's Junction Shopping Centre. Excavations revealed, among other artefacts of the workhouse, the skeletal remains of close to 1,000 Famine-era dead, where overcrowding in local graveyards had necessitated burial pits on the workhouse grounds. Jonny Geber, *Victims of Ireland's Great Famine: the Bioarchaeology of Mass Burials at Kilkenny Union Workhouse* (Gainesville, 2015).
45. Willie Nolan, 'Land Reformation in Post-Famine Ireland', in J. Crowley, W.J. Smyth and M. Murphy (eds), *Atlas of the Great Irish Famine* (Cork, 2012), p. 571.
46. Afri (Action from Ireland) are an NGO, who self-describe as 'a group of committed and creative people who seek to promote debate and influence policy and practice in Ireland and internationally on human rights, peace and justice issues'. www.afri.ie/ Accessed 8 September 2017. They began a 'Great Famine Project' in 1984, which has included the promotion of a number of memorial sites and events. Emily Mark-FitzGerald, *Commemorating the Irish Famine: Memory and the Monument* (Liverpool, 2013), p. 134.
47. The local context is qualified in the text beneath a small portrait image: 'Erected by Afri's Great Famine Project during the 150th anniversary of the death of Fr Edmund Rice, Good Friday 1844.' Born locally, Rice was the founder of the Christian Brothers in Ireland, which ran many schools

for boys. The Gaelic text on the stones translates as 'may God have mercy on their souls'. There are also two small cruciform icons, which are traditional Irish St Brigid's crosses. These are usually made of rushes and were reputedly first made by the sixth-century Irish saint.

48. Jonathan Bordo, 'Picture and Witness at the Site of Wilderness', in W.J.T. Mitchell (ed.), *Landscape and Power* (Chicago and London, 2002), p. 292.
49. Ibid., p. 300.
50. Ibid., p. 308.
51. Ibid., p. 309.
52. Giorgio Agamben, *Remnants of Auschwitz* (New York, 2008). Agamben discusses the writings of Primo Levi in this regard.
53. Roland Barthes, *Camera Lucida* (London, 2000), p. 87.
54. This is discussed in Susan Sontag, *On Photography* (London, 2002), pp. 14–15.
55. Batchen writes: '[...] photographs remind us that memorialization has little to do with recalling the past; it is always about looking ahead toward that terrible, imagined, vacant future in which we ourselves will have been forgotten'. Geoffrey Batchen, *Forget Me Not – Photography and Remembrance* (New York, 2004), p. 98.
56. Abigail Solomon-Godeau, *Photography at the Dock* (Minneapolis, 1997), p. 172.
57. Walter Benjamin, 'Little History of Photography', in M.W. Jennings, H. Eiland and G. Smith (eds), *Walter Benjamin: Selected Writings Volume 2, 1927–1934* (Cambridge, MA and London, England, 1999), p. 515.
58. Liam Kelly, *Photographs and Photography in Irish Local History* (Dublin, 2008), p. 28.
59. Justin Carville, *Photography and Ireland* (Exposure Series) (London, 2011), p. 18.
60. Ibid., p. 65.
61. Ibid., pp. 67–8.
62. Ibid., p. 64.
63. Ibid.
64. Alanna O'Kelly's work discussed in Chapter 4 is one example in art practice.
65. Ulrich Baer, 'To Give Memory a Place: Holocaust Photography and the Landscape Tradition', *Representations* 69 (2000), p. 55. The images discussed are Dirk Reinartz, *Sobibór: Extermination Camp Grounds*, published in 1995, and Mikael Levin, *Nordlager Ohrdruf, 1995*. Baer also writes that such photographs, connected to the appearance of trauma, 'can visually stage experiences that would otherwise remain forgotten because they were never fully lived', and '[p]hotography and trauma dispel the illusory certainty that what is seen is what can be known'. Ulrich Baer, *Spectral Evidence* (Cambridge, MA and London, 2002), pp. 2, 182.
66. Ó Gráda, *Famine*, p. 39. He also suggests that '[f]olklore is prone to forget the more distant past, however, and suffers from chronological

confusion. It is also the subject of hidden biases and evasion'. Ibid., p. 42.

67. An example is described by 'Dáithí Ó Ceanntabhail, national teacher, Croom, County Limerick'. Póirtéir, *Famine*, p. 187.
68. Póirtéir, *Famine*.
69. Mícheál Briody, *The Irish Folklore Commission: 1935–1970: History, Ideology, Methodology* (Helsinki, 2008), pp. 336–7.
70. Ibid., p. 336.
71. Seamas Mac Philib, 'Obituaries: Kevin Danaher (Caoimhín Ó Danachair)', *The Journal of the Royal Society of Antiquaries of Ireland* cxxxii (2002), p. 153.
72. Briody, *The Irish Folklore Commission*, pp. 245–6.
73. This image is discussed further in Niamh Ann Kelly, *Ultimate Witnesses: The Visual Culture of Death, Burial and Mourning in Famine Ireland* (Hamden, CT, 2017).
74. Discussed in Eileen M. Murphy, 'Children's Burial Grounds in Ireland (*cilliní*) and Parental Emotions Toward Infant Death International'. *International Journal of History & Archaeology* 15 (2011).
75. Kelly, *Photographs*, 87.
76. For an analysis of the evolution of photography criticism, see Susie Linfield, *The Cruel Radiance: Photography and Political Violence* (Chicago and London, 2009), pp. 3–31.
77. Baer, 'To Give', p. 51.
78. Ibid., p. 54.
79. Judith Butler, *Precarious Life: The Powers of Mourning and Violence* (London and New York, 2004), p. 150.

6 Beautiful Places: Commemorative Tourism and Grievous History

1. www.afri.ie. Accessed 8 September 2017.
2. Ó Murchadha writes that about 500 undertook the overnight walk. Ciarán Ó Murchadha, *The Great Famine: Ireland's Agony 1845–1852* (London and New York, 2011), p. 165.
3. Ibid.
4. Ó Murchadha suggest scores of persons 'of both sexes and all ages, died of hunger-related exhaustion or hypothermia or by drowning'. Ibid., p. 166.
5. The letter, dated 13 April 1849, was signed 'A Ratepayer'. Reproduced in William J. Smyth, 'The Province of Connacht and the Great Famine, in J. Crowley, W.J. Smyth and M. Murphy (eds), *Atlas of the Great Irish Famine* (Cork, 2012), p. 287.
6. Charlie Connelly, *And Did Those Feet: Walking Through 2,000 Years of British and Irish History* (London, 2009), pp. 293–4.
7. Co-organized by Afri and the Louisburgh Community Project, the walks are themed annually.

8. Others have included 'the cellist Vedran Smailovic, who played his instrument in the streets of Sarajevo during the siege of the early nineties, and Kim Phúc, the woman made famous by the photograph of her as a little girl, running naked and burned raw by napalm during the Vietnam War'. Connelly, *And Did*, p. 294.

9. Ibid.

10. Christine Kinealy, *The Great Irish Famine – Impact, Ideology and Rebellion* (Basingstoke and New York, 2002), p. 80. Kinealy draws attention to how this action by the Choctaw was construed in the press as proof of the success of Christian missionary project, in a religiously inspired racial assumption that aid or charity is a primarily Christian virtue. Ibid.

11. Kinealy, *The Great Irish Famine*, p. 80; Cormac Ó Gráda, *Famine: A Short History* (Princeton, NJ and Oxford, 2009), p. 218; Emily Mark-FitzGerald, *Commemorating the Irish Famine: Memory and the Monument* (Liverpool, 2013), p. 136.

12. Discussed in Barry Roche, 'Cork Sculpture Recalls Generosity of Choctaw Nation During the Famine', *Irish Times*, 13 June 2017.

13. See: Luke Gibbons, 'Doing Justice to the Past', in T. Hayden (ed.), *Irish Hunger – Personal Reflections of the Famine* (Boulder, CO, 1998), pp. 257–60, and Margaret Kelleher, 'The Female Gaze: Asenath Nicholson's Famine Narrative', in C. Morash and R. Hayes (eds), *Fearful Realities – New Perspectives on the Famine* (Dublin, 1996), p. 126.

14. William Logan and Keir Reeves, 'Introduction: Remembering Places of Pain and Shame', in W. Logan and K. Reeves (eds), *Places of Pain and Shame: Dealing with 'Difficult Heritage'* (Abingdon and New York, 2009), p. 2.

15. Benedict Anderson, *Imagined Communities: Reflections on the Origin and Spread of Nationalism* (London, 1983).

16. David Rieff, *In Praise of Forgetting: Historical Memory and its Ironies* (New Haven, CT and London, 2016), p. 35. Rieff has referred to Ireland's collective memory of the Famine as 'constructed and politicized imaginative political geography'. Ibid., p. 8.

17. David Brett, 'The Construction of Heritage', in B. O'Connor and M. Cronin (eds), *Tourism in Ireland: A Critical Analysis* (Cork, 1993), p. 183.

18. Ibid., p. 201.

19. Connelly, *And Did*, p. 297.

20. Homi K. Bhabha, 'DissemiNation: Time, Narrative, and the Margins of the Modern Nation', in Homi K. Bhabha (ed.), *Nation and Narration* (London and New York, 1999), pp. 291–322.

21. Ibid., p. 314.

22. Bronwyn Batten, 'The Myall Creek Memorial: History, Identity and Reconciliation', in W. Logan and K. Reeves (eds), *Places of Pain and Shame: Dealing with 'Difficult Heritage'* (Abingdon and New York, 2009), p. 88.

23. Ibid., p. 93.

24. Terri Kearney and Philip O'Regan, *Sibbereeen: The Famine Story* (Skibereeen, 2015).

25. Daniel O'Connell promoted the repeal of the Act of Union (1800) between Ireland and Britain as a means to gain an independent parliament for Ireland. He sought and achieved Catholic Emancipation for Ireland in 1829 and went on to win a seat in the House of Commons in 1830.

26. The visitors' centre also suggests that the Famine can be read as a founding understanding of later political struggles, and following the Famine exhibition area, there are representations of the Irish Republican political movement and the Orange Order.

27. The site's website notes that one of Doherty's inaugural aims was to provide employment for the then economically hard-hit local area. www.doaghfamilnevillage.com. Accessed 19 March 2017.

28. Mass rocks are generally associated with the times of the Penal Laws, predating the Famine.

29. In 2009 the site incorporated a 'Boom to Bust' section with mocked-up streetscapes and text panels of economic and social statistics charting a climate of economic recession.

30. Kernan Andrews, 'Famine Victims Should not be Forgotten by this Generation: Shooting the Breeze - Mark Kennedy', *Galway Advertiser*, 21 April 2011. Kennedy suggests that up to 250,000 people may have emigrated from Galway Port during the Famine. He comments that an impetus behind the drive to have the memorial elements completed was a desire to have the park open for the return of the Volvo Ocean Race, which Galway hosted in the summer of 2012, in the form of a large-scale lively port and city festival. Ibid.

31. Donal Carey, then Minister of State who unveiled it, noted the memorial as the first national monument to the Famine in Ireland. http://clarechampion.ie/call-for-ennistymon-famine-memorial-refurbishment/. Accessed 20 November 2017

32. Though on the Clare County Library website, a link to the Ennistymon workhouse records, Return of Deaths, lists the death of a Michael Rice, aged 9, from Fever on 14 June 1850, following admittance to the workhouse on 24 February 1850, common discrepancies in recordings of names and ages suggest this may be a coincidence. Nonetheless, the online records, by scale of description, are a powerful meditation on the painful breadth of workhouse deaths. http://www.clarelibrary.ie/eolas/coclare/history/kr_et_workhouses/kr_et_workhouses.htm. Accessed 14 January 2018.

33. Tim Robinson, *Stones of Aran: Pilgrimage* (London, 2008), p. 42.

34. Quoted in Noel Kissane, *The Irish Famine: A Documentary History* (Dublin, 1995), p. 99.

35. Description from John Crowley, 'Thomas Carlyle and Famine Ireland', in J. Crowley, W.J. Smyth and M. Murphy (eds), *Atlas of the Great Irish Famine* (Cork, 2012), p. 482. Quote ibid., p. 486.

36. From August 1846, all public employment schemes were administrated by the Board of Works, with Trevelyan controlling the revised programme 'with extraordinary thoroughness [...] keeping an iron grip on the whole operation'. Enda Delaney, *The Curse of Reason: The Great Irish Famine* (Dublin, 2012), p. 125. Gray notes that in the latter years of the Famine, from 1848 onwards and to varying degrees in different regions, there was a marked withdrawal of state intervention, leaving the Poor Law to take the burden of relief measures. Gray, 'British Relief Measures', in J. Crowley, W.J. Smyth and M. Murphy (eds), *Atlas of the Great Irish Famine* (Cork, 2012), p. 84.
37. Quoted in Kissane, *The Irish Famine*, p. 50.
38. Crowley, 'Thomas Carlyle', p. 485.
39. Stuart McLean, *The Event and its Terrors – Ireland, Famine, Memory* (Stanford, CA, 2004), p. 165.
40. Kissane, *The Irish Famine*, p. 98.
41. McLean, *The Event*, p. 59.
42. John O'Connor, *The Workhouses of Ireland: The Fate of Ireland's Poor* (Dublin, 1995), p. 80.
43. For example, the Ballinrobe Workhouse was described in these terms in an article in *The Mayo Constitution*, on 23rd March, 1847. Mayo County Library, *The Famine*, pp. 80–2.
44. The Irish Workhouse Centre, launched in 2011, is housed in Portumna Workhouse, County Galway, which opened 1852 in one of 33 new unions formed in the post-Famine era. The centre hosts guided tours of the site, with multi-lingual information available.
45. Macroom in County Cork has a plaque on a new hospital building that is the only overt clue to the community hospital's predecessor at that location. In Cellbridge, County Kildare, a paint factory now occupies the former workhouse, while in Ballinrobe, County Mayo, the remaining workhouse buildings are now local council depot and offices. Dunsaughlin workhouse in County Meath was restored under private ownership and was for a time opened as a guesthouse. Others are even less visible, as the demise of the workhouse in Westport, County Mayo exemplifies, since the location of a housing estate. Commemorating such places are now reliant on local tourist information interests and the enthusiasm of local historians. This is also true in regard to workhouse records, which are, widely, randomly and partially preserved by interested constituents.
46. For more on Dunfanaghy and Donoghmore workhouses see: Niamh Ann Kelly, 'Narrating Sites of History: Workhouses and Famine Memory', in O. Frawley (ed.), *Memory Ireland Volume III: Cruxes in Irish Cultural Memory – The Famine and the Troubles* (Syracuse, NY, 2014), pp. 152–73.
47. Workhouses were viewed as places of absolute last resort when, following a fever epidemic, the average weekly mortality rates in workhouses rose in a matter of months from four per thousand in October 1846 to 24 per thousand by April 1847. Kissane, *The Irish Famine*, p. 89.
48. Ibid.

49. Ibid., pp. 172–3. Kissane reproduces of a table from Joel Mokyr's *Why Ireland Starved: a Quantitative and Analytical History of the Irish economy, 1800–1850* (1983) and a map from Dudley Edwards and T. Desmond Williams' *The Great Famine: studies in Irish History, 1845–52* (1956), and also points out that prior to the Famine the population was increasing, and that due to Famine emigration and conditions in Ireland, the fall in birth-rate can be read as a constituent of population decline. Ibid., p. 172.
50. McLean, *The Event*, p. 166.
51. Ibid., pp. 165–6.
52. Mary Daly, 'The Operations of Famine Relief, 1845–57', in C. Póirtéir (ed.), *The Great Irish Famine – The Thomas Davis Lecture Series* (Cork, 1995), p. 128.
53. O'Connor, *The Workhouses of Ireland*, p. 125.
54. Gray, 'British Relief Measures', p. 79.
55. Ibid.
56. 'This range of hills is a favourite walking destination. Offering spectacular views [...]'. Lonely Planet, *Walking in Ireland: The Best Walks in the Republic and Northern Ireland* (Melbourne, Oakland, CA and London and Paris, 1999), p. 181.
57. Edmund O'Riordan, *Famine in the Valley* (Tipperary Free Press, 2010), p. 54.
58. Bob Montgomery, 'Great Irish Roads? Is this our Stelvio?, *Irish Times*, 6 July 2005.
59. www.wildatlanticway.com. Accessed 10 November 2017.
60. Ibid.
61. Hannah Arendt, *Between Past and Future: Eight Exercises in Political Thought* (New York, 1968).
62. Ibid., p. 13. Arendt was referring to large moments in historical time, where there is a sort of lull between seismic or identity-altering shifts in collective experiences. This subjective approach has relevance in terms of contemplating a past era as vast as the Famine, where it is understood as an event that shaped identities in modern Ireland. As a critique of how time is perceived in historical analysis, she quoted William Faulkner: 'the past is never dead, it is not even past'. Ibid., p. 10.

Conclusion   Imaging the Great Irish Famine

1. Willis was described by O'Rourke, in his account of the Famine, first published in 1874, as: '[a] physician, an excellent, kind-hearted man who had been sent on duty to Bantry in the later stages of the Famine' Canon John O'Rourke, *The History of the Great Irish Famine of 1847*, with Notices of Earlier Famines (Dublin, 1874) (1994), p. 211. Before working in Bantry, Willis published a pamphlet in 1845, 'Facts connected with social and sanitary conditions of the

working classes of the city of Dublin: with tables of sickness, medical attendance, deaths, expectation of life'.

2. Canon John O'Rourke, *On a Cross*, Pamphlet (*c.* 1885), p. 3.

3. James Gerard Martin, 'The Society of the St Vincent de Paul as an emerging social phenomenon in mid-nineteenth century Ireland', MA thesis, National College of Industrial Relations NCEA (Dublin, 1993), p. 71.

4. Ibid., p. 147.

5. John O'Connor, *The Workhouses of Ireland: The Fate of Ireland's Poor* (Dublin, 1995), p. 234.

6. Martin, 'The Society', p. 147.

7. O'Connor, *The Workhouses*, p. 147.

8. Martin, 'The Society', p. 147.

9. Born in Cork, Cross (1956-) studied art in Cork, Leicester and San Francisco. A member of Aosdána, her work is in collections worldwide, including IMMA and the Tate Modern, London. Yvonne Scott writes that *Endarken* 'represents the artist's frustration at the erosion of the remaining fragments of the past'. Yvonne Scott, 'Dorothy Cross', in C. Marshall and P. Murray (eds), *Art and Architecture of Ireland (AAI), Vol. V. Twentieth-Century Art and Artists* (New Haven, CT and London, 2014), p. 100.

10. Gill Perry, *Playing at Home: The House in Contemporary Art* (London, 2013), p. 67.

11. Ralph Rugoff, 'Corrosive Vision', in IMMA (ed.), *Dorothy Cross* (Italy, 2005), p. 69.

12. Mieke Bal, *Travelling Concepts in the Humanities – A Rough Guide* (Toronto, Buffalo, NY and London, 2002), p. 173.

13. Judith Butler and Athena Athanasiou, *Dispossession: The Performative in the Political* (Cambridge and Malden, MA, 2013), p. xi.

14. This was first discussed by Butler on undoing masculinist constructions of an identity-seeking self. The content referenced here is from a lecture Butler gave at Trinity College Dublin, 'Vulnerability and Resistance Revisited', 5 February 2015, and relates to theories raised in: Judith Butler, *Precarious Life: The Powers of Mourning and Violence* (London and New York, 2004); Judith Butler, *Frames of War: When is Life Grievable?* (London and New York, 2010); and Butler and Athanasiou, *Dispossession*.

15. Butler and Athanasiou, *Dispossession*, p. xi.

16. Christine Kinealy, *Apparitions of the Death and Disease: The Great Hunger in Ireland* (Hamden, CT, 2014), p. 28.

17. Thomas Bartlett, *Ireland: A History* (Cambridge, 2010), p. 282.

18. This is apparent, for example, in the tone of some submissions to Tom Hayden's book *Personal Reflections on the Legacy of the Famine* (1998) such as those by John Waters and Nell McCafferty. The legacy of fraught land ownership in the early twenty-first century is implied in Fintan O'Toole's

book *Ship of Fools – How Corruption and Stupidity Killed the Celtic Tiger* (London, 2009), which reads land hunger in Ireland as an attempted reversal of fortunes.

19. Debbie Lisle, *Holidays in the Danger Zone: Entanglements of War and Tourism* (Minneapolis and London, 2016) p. 285.

20. David Rieff, *The Reproach of Hunger: Food, Justice and Money in the 21st Century* (London and New York, 2016), p. 154. Contrasting proportions of incomes spent on food at the start of the twenty-first century, Rieff notes that the poorest billion of the world's population spend an average of 60–80 per cent of their income on food, while in the US, in his example, the average spend on food is 13–15 per cent of incomes. Ibid., p. 69.

21. Jill Treanor, 'Half of world's wealth now in hands of 1% of population', *Guardian*, 13 October 2015.

22. Elaine Scarry, *The Body in Pain* (New York and Oxford, 1985), p. 286.

Bibliography

Agamben, Giorgio, *Remnants of Auschwitz* (New York, 2008).

Alpers, Svetlana, 'Is art history?', in S. Kemal and I. Gaskell (eds), *Explanation and Value in the Arts* (Cambridge, 1993), pp. 109–26.

Anderson, Benedict, *Imagined Communities: Reflections on the Origin and Spread of Nationalism* (London, 1983).

Andrews, Kernan, 'Famine Victims Should not be Forgotten by this Generation: Shooting the Breeze - Mark Kennedy', *Galway Advertiser*, 21 April 2011.

Apel, Dora, *Memory Effects: The Holocaust and the Art of Secondary Witnessing* (New Brunswick, NJ and London, 2002).

Archive Consultancy for Dublin City Council, History of Monuments: O'Connell Street Area, Report (Dublin, 2003).

Arendt, Hannah, *Between Past and Future: Eight Exercises in Political Thought* (New York, 1968).

Arnold-de Simine, Silke, *Trauma, Empathy, Nostalgia* (Basingstoke and New York, 2013).

Astill, James, 'The Hidden Disaster', in 'Famine in Africa'. *Supplement, Guardian, in association with Concern*, 30 November 2002.

Baer, Ulrich, 'To Give Memory a Place: Holocaust Photography and the Landscape Tradition'. *Representations* 69 (2000), pp. 38–62.

—— *Spectral Evidence* (Cambridge, MA and London, 2002).

Bal, Mieke, *Double Exposures: The Subject of Cultural Analysis* (New York and London, 1996).

—— *Travelling Concepts in the Humanities – A Rough Guide* (Toronto, Buffalo and London, 2002).

Balme, Christopher, 'Staging the Pacific: Framing Authenticity in Performances for Tourists at the Polynesian Cultural Center', *Theatre Journal* 1/4 (1998), pp. 53–70.

Bann, Stephen, 'Art History & Museums', in M.A. Cheetham, M.A. Holly and K. Moxley (eds), *The Subjects of Art History – Historical Objects in Contemporary Perspective* (Cambridge, 1998).

Barber, Fionna, *Art in Ireland since 1910* (London, 2013).

Barthes, Roland, *Camera Lucida* (London, 2000).

Bartlett, Thomas, *Ireland: A History* (Cambridge, 2010).

Bibliography

Batchen, Geoffrey, *Forget Me Not – Photography and Remembrance* (New York, 2004).

Batten, Bronwyn, 'The Myall Creek Memorial: History, Identity and Reconciliation', in W. Logan and K. Reeves (eds), *Places of Pain and Shame: Dealing with 'Difficult Heritage'* (Abingdon and New York, 2009).

Beiner, Guy, 'Commemorative Heritage and the Dialectic of Memory', in M. McCarthy (ed.), *Ireland's Heritages – Critical Perspective on Memory and Identity* (Farnham and Burlington, VT, 2005).

—— 'Recycling the Dustbin of Irish History: The Radical Challenge of "Folk Memory"', *History Ireland* xiv/1 (2006), pp. 42–7.

Bell, Desmond, 'Interview with Filmmaker Pat Murphy', *Kinema* Spring (2007).

Benjamin, Walter, 'Little History of Photography', in M.W. Jennings, H. Eiland and G. Smith (eds), *Walter Benjamin: Selected Writings Volume 2, 1927–1934* (Cambridge, MA/London, England, 1999).

Bennett, Jill, *Empathic Vision: Affect, Trauma, and Contemporary Art* (Stanford, CA, 2005).

—— 'Aesthetics of Intermediality', *Art History* xxx/3 (2007), pp. 432–50.

Bennett, Tony, 'The Exhibitionary Complex', *New Formations* 4 (1988), pp. 73–102.

Bhabha, Homi K., 'DissemiNation: Time, Narrative, and the Margins of the Modern Nation', in Homi K. Bhabha (ed.), *Nation and Narration* (London and New York, 1999).

Bhreathnach-Lynch, Sighle, 'Framing the Irish: Victorian Paintings of the Irish Peasant', *Journal of Victorian Culture* ii/2 (1997), pp. 245–60.

Blom, Thomas, 'Morbid Tourism – A Postmodern Market Niche with an Example from Althrop', *Norwegian Journal of Geography*, liv/1 (2000), pp. 29–36.

Boland, Eavan, *New Collected Poems* (Manchester, 2005).

Bonnell, Jennifer and Simon, Roger L., '"Difficult" Exhibitions and Intimate Encounters', *Museum and Society* v/2 (2007), pp. 65–8.

Bordo, Jonathan, 'Picture and Witness at the Site of Wilderness', in W.J.T. Mitchell (ed.), *Landscape and Power* (Chicago and London, 2002).

Bourke, Marie, *The Story of Irish Museums 1970–2000 – Culture, Identity and Education* (Cork, 2011).

Brett, David, 'The Construction of Heritage', in B. O'Connor and M. Cronin (eds), *Tourism in Ireland: A Critical Analysis* (Cork, 1993).

—— 'Things in Their Places', *Visual Culture in Britain* x/2 (2009), pp. 125–38.

Briody, Mícheál, *The Irish Folklore Commission: 1935–1970: History, Ideology, Methodology* (Helsinki, 2008).

Butler, Judith, *Precarious Life: The Powers of Mourning and Violence* (London and New York, 2004).

—— *Frames of War: When is Life Grievable?* (London and New York, 2010).

Butler, Judith and Athena Athanasiou, *Dispossession: The Performative in the Political* (Cambridge and Malden, MA, 2013).

Burke-Kennedy, Eoin, 'Inventor of "Celtic Tiger" phrase bails out of bank job', *Irish Times*, 21 March 2014.

Cahill, Katherine, 'In the Mainstream of Irish Naturalism: The Art of Lilian Lucy Davidson', *Irish Arts Review Yearbook* xv (1999), pp. 34–45.

Campbell, David, 'Geopolitics and Visuality: Sighting the Darfur Conflict', *Political Geography* xxvi (2007), pp. 357–82.

Campbell, Julian, 'The Artist as Witness: James Mahony', in J. Crowley, W.J. Smyth and M. Murphy (eds), *Atlas of the Great Irish Famine* (Cork, 2012).

Campbell, Myles, 'Carolyn Mulholland', in A. Carpenter and P. Murphy (eds), *Art and Architecture of Ireland Volume III – Sculpture 1600–2000* (Dublin, 2015).

Campbell, Stephen J., *The Great Irish Famine: Words and Images from the Famine Museum Strokestown Park, County Roscommon* (Roscommon, 1994).

Carville, Justin, 'Photography, Tourism and Natural History: Cultural Identity and the Visualisation of the Natural World', in M. Cronin and B. O'Connor (eds), *Irish Tourism: Image, Culture and Identity* (Clevedon, Buffalo, NY, Toronto and Sydney, 2003).

—— 'Resisting Vision: Photography, Anthropology and the Production of Race in Ireland', in C. Breathnach and C. Lawless (eds), *Visual, Material and Print Culture in Nineteenth-Century Ireland* (Dublin and Portland, OR, 2010).

—— *Photography and Ireland* (Exposure Series) (London, 2011).

Cavarero, Adriana, *Horrorism: Naming Contemporary Violence* (New York, 2011).

Chambers, Iain, 'Afterword: After the Museum', in I. Chambers, A. De Angelis, C. Ianniciello, M. Orabona and M. Quadraro (eds), *The Postcolonial Museum: The Arts of Memory and the Pressures of History* (Abingdon and New York, 2016).

Chen, Nancy, '"Speaking Nearby": A Conversation with Trinh T. Minh-ha', *Visual Anthropology Review* viii /1 (1992), pp. 82–91.

Coffey, Petra, 'George Victor du Noyer 1817-1869, Artist, Geologist and Antiquary', *The Journal of the Royal Society of Antiquaries of Ireland* 123 (1993), pp. 102–19.

Connelly, Charlie, *And Did Those Feet: Walking Through 2,000 Years of British and Irish History* (London, 2009).

Corless, Kieron, 'Hunger: Interviews', *Sight and Sound* (November 2008), pp. 26–7.

Corporaal, Marguérite and Jason King (ed.), *Irish Global Migration and Memory: Transatlantic Perspectives of Ireland's Famine Exodus* (London, 2016).

Coulter, Riann, 'Hibernian Salon des Refuses', *Irish Arts Review* xx/3 (2003), pp. 80–5.

Crane, David, *Empires of the Dead: How One Man's Vision Led to the Creation of WW1's War Graves* (London, 2013).

Crawford, Donald W., 'Comparing Natural and Artistic Beauty', in S. Kemal and I. Gaskell (eds), *Landscape, Natural Beauty and the Arts* (Cambridge, 1993).

Crawford, Margaret E., 'Subsistence Crises and Famines in Ireland: A Nutritionist's View', in M.E. Crawford (ed.), *Famine: The Irish Experience, 900–1900* (Edinburgh, 1989).

Crofts, Susan, 'Maurice MacGonigal PRHA (1900–1979) and his Western Paintings', *Irish Arts Review Yearbook* xiii (1997), pp. 135–42.

Crookshank Anne and the Knight of Glin, *Ireland's Painters 1600–1940* (Yale, 2002).

Crowdus, Gary, 'The Human Body as Political Weapon: An interview with Steve McQueen', *Cineaste* (Spring 2009), pp. 22–5.

Crowley, John, 'Exhibiting the Great Famine', in N. Buttimer, C. Rynne and H. Guerin (eds), *The Heritage of Ireland – Natural, Man-Made and Cultural Heritage. Conservation and Interpretation* (Cork, 2000).

—— 'Thomas Carlyle and Famine Ireland', in J. Crowley, W.J. Smyth and M. Murphy (eds), *Atlas of the Great Irish Famine* (Cork, 2012).

Bibliography

Crowley, J., W.J. Smyth and M. Murphy (eds), *Atlas of the Great Irish Famine* (Cork, 2012).

Cullen, Fintan (ed.), *Sources in Irish Art – A Reader* (Cork, 2000).

Curtis, L. Perry Jr, *Apes and Angels: The Irishman in Victorian Caricature* (Washington, DC, 1997).

—— *Notice to Quit: The Great Irish Famine Evictions* (Hamden, CT, 2015)

Daly, Mary, 'The Operations of Famine Relief, 1845–57', in C. Póirtéir (ed.), *The Great Irish Famine – The Thomas Davis Lecture Series* (Cork, 1995).

—— 'Historians and the Famine: A Beleaguered Species?', *Irish Historical Studies* xxx/120 (1997), pp. 591–601.

Davis, Colin, 'Can the Dead Speak to Us? De Man, Lévinas and Agamben', *Culture, Theory and Critique* xlv/10 (2004), pp. 77–89.

Deepwell, Katy, *Dialogues: Women Artists from Ireland* (London, 2005).

Delaney, Enda, *The Curse of Reason: The Great Irish Famine* (Dublin, 2012).

—— *The Great Irish Famine: a History in Four Lives* (Dublin 2014).

Department of Irish Folklore, *Folk Tradition in Irish Art: An Exhibition of Paintings from the Collection of the Department of Irish Folklore, University College Dublin* (Dublin, 1993).

Digby, Marie Claire, 'Irish Hunger Memorial in NYC reopens after €4.5m renovation', *Irish Times*, 3 August 2017.

Donnelly, James S. Jnr, *The Great Irish Potato Famine* (Stroud, 2002).

Dunlevy, Mairead, *Dress in Ireland: A History* (Cork, 1999).

Dunne, Tom, 'The Dark Side of the Irish Landscape: Depictions of the Rural Poor, 1760–1850', in Crawford Art Gallery and Gandon Editions (eds), *Whipping the Herring, Survival and Celebration in Nineteenth Century Irish Art* (Cork, 2006).

Famine Commemoration Committee, Department of the Taoiseach and European Community Humanitarian Office, *Ireland's Famine: Commemoration and Awareness* (Dublin, 1997).

Feehan, John, 'The Potato: Root of the Famine', in John Crowley, William J. Smyth and Mike Murphy (eds), *Atlas of the Great Irish Famine* (Cork, 2012).

Feith, Jesse, 'Coderre says Black Rock Memorial Plan is on Track', Montreal Gazette, 7 October 2017.

Ferguson, Ciara, 'Horror and Hope', *The Sunday Independent*, 1 June 1997.

Findlen, Paula, 'The Two Cultures of Scholarship?', *The History of Science* xcvi/2 (2005), pp. 230–7.

Fitzpatrick, David, *Oceans of Consolation: Personal Accounts of Irish Migrations to Australia* (Cork, 1995).

Foley, Michael, *Death in Every Paragraph* (Hamden, CT, 2015).

Foster, Roy F., *The Irish Story: Telling Tales and Making it Up in Ireland* (London, 2001).

Foynes, Peter, *The Great Famine in Skibbereen and District* (Skibbereen, 2004).

Furlong, Elaine, 'Dunbrody May Not Sail Again – It's Not Worth It', *The Irish Independent*, 17 February 2010.

Geary, Laurence M., '"The Late Disastrous Epidemic": Medical Relief and the Great Famine', in C. Morash and R. Hayes (eds), *Fearful Realities – New Perspectives on the Famine* (Dublin, 1996).

—— 'Medical Relief and the Great Famine', in J. Crowley, W.J. Smyth and M. Murphy (eds), *Atlas of the Great Irish Famine* (Cork, 2012).

271

—— '"The Noblest Offering That Nation Ever Made to Nation": American Philanthropy and the Great Famine in Ireland', *Éire-Ireland* 48/3&4 (2013) pp. 103–28.

Geber, Jonny, 'Burying the Famine Dead: Kilkenny Union Workhouse', in J. Crowley, W.J. Smyth and M. Murphy (eds), *Atlas of the Great Irish Famine* (Cork, 2012).

—— *Victims of Ireland's Great Famine: the Bioarchaeology of Mass Burials at Kilkenny Union Workhouse* (Gainesville, 2015).

George Moore Society, *Famine* (Exhibition Catalogue) (Claremorris, 1995).

Gerrish Nunn, Pamela, *Problem Pictures, Women and Men in Victorian Painting* (Menston, 1995).

Gibbons, Luke, 'Doing Justice to the Past', in T. Hayden (ed.), *Irish Hunger – Personal Reflections of the Famine* (Boulder, CO, 1998).

—— 'The Global Cure? History, Therapy and the Celtic Tiger', in P. Kirby, L. Gibbons and M. Cronin (eds), *Reinventing Ireland: Culture, Society and the Global Economy* (London and Sterling, VA, 2002).

Gilroy, Paul, *The Black Atlantic: Modernity and Double Consciousness* (London/New York, 1993).

Graham, Colin, '"... maybe that's just Blarney": Irish Culture and the Persistence of Authenticity', in C. Graham and R. Kirkland (eds), *Ireland and Cultural Theory: The Mechanics of Authenticity* (Basingstoke and London, 1999).

Gray, Peter, '*Punch* and the Irish Famine', *History Ireland* i/2 (1993), pp. 26–32.

—— *The Irish Famine* (London, 1995).

—— 'Memory and the Great Irish Famine', in P. Gray and K. Oliver (eds), *The Memory of Catastrophe* (Manchester and New York, 2004).

—— 'British Relief Measures', in J. Crowley, W.J. Smyth and M. Murphy (eds), *Atlas of the Great Irish Famine* (Cork, 2012).

Greene, Ted, *Drogheda: Its Place in Local History* (Julianstown, 2006).

Harbison, Peter, *Irish High Crosses with the Figure Sculptures Explained* (Drogheda, 1994).

Herzfeld, Michael, *A Place in History – Social and Monumental Time in a Cretan Town* (New Jersey, 1991).

Hill, Judith, *Irish Public Sculpture* (Dublin, 1998).

Hirsch, Marianne, 'Projected Memory: Holocaust Photographs in Personal and Public Fantasy', in M. Bal, J. Crewe and L. Spitzer (eds), *Acts of Memory: Cultural Recall in the Present* (Hanover, NH, 1999).

Hobsbawm, Eric and Ranger, Terence (eds), *The Invention of Tradition* (Cambridge, UK, New York, Melbourne and Madrid, 2000).

Hofmeyr, Benda, '"Isn't Art an Activity that Gives Things a Face?" Lévinas on the Power of Art', *Image and Narrative, Online Magazine of the Visual Narrative* (18: Thinking Pictures) viii/1 (2007).

Hohenhaus, Peter, 'Commemorating and Commodifying the Rwandan Genocide', in L. White and E. Frew (eds), *Dark Tourism and Place Identity: Managing and Interpreting Dark Places* (London and New York, 2013).

Holly, Michael Ann, 'Past Looking', in S. Melville and B. Readings (eds), *Vision and Textuality* (London, 2005).

Bibliography

Hooper-Greenhill, Eilean, *Museums and the Interpretation of Visual Culture* (London and New York, 2000).
—— 'Interpretative Communities, Strategies and Repertoires', in S. Watson (ed.), *Museums and Their Communities* (New York and Abingdon, 2007).
Huyssen, Andreas, *Present Pasts: Urban Palimpsests and the Politics of Memory* (Stanford, CA, 2003).
Irish Times, 'State to Part-Fund Famine Ship Replica', *Irish Times*, 29 March 2000.
Jackson, Alvin, *Ireland 1798–1998* (Malden, MA, Oxford and Victoria, 1999).
Johnson, Lewis, 'Pre-Raphaelitism, Personification, Portraiture', in M. Pointon (ed.), *Pre-Raphaelites Re-viewed* (Manchester and New York, 1989).
Johnston, R.J., *A Question of Place: Exploring the Practice of Human Geography* (Oxford and Cambridge MA, 1991).
Kearney, Terri and O'Regan, Philip, *Sibbereeen: The Famine Story* (Skibereeen, 2015).
Keil, Chris, 'Sightseeing in the Mansions of the Dead', *Social and Cultural Geography* vi/4 (2005), pp. 479–94.
Kelleher, Margaret, 'The Female Gaze: Asenath Nicholson's Famine Narrative', in C. Morash and R. Hayes (eds), *Fearful Realities – New Perspectives on the Famine* (Dublin, 1996).
—— *The Feminization of Famine – Expressions of the Inexpressible?* (Cork, 1997).
Kelly, John, *The Graves are Walking: A History of the Great Irish Famine* (London and New York, 2012).
Kelly, Liam, *Photographs and Photography in Irish Local History* (Dublin, 2008).
Kelly, Niamh Ann, 'The Irish Cottage in Famine Remembrance', in D.A. Valone (ed.), *Ireland's Great Hunger, Volume 2* (Lanham, MD, Boulder, CO, New York, Toronto and Plymouth, 2010).
—— 'Similarity and Difference: The Appearance of Suffering at the Strokestown Famine Museum', in A. Hoffman and E. Peeren (eds), *Representation Matters: (Re) Articulating Collective Identities in a Postcolonial World* (Amsterdam, 2010).
—— 'Transgressing Time: Imagining an Exhibition of Works by Alanna O'Kelly and Phil Collins', in M. Bal and M.A. Hernández-Navarro (eds), *Art and Visibility in Migratory Culture – Conflict, Resistance, and Agency* (Amsterdam and New York, 2011).
—— 'Narrating Sites of History: Workhouses and Famine Memory', in O. Frawley (ed.), *Memory Ireland Volume III: Cruxes in Irish Cultural Memory – The Famine and the Troubles* (Syracuse, NY, 2014).
—— *Ultimate Witnesses: The Visual Culture of Death, Burial and Mourning in Famine Ireland* (Hamden, CT, 2017).
Kelly, Olivia, 'Replica Famine Ship "Jeanie Johnston" Sinks in Value', *Irish Times*, 22 May 2015.
Kenneally, Thomas, *Three Famines – Starvation and Politics* (New York, 2011).
Kennedy, Liam, Paul S. Ell, E.M. Crawford and L.A. Clarkson, *Mapping the Great Irish Famine* (Dublin, 1999).
Kennedy, S.B., *Irish Art and Modernism 1880–1950* (Belfast, 1991).
Kennedy, Róisín, 'Searching for the Vital Form', in Royal Hibernian Academy (ed.), *Edward Delaney – Bronzes from the Sixties* (Dublin, 2004).

Kidd, Jenny, 'Introduction: Challenging History in the Museum', in J. Kidd, S. Cairns, A. Drago, A. Ryall and M. Stearn (eds), *Challenging History in the Museum* (Abingdon and New York, 2016).

Kinealy, Christine, 'The Role of the Poor Law during the Famine', in C. Póirtéir (ed.), *The Great Irish Famine: The Thomas Davis Lecture Series* (Cork, 1995).

—— 'The Great Irish Famine – A Dangerous Memory?' in A. Gribben (ed.), *The Great Famine and the Irish Diaspora in America* (Amherst, MA, 1999).

—— *The Great Irish Famine – Impact, Ideology and Rebellion* (Basingstoke and New York, 2002).

—— 'The Operation of the Poor Law during the Famine', in J. Crowley, W.J. Smyth and M. Murphy (eds), *Atlas of the Great Irish Famine* (Cork, 2012).

—— *Apparitions of the Death and Disease: The Great Hunger in Ireland* (Hamden, CT, 2014).

King, Jason, 'Remembering and Forgetting the Famine Irish in Quebec: Genuine and False Memories, Communal Memory and Migration', *The Irish Review* 44 (2012), pp. 20–41.

Kirshenblatt-Gimblett, Barbara, *Destination Culture* (Berkeley, CA, Los Angeles and London, 1998).

Kissane, Noel, *The Irish Famine: A Documentary History* (Dublin, 1995).

Kohn, Roger, *Rowan Gillespie: Looking for Orion* (Dublin, 2007).

Landsberg, Alison, *Prosthetic Memory – The Transformation of American Remembrance in the Age of Mass Culture* (New York, 2004).

Laqueur, Thomas W., 'Introduction', *Representations (Grounds for Remembering)* 69/ Special Issue (2000), pp. 1–8.

Leach, Cristín, 'Muriel Brandt's 1916 Breadline', *Sunday Times (Ireland)*, 17 March 2016.

Lee Dunn, Mary, *Ballykilcline Rising: From Famine Ireland to Immigrant America* (Amherst, MA, 2008).

Leerssen, Joep, *Mere Irish and the Fíor-Ghael: Studies in the Idea of Irish Nationality, Its Development and Literary Expression Prior to the Nineteenth Century* (Cork, 1997).

Lennon, John and Foley, Malcolm, *Dark Tourism: The Attraction of Death and Disaster* (London and New York, 2000).

Levi, Primo, *If This is a Man* and *The Truce* (London, 1994).

Lévinas, Emmanuel, 'Ethics of the Infinite', in R. Kearney, *States of Mind: Dialogues with Contemporary Thinkers on the European Mind*ed (Manchester, 1995).

Linfield, Susie, *The Cruel Radiance: Photography and Political Violence* (Chicago and London, 2009).

Lisle, Debbie, *Holidays in the Danger Zone: Entanglements of War and Tourism* (Minneapolis and London, 2016).

Litton, Helen, *The Irish Famine: An Illustrated History* (Dublin, 1994).

Lloyd, David, 'The Memory of Hunger', in D.E. Eng and D. Kazanjian (eds), *Loss: The Politics of Mourning* (Berkeley, CA, Los Angeles and London, 2003).

—— 'The Political Economy of the Potato', *Nineteenth-Century Contexts* (29 June/September 2007), pp. 311–35.

Bibliography

Logan, William and Reeves, Keir, 'Introduction: Remembering Places of Pain and Shame', in W. Logan and K. Reeves (eds), *Places of Pain and Shame: Dealing with 'Difficult Heritage'* (Abingdon and New York, 2009).

Lonely Planet, *Walking in Ireland: The Best Walks in the Republic and Northern Ireland* (Melbourne, CA, Oakland, CA, London and Paris, 1999).

Lynch, John, 'Hunger: Passion of the Militant', *Nordic Journal of English Studies* xiii/2 (2014), pp. 184–201.

Lysaght, Patricia, 'Hospitality at Wakes and Funerals in Ireland from the Seventeenth to the Nineteenth Century: Some Evidence from the Written Record', *Folklore* 114 (2003), pp. 403–26.

MacCurtain, Margaret, 'The Real Molly Macree', in A.M. Dalsimer (ed.), *Visualizing Ireland: National Identity and the Pictorial Tradition* (Boston, MA and London, 1993).

McClaughlin, Trevor, *Barefoot and Pregnant? Irish Famine Orphans in Australia* (2 vols) Documents and Register (Victoria, 1991).

McDonagh, Marese, 'Strokestown House and Famine Museum to Begin Fresh Chapter', *Irish Times*, 5 October 2015.

Macdonald, Sharon, *Difficult Heritage: Negotiating the Nazi Past in Nuremberg and Beyond* (London/New York, 2009).

—— *Memorylands: Heritage and Identity in Europe Today* (London and New York, 2013).

Mac Philib, Séamas, 'Obituaries: Kevin Danaher (Caoimhín Ó Danachair)', *The Journal of the Royal Society of Antiquaries of Ireland* cxxxii (2002), p. 153.

Mac Suibhne, Breandán, *Subjects Lacking Works? The Gray Zone of the Great Famine* (Hamden, CT, 2017).

—— *The End of Outrage: Post-Famine Adjustment in Rural Ireland* (Oxford, 2017).

Mahoney, Paschal, *Grim Bastilles of Despair: The Poor Law Union Workhouses in Ireland* (Hamden, CT, 2016).

Mark-FitzGerald, Emily, *Commemorating the Irish Famine: Memory and the Monument* (Liverpool, 2013).

Marks, Kathy, 'Blair Issues Apology for Irish Potato Famine', *Independent*, 2 June 1997.

Marshall, Catherine, 'History and Memorials: Fine Art and the Great Famine in Ireland', in C. Breathnach and C. Lawless (eds), *Visual, Material and Print Culture in Nineteenth-Century Ireland* (Dublin and Portland, OR, 2010).

—— *Monuments and Memorials of the Great Famine* (Hamden, CT, 2014).

Mayo County Library, *The Famine in Mayo: A Portrait from Contemporary Sources, 1845–1850* (Castlebar, 2004).

McCain, Gary and Nina M. Ray, 'Legacy Tourism: The Search for Personal Meaning in Heritage Travel', *Tourism Management* xxiv (2003), pp. 713–17.

McGarry, Patsy, 'Famine Memorial, Jim Callery recognized by EU for History Role', *Irish Times*, 18 April 2017.

McGowan, Mark, 'Famine, Facts and Fabrication: An Examination of Diaries from the Irish Famine Migration to Canada', *The Canadian Journal of Irish Studies* xxxiii/2 (2007), pp. 48–55.

McLean, Stuart, *The Event and its Terrors – Ireland, Famine, Memory* (Stanford, CA, 2004).

McMahon, Colin, 'Montreal's Ship Fever Monument: An Irish Famine Memorial in the Making', *The Canadian Journal of Irish Studies* xxxiii/1 (2007).

Meghen, P.J., 'Stephen de Vere's Voyage to Canada, 1847', *The Old Limerick Journal: Famine Edition* 32 (1995), pp. 136–40.

Minh-ha, Trinh T., 'The Totalizing Quest of Meaning', in N. Wheale (ed.), *The Postmodern Arts* (London/New York, 1995).

Montgomery, Bob, 'Great Irish Roads? Is this our Stelvio?, *The Irish Times*, 6 July 2005.

Moreno, Barry, *Images of America: Castle Garden and Battery Park* (Charleston, SC, Chicago, Portsmouth and San Francisco, 2007).

Moroney, Mic, 'Images of Erin', *Irish Times*, 18 November 2000.

Murphy, Derville, 'Margaret Allen, Social Commentator', *Irish Arts Review* xxvii/1 (2010), pp. 88–91.

Murphy, Eileen M., 'Children's Burial Grounds in Ireland (*cillíní*) and Parental Emotions Toward Infant Death International', *International Journal of History & Archaeology* 15 (2011).

Murphy, Maureen, *Compassionate Stranger: Asenath Nicholson and the Great Irish Famine* (Syracuse, CA, 2015).

Murphy, Paula, 'Madonna and Maiden, Mistress and Mother: Woman as Symbol of Ireland and Spirit of the Nation', in J. Steward (ed.), *When Time Began to Rant and Rage, Figurative Painting from Twentieth Century Ireland* (London and Berkeley, CA, 1998), pp. 90–101.

Murray, Peter (compiler), *Catalogue of The Crawford Municipal Art Gallery* (Cork, 1992).

——— 'Refiguring Delaney', *Irish Arts Review* xxii/4 (2004), pp. 80–5.

National College of Art (Ireland) *Thomas Davis and the Young Ireland Movement Centenary: Exhibition of Pictures of Irish Historical Interest*, (Exhibition Catalogue) (Dublin 1946).

Netzer, Nancy, 'Picturing an Exhibition: James Mahony's Watercolours of the Irish Industrial Exhibition of 1853', in A.M. Dalsimer (ed.), *Visualizing Ireland: National Identity and the Pictorial Tradition* (Boston and London, 1993).

Newton, Douglas, 'Old Wine in New Bottles, and the Reverse', in F.S. Kaplan (ed.), *Museums and the Making of 'Ourselves': The Role of Objects in National Identity* (London and New York, 1994).

Nolan, Willie, 'Land Reformation in post-Famine Ireland', in J. Crowley, W.J. Smyth and M. Murphy (eds), *Atlas of the Great Irish Famine* (Cork, 2012).

Nora, Pierre, *Realms of Memory: Rethinking the French Past. Volume I: Conflicts and Divisions* (New York, 1996).

O'Brien, Kathleen, 'Famine Commemorations: Visual Dialogues, Visual Silences', in D.A. Valone and C. Kinealy (eds), *Ireland's Great Hunger: Silence, Memory and Commemoration* (Lanham, MD and Oxford, 2002).

Ó Ciosáin, Niall, 'Famine Memory and the Popular Representation of Scarcity', in I. McBride (ed.), *History and Memory in Modern Ireland* (Cambridge, 2001).

——— 'Approaching a Folklore Archive: The Irish Folklore Commission and the Memory of the Great Famine', *Folklore* 115 (2004), pp. 222–32.

O'Connor, John, *The Workhouses of Ireland: The Fate of Ireland's Poor* (Dublin, 1995).

O'Connor, Joseph, *Star of the Sea* (London, 2002).

Bibliography

O Crualaóich, Gearóid, 'The Merry Wake', in J.S. Donnelly and K.A. Miller (ed.), *Irish Popular Culture 1650–1850* (Dublin, 1998).

O'Flaherty, Liam, *Famine* (Dublin, 1979).

O'Gallagher, Marianna, *Grosse Ile: Gateway to Canada 1832–1937* (Ste. Foy, 1984).

Ó Gráda, Cormac, 'Making History in the 1940s and 1950s: The Saga of the Great Famine', *The Irish Review* xii (1992), pp. 87–107.

—— *Black '47 and Beyond: The Great Irish Famine in History, Economy and Memory* (Princeton, NJ, 1999).

—— *Famine: A Short History* (Princeton, NJ/Oxford, 2009).

O'Grady, Donal, 'Carrick Workhouse Attic Memorial Opened', *Leitrim Observer*, 12 September 2008.

O'Kelly, Alanna and Jean Fisher, *Alanna O'Kelly: 23rd São Paulo Biennal* (Dublin, 1996).

Ó Murchadha, Ciarán, *The Great Famine: Ireland's Agony 1845–1852* (London/New York, 2011).

O'Riordan, Edmund, *Famine in the Valley*. (Tipperary Free Press/online, 2010).

O Riordan, Tomás, 'The Introduction of the Potato into Ireland', *History Ireland* ix (2001), pp. 27–31.

O'Rourke, Canon John, *On a Cross*, Pamphlet (c. 1885).

—— *The History of the Great Irish Famine of 1847*, with Notices of Earlier Famines (Dublin, 1874) (1994).

Ó Súilleabháin, Seán, *Irish Folk Custom and Belief* (Dublin, 1967).

O'Sullivan, Niamh, *The Tombs of a Departed Race: Illustrations of Ireland's Great Hunger* (Hamden, CT, 2014).

—— *In the Lion's Den – Daniel Macdonald, Ireland and Empire* (Hamden, CT, 2016).

—— (ed.), *Coming Home: Art and the Great Hunger* (Hamden CT, 2018).

O'Toole, Fintan, *The Ex-Isle of Erin* (Dublin, 1996).

—— *Ship of Fools – How Corruption and Stupidity Killed the Celtic Tiger* (London, 2009).

Pearce, Susan M., 'Collecting Reconsidered', in S.M. Pearce (ed.), *Interpreting Objects and Collections* (London/New York, 1994).

Perry, Gill, *Playing at Home: The House in Contemporary Art* (London, 2013).

Poe, Simon, 'The Cult of Beauty: The Aesthetic Movement 1860–1900, Exhibition Review', *The British Art Journal* xii/1 (2011), pp. 79–80.

Póirtéir, Cathal, *Famine Echoes* (Dublin, 1995).

Pollack, Barbara, 'Film: Body and Soul', *Art in America*, March 2009, pp. 75–8.

Quigley, Michael, 'Grosse Île: Canada's Famine Memorial', in A. Gribben (ed.), *The Great Famine and the Irish Diaspora in America* (Amherst, MA, 1999).

Rancière, Jacques, *The Politics of Aesthetics* (London, 2004).

Reilly, Ciaran, *Strokestown and the Great Irish Famine* (Dublin, 2014).

Richardson, Hilary and Scarry, John, *An Introduction to Irish High Crosses* (Cork 1990).

Ricoeur, Paul, *Time and Narrative, Volume 2* (Chicago and London, 1985).

—— *Time and Narrative, Volume 3* (Chicago, 1988).

Rieff, David, *In Praise of Forgetting: Historical Memory and its Ironies* (New Haven, CT and London, 2016).

—— *The Reproach of Hunger: Food, Justice and Money in the 21st Century* (London and New York, 2016).

Riegel, Henrietta, 'Into the Heart of Irony: Ethnographic Exhibitions and the Politics of Difference', in S, Macdonald and G. Fyfye (eds), *Theorizing Museums* (Oxford and Cambridge, MA, 2004).

Richardson, Hilary and John Scarry, *An Introduction to Irish High Crosses* (Cork 1990).

Rigney, Ann, 'Plentitude, Scarcity and the Circulation of Cultural Memory', *Journal of European Studies* 35/1 (2005), pp. 12–28.

Ringer, Greg, *Destinations – Cultural Landscapes of Tourism* (London/New York, 2005).

Robinson, Tim, *Stones of Aran: Pilgrimage* (London, 2008).

Roche, Barry, 'Cork Sculpture Recalls Generosity of Choctaw Nation During the Famine', *Irish Times*, 13 June 2017.

Rolston, Bill, 'Political Murals in Northern Ireland', *Museum International* lvi/3 (2004).

Rooney, Brendan, 'Erskine Nicol R.S.A. A.R.A. 1825–1904', in N. Figgis and B. Rooney (eds), *Irish Paintings in the National Gallery of Ireland, Vol. I* (Dublin, 2001).

Rugoff, Ralph, 'Corrosive Vision', in Irish Museum of Modern Art (ed.), *Dorothy Cross* (Italy, 2005).

Said, Edward, 'Invention, Memory, and Place', in W.J.T. Mitchell (ed.), *Landscape and Power* (Chicago and London, 2002).

Salgado, Sebastiâo, *Sahel, the End of the Road* (Berkeley, Los Angeles and London, 2004).

Scarry, Elaine, *The Body in Pain* (New York and Oxford, 1985).

Scott, Yvonne, 'Dorothy Cross', in C. Marshall and P. Murray (eds), *Art and Architecture of Ireland (AAI), Vol. V. Twentieth-Century Art and Artists* (New Haven, CT and London, 2014).

Sheller, Mimi and John Urry, 'Places to Play, Place in Play', in M. Sheller and J. Urry, *Tourism Mobilities: Places to Play, Place in Play* (London and New York, 2004).

Shklar, Judith N., *The Faces of Injustice* (New Haven, CT, 1990).

Smyth, William J., 'The Province of Connacht and the Great Famine, in J. Crowley, W.J. Smyth and M. Murphy (eds), *Atlas of the Great Irish Famine* (Cork, 2012).

—— '"Variations in Vulnerability": Understanding Where and Why the People Died', in J. Crowley, W.J. Smyth and M. Murphy (eds), *Atlas of the Great Irish Famine* (Cork, 2012).

Solomon-Godeau, Abigail, *Photography at the Dock* (Minneapolis, 1997).

Sontag, Susan, *On Photography* (London, 2002).

—— *Regarding the Pain of Others* (London, 2003).

Stewart, David, 'Deconstruction or Reconstruction? The Victorian Paintings of George Frederic Watts', Southeast College Art Conference Review xii/3 (1993), pp. 181–6.

Steyn, Juliet, 'Vicissitudes of Representation: Remembering and Forgetting', in J. Kidd, S. Cairns, A. Drago, A. Ryall and M. Stearn (eds), *Challenging History in the Museum* (Abingdon and New York, 2016).

Stone, Philip R., 'A Dark Tourism Spectrum: Towards a Typology of Death and Macabre Related Tourist Sites, Attractions and Exhibitions', *Tourism* liv/2 (2006), pp. 145–60.

Sturken, Marita, 'Tourists of History: Souvenirs, Architecture and the Kitschification of Memory,' in L. Plate and A. Smelik (eds), *Technologies of Memory in the Arts* (Basingstoke and New York, 2009), pp. 18–35.

Bibliography

Tóibín, Colm and Diarmuid Ferriter, *The Irish Famine* (London, 2004).

Toussaint, Stéphanie and Alain Decrop, 'The Père-Lachaise Cemetery: Between Dark Tourism and Heterotopic Consumption', in L. White and E. Frew (eds), *Dark Tourism and Place Identity: Managing and Interpreting Dark Places* (New York, 2013).

Treanor, Jill, 'Half of world's wealth now in hands of 1% of population', *Guardian*, 13 October 2015.

Trodd, Colin, 'Before History Painting: Enclosed Experience and the Emergent Body in the Work of G.F. Watts', *Visual Culture in Britain* vi/1 (2005), pp. 37–57.

Turner, Bryan S., *The Body and Society* (London, 1996).

Valone, David A., 'Economic Identity and the Irish Peasantry on the Eve of the Great Hunger', in D.A. Valone and J.M. Bradbury (eds), *Anglo-Irish Identities, 1671–1845* (Lewisburg, PA, 2008).

Vergès, Françoise, 'A Museum without Objects', in I. Chambers, A. De Angelis, C. Ianniciello, M. Orabona and M. Quadraro (eds), *The Postcolonial Museum: The Arts of Memory and the Pressures of History* (Abingdon and New York, 2016).

Warner, Marina, *Monuments and Maidens: The Allegory of the Female Form* (London, Sydney, Auckland and Bergvlei, 1996).

Wells, Karen, 'Melancholic Memorialisation: The Ethical Demands of Grievable Lives', in G. Rose and D.P. Tolia-Kelly (eds), *Visuality/Materiality: Images, Objects and Practices* (Farnham and Burlington, VT, 2012).

Whelan, Irene, 'The Stigma of Souperism', in Cathal Póirtéir (ed.), *The Great Irish Famine: The Thomas Davis Lecture Series* (Cork, 1995).

Whelan, Kevin, 'Pre and Post-Famine Landscape Change', in C. Póirtéir (ed.), *The Great Irish Famine: The Thomas Davis Lecture Series* (Cork, 1995).

—— 'Immoral Economy: Interpreting Erskine Nicol's *The Tenant*', in Boston College Museum of Art (ed.), *America's Eye: The Irish Art of Brian P. Burns* (Chestnut Hill, MA, 1996).

—— 'Between Filiation and Affiliation: The Politics of Postcolonial Memory', in C. Carroll and P. King (eds), *Ireland and Postcolonial Theory* (Cork, 2003).

White, Geoffrey M., 'Is Paris Burning – Touring Americas "Good War" in France', *History & Memory* xxvii/2 (2015), pp. 74–103.

White, Leanne and Elspeth Frew, 'Exploring Dark Tourism and Place Identity', in L. White and E. Frew (eds), *Dark Tourism and Place Identity: Managing and Interpreting Dark Places* (London and New York, 2013).

Williams, Paul, *Memorial Museums: The Global Rush to Commemorate Atrocities* (Oxford and New York, 2007).

Willis, Emma, *Theatricality, Dark Tourism and Ethical Spectatorship: Absent Others* (Basingstoke and New York, 2014).

Wilson, David, 'Tourism, Public Policy and the Image of Northern Ireland since the Troubles', in B. O'Connor and M. Cronin (eds), *Tourism in Ireland: A Critical Analysis* (Cork, 1993).

Young, James, 'The Holocaust as Vicarious Past: Art Spiegleman's "Maus" and the Afterimages of History', *Critical Inquiry* xxiv/3 (1998), pp. 666–99.

—— *At Memory's Edge: After-Images of the Holocaust in Contemporary Art and Architecture* (New Haven, CT and London, 2000).

Other Sources

Butler, Judith, '*Vulnerability and Resistance Revisited*' Lecture (Trinity College Dublin, 5 February 2015).
Dáil Éireann, Archives: Vol. 456, No. 5 (5 October 1995).
Dáil Éireann, Archives: Vol. 477, No. 1 (26 March 1997).
Marshall, Catherine, Personal Research File (2005).
O'Connor, Sinéad et al, *Famine Song Lyrics* (1995).
O'Kelly, Alanna, *Winter Lecture* (Irish Museum of Modern Art, 4 December 2001). Audio courtesy of IMMA.
Tourism Ireland, The Jeanie Johnston Walk-Around Guide (n.d.).

Press Releases:

Irish Museum of Modern Art (IMMA), *Representations of the Famine*, (1998).
Irish Museum of Modern Art (IMMA), *Súil Eile: Selected Works from the IMMA Collection at Ballina Arts Centre, Co Mayo*, (2007).
Teagasc, Exhibition Press Release (1995).

MA Thesis:

Martin, James Gerard, 'The Society of the St. Vincent de Paul as an emerging social phenomenon in mid-nineteenth century Ireland', MA thesis, National College of Industrial Relations NCEA (Dublin, 1993), p. 71.

Websites:

//www.strokestownpark.ie/.
//www.museum.ie/Country-Life.
//oireachtasdebates.oireachtas.ie/debates.
www.afri.ie/.
mcny.org.
www.croagh-patrick.com/.
//jeaniejohnston.ie/.
www.irishfaminememorial.org/en/orphans/database/.
www.dunbrody.com.
//clarechampion.ie/call-for-ennistymon-famine-memorial-refurbishment/.
www.wildatlanticway.com.
area.www.doaghfamilnevillage.com.
www.ucd.ie/irishfolklore/en/.
www.iln.co.uk/heritage.
//irelandparkfoundation.com/.
www.pc.gc.ca/eng/lhn-nhs/qc/grosseile/index.aspx.
www.teagasc.ie/.
www.opw.ie/en/nhp/.
ighm.org.
carrickheritage.com.

Bibliography

www.discoverireland.ie/.

Independent.ie, 'Rowan's Found a Niche', 24 May 2009, https://www.independent.
ie/entertainment/books/rowans-found-a-niche-26538489.html.

http://www.decadeofcentenaries.com/.

http://www.clarelibrary.ie/eolas/coclare/history/kr_et_workhouses/kr_et_
workhouses.htm.

Film:

Black 47, 2018, Dir. Lance Daly, 100 mins.
Hunger, 2008, Dir. Steve McQueen, 96 mins.
Wide Open Spaces, 2009, Dir. Tom Hall, 85 mins.

TV:

When Ireland Starved, 1995, Radharc Four-Part Documentary Series.
The Hanging Gale, 1995, BBC and RTE, Drama Mini-series.

Index

Index

Index

Index

Index

Index

public mourning, 23
public works schemes, 5, 6, 7, 188
Punch, 44, 234

Quadraro, Michaela, 9
Quakers (Society of Friends), 96–7,
    182, 246
Quarter Acre Clause, 6
Quigley, Michael, 62

racial identity, 84
racial stereotypes, 33, 44, 47, 59,
    198, 231
Rahmato, Dessalegn, 163
Rancière, Jacques, 143, 145
Rating Clause, 6
Rebellion (1798), 21, 227
Reeves, Keir, 91, 115, 183
relief works, 5, 6, 7, 26, 95, 188,
    196–208, 209, 210, 240 *see also*
    soup kitchens; workhouses
religious sectarianism, 7, 33
Rembrant van Rijn, 38
replica famine ships, 75–82, 93
Representations of the Famine
    (IMMA, 1998), 130, 138–43, 145
Republicanism, 188
revisionism, 18, 20, 22, 120, 132
Rice, Edmund, 164, 259
Rice, Michael, 193, 195, 263
Richtin, Fred, 236
Ricoeur, Paul, 129–30, 136, 252, 253
Rieff, David, 183, 218, 267
Riegal, Henrietta, 116
Rigney, Ann, 122, 146
Ringer, Greg, 24, 25
Robins, Alannah, 138
Robinson, Tim, 196, 206
Rolston, Bill, 58
Romanticism, 33, 35, 36, 161, 175, 218
Routh, Sir Randolph, 198
Royal Hibernian Academy (RHA),
    127–8, 242
Rugoff, Ralph, 214

rural landscapes, 23, 68–70
    commemorative walks, 179–84
    graveyards, 160–70, 173, 175
    heritage trails, 185–96
    historic roads and walls, 203–6, 207
    landscapes of remembrance, 23,
        68–70, 208–10
    picturesque art forms, 36, 37, 39,
        161, 171
Russell, John, 6, 197, 198
Rwandan Genocide, 25–6

Said, Edward, 244
Salgado, Sebastiâo, 236–7
Salisbury, Robert Gascoyne-Cecil,
    Lord Salisbury, 142
Sands, Bobby, 29–30, 31, 230
scalps/scalpeens, 15, 189
Scarry, Elaine, 11, 31, 36, 51, 59, 218
sculptures, 49, 52–8, 60, 68, 69, 68–70,
    71, 85–7, 182
secondary witnessing, 123, 146, 217–19
Sharpley, Richard, 9
Sheller, Mimi, 24
Ship Fever Monument, Montreal,
    63–4, 149
ships
    artistic motif, 68–75
    conditions on board, 61–2, 67–8
    replica famine ships, 75–82, 93
    slave ships, 84
Shklar, Judith, 21
Simon, Roger, 103
sites of Famine memory, 9, 10, 22, 23,
    65, 105 *see also* heritage sites
Skibbereen Heritage Centre, 97, 98,
    100, 104
Skibbereen Trail, 186–8, 195, 209
slavery, 83–4
Smailovic, Vedran, 181, 262
Smith O'Brien, William, 110, 111, 248
Smurfit, Norma, 55
Smyth, William J., 65
social breakdown, 29, 44

Index

Lightning Source UK Ltd.
Milton Keynes UK
UKHW051134070821
388360UK00006B/10